"Recall, Recoil, Rejoice"

By

Mary M Zaharko

Table of Contents

Dedication

To my patient, loving family, Stephen, Peter, niece Mary, and Manya, who inspired me to write this Bio/Memoir, and my inquisitive grandchildren, Jamison and Jadyn.

About the Author

Mary Zaharko's life journey has been as diverse as it is fascinating. She transformed from a model to a secretary, then became a policewoman and detective with the NYPD, and later pursued careers as a gemologist, antique dealer, and author. Her first book, a children's story titled "The Mystical Computer," marked the beginning of her writing career.

Never "The Rocking Chair" type, her advanced years did not hold her back from writing again, her autobiography detailing decades of her interesting, often exciting life. Thus, "Recall, Recoil, Rejoice" was born, a book in which she reveals a haunting secret, death threats, etc.

Encompassing nearly a century of an extraordinary life!

WOW!

.

Chapter One:
Early Childhood

I was born in Norwich, Connecticut, in 1925. When I was a toddler, we moved to Central Falls, Rhode Island. I remember living on Earle Street, where we shared a large plot of land with another family. We lived on the second floor of a two-story house. There was a huge black iron stove in the kitchen/living room. The stove had a vent pipe going through the wall to the outside. On cold days, when it was snowing or raining, I used to sit behind the stove, and my sister, Hanya, would read to me. My brother Ted often joined us in playing Jacks or Pick-up-Sticks. Hanya was five years older than me, and Ted was seven years older.

One favorite memory of mine was Christmas in Central Falls when Mama took us to the American Legion Post for their annual gift-giving to the neighborhood children. I not only got a Christmas box loaded with candy and cookies but received my first teddy bear. He was golden-colored, had amber-colored eyes, and gave a soft growl when turned over. Even his hands and feet and head turned. I never had a teddy bear before and I just loved him. I still love teddy bears to this day! Hanya also received a Christmas Box along with a copy of Charles Dickens's "David Copperfield." Ted received a Christmas Box and a football as well.

We later moved to a three-story building on Garfield Street. We lived on the second floor, but this time, we had a balcony that extended to the length of the apartment. All the tenants had a section of the basement designated for their personal use. My father used to make kielbasa there. He would stuff casings and then hang them on a clothesline to cure. He was very clever. He also made a big wooden box with two sections. The bottom half had shelving, while the upper half had a metal wall installed. A pipe extended down to the bottom so that melted ice water would drain into a bucket. He would buy a block of ice, which he then placed inside the metal-sided section. The shelf portion would hold the kielbasa. When the ice melted, he would empty the bucket and buy a new block of ice. This was our homemade refrigerator, which allowed Mama to preserve lots of food.

On Sunday mornings, I would hear my brother (pulling a cart loaded with newspapers) in the street calling out, "Get your Sunday papers, Boston American." Ted loved selling the newspapers because he often received tips along with a percentage of the sales.

Mama and Papa were active members of the Ukrainian Social Club, and every month, we would go there and mingle with friends. There was a recreation room with a pool table, card table, and a miniature bowling alley for the kids. Another room was spacious and had a stage where dances were often held. Frequently, members performed in plays. Mama was always selected for a play. I remember once leaving the recreation room and standing in the back, watching the actors perform. One scene involved Mama, who looked lovely in a flowing yellow gown. She was being pushed by her fellow actor, who at one point raised his hand as though to strike her. It was a tense scene, and I cried out, "Neh bey moyah Mama!" (Don't hit my Mama) Needless to say, I ruined the scene. The audience was laughing and clapping. Papa grabbed me and took me back to the recreation room. I guess poor Mama just carried on. Papa told me that it was acting and Mama was not going to get hurt. I was not allowed to go into the room again whenever there was a play with Mama in it.

We often went to the local theater in Pawtucket, where I was introduced to movies. We saw Flash Gordon, Rin Tin Tin, Buck Jones, etc., but what made it really interesting was a man playing the organ whenever there was an exciting action scene. One time Papa took us to Pawtucket to the Leroy Theater to see King Kong. I sat next to Papa. When King Kong appeared on the screen, I, like many others, screamed and leaped off my seat onto his lap for protection, burying my head on his chest. Papa laughed and said it was only make-believe and told me to enjoy the movie. After the movie, Papa took us for a treat at Woolworth's 5&10 cent store, where we had ice cream. I had my usual strawberry ice cream soda, and Ted and Hanya shared a huge banana split. Ahhhh, those were the days!

I was eight years old when we moved to Sumner Avenue. We had a spacious house complete with a full basement on a large lot. One beautiful spring day, my brother and his friends decided to play Cowboys and Indians. I was sitting in a swing under the shade of a huge umbrella-shaped oak tree when two of his friends who said they were "Cowboys" grabbed me off the swing and said, "You are our prisoner, Indian girl." They claimed they needed to hide me from the other Indians (my brother being one of them) and took me to our basement. I was tied to a pillar. The two boys stood back laughing and then one of them proceeded to lift up my skirt and placed his hand at my waist. He was about to pull my panties down when, thankfully, my brother opened the door and rushed down the stairs, yelling, "Get your hands off my sister, or I'll kill you!" They took off, needless to say, and my brother untied me. I started to cry. My brother put his arms around me and said, "I'll always protect you. Don't tell anyone what happened. It'll never happen again – I promise you!" NOT TRUE!! More on that later…

3

Shortly after that incident, we moved to New York City. It was the height of the Depression, and both my parents, who had worked in local factories, had been laid off. My father went to New York City to seek employment having been told it was the best place to find a job. He eventually found a job as a janitor in an apartment building. He felt that this was great because the family was given an apartment without paying rent! This was a challenge and a big change for him, doing repairs, collecting rent and catering to tenants, so different from being the electrician he had been before. We packed our belongings and were off to a new life in New York City (Manhattan).

Chapter Two:
Yiddish Theater

We moved to 60 Second Avenue, a six-story apartment building with an elevator located between Third and Fourth Streets next to a popular Yiddish theater. There was an Italian restaurant in front and a music store next door. Our apartment was on the ground floor behind the Italian restaurant. It was nice: roomy and light, with all the windows facing an alley on the side. The only problem with the apartment was that it smelled of garlic all the time because of the restaurant, and we were always killing roaches! Music blared daily from the record store, mostly blues and torch music. I loved "Stormy Weather" by Frances Langford. Many nights, I went to sleep humming the tunes I had heard that day.

The majority of the tenants in the building were Jewish. Most of them were nice, but some were really demanding and aloof. My brother was in high school and would often run the elevator, giving the elevator man a break now and then. I started to learn a few Yiddish phrases, especially any that might refer to me. I was referred to as the "Shayna Sehiksa" (the pretty gentile girl}. Mama told me that people complimented my looks because I was a pretty child with big green eyes, dimples, and sweet, full lips. My parents were referred to as "galitzyanes." They were Ukrainian Christians from Galicia, an area that encompassed parts of Poland and Western Ukraine. Once, one of my friends, Mendel, nicknamed Manny, was having a birthday party to which I was invited. I remember his "Bubby" (grandmother), an Orthodox Jew, saying, "Mendel, give the sehiksa a paper plate and paper cup," I suppose it was because I was a Christian. I saw everyone else using regular china and glasses.

One afternoon, a tenant dropped in to pay her rent and noticed me doing my homework. For purposes of this story, I will call her "Mrs. L." She asked me how old I was. I told her I was nine years old. She told Mama I was adorable and that she'd like to know me better. She had no children but always wanted a girl to love and spoil. She mentioned that she and her husband acted in the theater next door, but when not acting on a weekend, she'd love to take me to Central Park or to the Metropolitan Museum of Art or even Coney Island for some fun if that was all right with Mama. I guess Mama was flattered by this beautiful woman wanting to do something nice for me, so she agreed.

Our first outing was to the Central Park Zoo and afterward, of course, to Schrafft's for ice cream. Her husband was busy rehearsing for an upcoming show and, therefore, did not accompany us. When we returned home, she said we'd go backstage in the theater to meet her husband. I was thrilled to think of going backstage in a real theater_ Wow! As we walked down the aisle, I saw a man on stage moving his arms and legs, dancing and singing so beautifully and effortlessly. It was magic! His voice resonated without a microphone! When he stopped singing, he smiled and said, "Manya, Manya," and sort of made a gargling sound. "Come here, bubbeleh; so happy to finally meet you." He reached over and hugged me and said, "This makes my missus so happy and me too. I know there will be many more good times. Now go, I have more rehearsing to do." With that, he gave me a quick hug and a pat on my backside and said to his wife, "Take Manya to the dressing room and show her around."

We went to the dressing room, where she told me to sit in a chair in front of a mirror. She said, "I am going to doll you up just like we do when we go onstage." She applied makeup and put a wig on my head, then took an ostrich feather boa off the hook and draped it around my neck. "Now, Manya, you're an actress. Do you like it?" Like it? I was in heaven. She then said she would remove my makeup and take me home because she, too, needed to prepare for that evening's performance, but we would do this again, perhaps next week. That evening, I couldn't stop talking about my exciting, wonderful day and couldn't wait for our next outing. I raved about how sweet and gentle a person she was. I adored her and also thought her husband was nice.

Several weeks went by before she was free again to go out with me. This time, we went to the American Museum of Natural History. We were there for hours before it was time to head home. She asked if I wanted to go backstage to the dressing room again and be made up like the other time. I told her I would love it. When we arrived at the theater, her husband was sitting in a chair onstage, reading a script with another actor. We went to the dressing room, and again, she put makeup on me, a flowing wig, and again placed the ostrich boa around my neck. "Now," she said, go show them what you look like." I gladly went on stage, and he called my name, "Manya, Manya," making that funny gargling sound. He said, "You look so beautiful; you will be an actress one day. Come, give me a hug!" I went over, and he hugged me and again patted my backside and said "Scoot, I've work to do." I was so happy feeling loved. It was not that Mama didn't love me, but the affection they were showering me with was different. It felt good. Mama was happy for me because she could not take me to the places they showed me.

One evening everyone was excited about some very high-powered stars that were coming for a benefit performance. I saw Eddie Cantor, Molly Picon, and others, as well as Mrs. L and her husband, who were there to perform.

The next outing was going to be very special, and I was told there would be a surprise for me. Mrs. L picked me up, and we boarded a bus on Second Avenue. She asked for a transfer. We got off at Fiftieth Street and transferred to a crosstown bus, getting off at Fifth Avenue and Fiftieth Street. Saint Patrick's Cathedral was on one side, and across was Sak's Fifth Avenue, the department store. She told me we were going to Saks for a surprise. First, she took me to the shoe department and said she was buying me a pair of Mary Jane shoes because she could not stand my Buster Brown shoes with laces! After getting the shoes, shiny black patent leather with cross straps, I was so happy. We then headed to the dress department, where she picked out a beautiful green velvet dress with a lace collar and said,

"Now, your outfit is complete." I wore my new dress (she told me it matched my eyes) and my new shoes at home. When we got there, she told me she wanted to show me to her husband before we went to see Mama. We went inside the theater where he was singing on stage. When he saw us, he said, "Manya, Manya," (gargling, gargling) "Come here and let me look at you." A woman called Mrs.L. for something so both women left and headed for the box office. I went up on stage. He sat in a chair, reached over for me, and placed me on his lap. This time, instead of a hug, he placed his hand under my dress and reached into my panties, cradling my buttocks and moving his fingers. I froze, whimpered, slid off his lap, and quickly got off the stage. He said, "Manya, wait!" but I ran up the aisle without saying a word to him and without seeing his wife as she was still at the box office. Mama loved my beautiful dress and Mary Jane shoes, but I could hardly wait to get out of them. That evening, instead of being happy as I had been in the past after our outings, I felt afraid, ashamed, you name it. I hardly spoke at supper about the day's events, supposedly a happy day. I went to bed feeling miserable. In the past, I had thought nothing about his quick pats on my backside, but I was wrong; it only made him feel more comfortable going even further. I cried into my pillow, knowing that I would never ever go out with her again, even though she had done nothing wrong. I simply couldn't stand seeing him again. Fortunately, it was the height of the Yiddish theater season, so she didn't come for me again. I was glad because it really took time for me to realize my good times were over. One Saturday, she arrived and asked for me, but Mama told her I wasn't home and that I was out with my sister. She asked whether Sunday would be a good day for us to do something, and Mama said, "Why not?" not knowing how I felt. When my sister Hanya and I came home, Mama told me she had been there looking for me and that tomorrow I could go out with her. I told Mama that I did not want to go out with her anywhere anymore. I wanted to play with my friends. I told Mama that if she asked for me to say I have a cold, or that I wasn't home. Mama thought this was strange and asked what was wrong. I never told her (or, for that matter, anyone else) of my experience but said I wanted to be left alone. Fortunately for me, my father was offered a new job as a janitor in the Bronx, which he accepted. We happily moved. I never said goodbye or saw them again, although, over the years, I became aware of the husband's popularity and the adulation of his peers—if they only knew his dark side and my dark secret! He had a hit record, which was No. 1 for the longest time!

Chapter Three:
Early Bronx Years

We moved to Prospect Avenue in the East Bronx. We had a very large apartment on the sixth floor. It was large enough for my parents to rent out two bedrooms for extra income. I was thrilled because, for the first time, I was allowed to have a pet other than my canary Dickie. My new dog I called Minka.

To this day I marvel over the difficulties my father endured being a janitor. He was responsible for two buildings, shoveling coal into the furnaces, mopping the floors as well as tending to repairs. One incident I'll never forget is when he climbed a six-story pole in the backyard to install a clothesline for Mama. It was scary watching him scale the pole, but he did it, and Mama had her clothesline.

Prospect Avenue was similar to Second Avenue in that there were two theaters close by, but this time featuring American Films, not Yiddish Theater. I had a lot of friends: Susan, Althea, and then my best friend Evelyn, who lived next door. Her parents, like mine, were janitors. Evelyn had a big dog, a German Shepherd named Rex. Her father was Bohemian, and her mother was Austrian. Her mother was very strict and carried a wooden spoon in her apron pocket, which she would use to enforce her rules. Many a time, she struck Evelyn on the head and shoulders in front of me because she thought Evelyn was disobeying her. One good thing about her was her baking skills. She was a fantastic baker. I loved her strudel. Evelyn and I did lots of things together. We went to the movies and often headed to Crotona Park for a run. I enjoyed our time together.

One day we decided to go roller skating in the park and took Rex with us. After skating for a while, we sat on a bench near a cluster of trees and bushes. We heard a whistle and, when looking in the direction it had come from, saw a man exposing himself to us. Evelyn said to Rex, "Bootswick (bite him); go get him." Rex went after the man who took off like an express train. Evelyn called Rex and he came back to us. We laughed and roller-skated back home.

School was soon out, and it was summer vacation time! I went to visit my friend, Olga, in Norwich for a month and had a wonderful time, although we got ourselves into some dangerous situations. I called Olga my cousin, although we were not actually related. My father was her godfather, and her mother was my godmother. Olga's father had a butcher shop on Central Avenue. Chocha (Aunty) Sally was a wonderful cook and had an unusual sideline business; she made moonshine! She had a huge copper vat sitting on a shelf on top of the bathtub where the whiskey was distilled. The whiskey must have been good because she was never short of customers. We often went to Ocean Beach in New London. We had a great time swimming and collecting clams and seashells.

When we wanted to swim locally, we would swim at a forbidden spot called "the Dam." Olga's house was right across the street from railroad tracks and canals. The canals were used by factories to have barges float to their locations. They were quite deep and muddy. There was a long line of metal chain link fencing, supposedly to stop intruders. Someone managed to separate the fencing from its post, and thus, anyone could enter and swim across the canal or walk a distance to a pathway leading to the Dam. The Dam, when not overflowing, made it easy for us to cross over to the other side, where there was a section cleared of shrubbery so we could go swimming. If the Dam was overflowing, we had to walk under its waterfall and pray that we would not slip on the green slimy moss and fall to the rocks below. This was really dangerous, but our parents weren't aware of it. One of our friends drowned in a canal after diving in and getting stuck in the mud. Another friend tried to rescue him but didn't succeed. We stopped going to the Dam after that!

We also visited Olga's cousins who had a farm. One time, when we were there, we saw a goat tied to a broken tree, and I decided to have some fun, taunting it by saying, "Baran Baran Butz" and we both laughed as he strained to get loose. We were still teasing the goat when Olga's father appeared and said it was time to go home. The goat had managed to free himself by then and butted Olga's father's backside! We laughed hysterically until he managed to get the rope and retied the goat to the tree.

Those were wonderful memories, but it was time to go home to Prospect Avenue. One of the tenants had a cousin who was very wealthy and owned several new apartment buildings on the fashionable Grand Concourse (often compared to Park Avenue in Manhattan). She said they were looking for an honest and reliable superintendent for one of their buildings, and she highly recommended Papa to them. Once they interviewed Papa, he got the job. Now, he was a superintendent! Wow! No more janitor!

Chapter Four:
Ambush

We moved to a beautiful new building, the 1939 Grand Concourse, next door to a Jewish synagogue called Temple Zion on the north side of Tremont Avenue and Grand Concourse. Our building extended down from Grand Concourse, Tremont Avenue, to 178th Street, and on the south side of Tremont Avenue, there was a Catholic church and school called Saint Margaret Mary. Saint Margaret Mary extended from Grand Concourse to Morris Avenue and East 177th Street, where there were mostly Irish residents. There was a subway station next to the temple for the Independent Train "D and B" lines.

1939 Grand Concourse was a dramatic change for us, and particularly for Papa. The building not only had a doorman, but there was also a porter to assist the superintendent. This was a classy building! It had a beautifully furnished lobby and two elevators. For the first time, we had our own telephone as well as a house telephone, which tenants would call if they needed some work done. We had a beautiful apartment. It faced the backyard but was sunny and spacious. The tenants were predominately Jewish, doctors, dentists, lawyers, garment factory owners, etc. Unlike Prospect Avenue where I had many girlfriends, here I had none. Now, I was a tomboy playing with my Jewish friends, who were frequently taunted by a group of mean Irish kids from across the way. I also had a new dog whom I called Rexie, a mixed breed but smart and loving. My previous dog, Minka, had a serious illness and had to be put down, so my parents had kindly given me Rexie.

My sister Hanya was at that time being courted by two serious boyfriends. Hanya was stunning: five-ten, slim, and really good-looking. Even though she was already quite tall, she wore high-heeled shoes, which made her look even taller. One of her boyfriends, Arthur, ran an architecture school close to the beauty shop where Hanya worked as a beautician and hairdresser. Arthur was also good-looking, at over six feet tall, and together they made a striking pair. Her other beau, Nick, was a smooth-talking charmer who was a hairdresser in the same beauty shop where Hanya worked.

Nick was handsome as well, but short! Probably about five seven. To compensate for his height, he wore special shoes called Adler Elevator Shoes, which added two to three inches to his height. Both men proposed to Hanya. We were all rooting for Arthur because we felt she would be better off marrying him, but no, Nick won out! I had to admit that Nick was handsome, a good-looking Italian with dark hair, dimples, and truly a great wit. They were married in the Ukrainian Protestant Church. Nick's parents weren't too thrilled as they were Catholic. Hanya moved into Nick's parents' home in Astoria, a mostly Italian neighborhood. After living there for only a short while, Hanya noticed that there was a long crack in the middle of their bedroom door. She peeked into the crack and was shocked to see that it showed the entire bedroom, including the bed! When she spoke to Nick's mother about having it repaired, she answered, "I'll take care of it. You know I'm worried that with your long legs, you might strangle Nick." Hanya could not believe what she said! In other words, Nick's mother had apparently stood outside the door (who knows how many times) to watch them in bed. How terrible!

Hanya packed her bags that same day and came home to us. Nick was, of course, beside himself because Hanya refused to return to

Astoria! As fate would have it, his draft number was called up, and he was inducted into the Seabees. Off he went to the South Pacific. Thereafter, Hanya and I shared a bedroom. She was now working at a new beauty parlor where Nick had worked as the head hairstylist, located in the Madison Hotel at Forty-Eighth Street and Madison Avenue. I, on the other hand, went to an all-girls junior high school called the "Elizabeth Barret Browning School" on Ryer Avenue and 183rd Street. While there, I befriended an Irish girl named Coleen. She had gone to Saint Margaret Mary Catholic School but did not like their strict codes and thus transferred to "EBB." It was also at this time that I had my tonsils removed, and lo and behold, there was a stunning transformation! I could no longer be a tomboy and play with the boys as I had in the past, Stickball, baseball, points, touch football, etc. From being skinny and too flat-chested, I became curvaceous overnight! The boys couldn't get over my radical change and challenged me to play touch football, but those days were over. Instead, I spent time now with Coleen on the "Irish" side of the neighborhood and met a few of her friends.

One day, Coleen asked if I wanted to go to a farewell party for one of the boys who had enlisted. She said it would be a fun time. I always thought the Irish boys were handsome, so why not go? We went to the fifth floor of a building on the other side of the Grand Concourse. We entered and were greeted with cheers. The living room was jammed with people, mostly boys and a few girls. There was a table set up with loads of beer in an ice bucket, a bottle of rum, pretzels, potato chips, and Coca-Cola as well as other sodas. The party was already in full swing. Everyone was having a good time. Some of the boys had flushed faces, and few of them appeared to be woozy, their sparkling blue Irish eyes glazed. They all were friendly and really charming. We were told to drop off our coats on the bed in the bedroom and join the festivities. I was introduced to those I did not know and was offered a beer which I declined, taking a Cola instead. One of the boys was the brother of the one who enlisted. He was extremely good-looking, well built and appeared to be the leader of his group of friends. He came up to me and said he was glad Coleen brought me since she told him what a fun-loving person I was. He put his arm around my shoulders and said I smelled nice. They had a record player going, and several couples were dancing. He asked me to dance. I did the Lindy Hop with him. His friends egged us on to keep dancing. I noticed a few of the girls cuddling and smooching with boys, and I began to feel uncomfortable. Coleen was in one corner kissing a boy and totally ignored me. I started to feel uneasy and thought it best to leave.

I walked into the bedroom to get my coat off the bed, and as I was putting on my coat, I heard the door opening. My dance partner, along with two of his friends, came in and asked where I was going. I said I needed to get home. My dance partner laughed and said, "Not before you're initiated by us!" He then pushed me down atop the pile of clothing on the bed and climbed on top of me. Having been a tomboy, I was strong for a girl and pulled my legs up and thrust them against his chest. He fell backward onto the floor laughing and said, "Come on, let's get her!" I got off the bed, headed to the window and stood on the windowsill, all the while hoping there was a fire escape, but there was none! I thought they were going to rape me. I screamed, "Help, help!" and mercifully, the door opened. It was the boy's mother. She yelled, "What the hell is going on here?" The boys quickly left the bedroom, and I stepped down from the windowsill, trembling and crying. She embraced me and apologized, saying, "Boys will be boys." Really? I left and once again told no one, but it brought back repressed memories of my early traumatic experience in the Rhode Island "Cowboys and Indians" game and the Yiddish theater. Needless to say, I dumped Coleen. She left EBB midterm when her family moved away. Rumor had it that Coleen was pregnant, which did not surprise me, recalling the party we had been to.

Years later, when I was a detective in the New York City Police Department and went to court, I was amused to find my Irishman (aspiring rapist) to be a criminal lawyer; how ironic. I guess he was surprised to learn of my occupation. Even though we didn't speak, I caught him glancing at me. He appeared to be a trifle uncomfortable. Small wonder!

Chapter Five:
War Years

After leaving junior high school, I went to Walton High School (again an all-girls school) on Kingsbridge Road and Reservoir Avenue. It was referred to as "Dr. Cahill's Sing Sing on the Reservoir." Dr. Cahill was a strict disciplinarian, although very fair and actually quite a good principal. Walton High School was next to the Kingsbridge Armory, and on the other side were two boys' high Schools, The Bronx High School of Science and De Witt Clinton High School. Whenever we went outside for gym, we were always greeted with whistles and howls from the boys. Eventually, all gym activities were held back inside our regular gymnasium. The school had two sessions. I attended the early session, and it was at this time, usually between eight and eight thirty am. that the soldiers from the armory would march down Reservoir Avenue. I remember going up to the window to sharpen my pencil in the steno-typing class and hearing the drill sergeant calling out, "Hep, two, three, four, hep, two, three, four," and my teacher, Mrs. Blaustein, calling out, "Miss Mary, kindly take your seat. Your pencil is sharpened down to the eraser."

I made a lot of friends at Walton, some lasting a lifetime. I was active in the drama club and frequently appeared in plays onstage. One time, after acting in a play, we were told a member of the audience was coming backstage to congratulate us. It was Eva Le Galliene! She was very gracious and told me to pursue acting because I seemed so natural and effective. I was thrilled to hear that, for I truly loved acting and singing, having been introduced to the stage by my

"Yiddish actor/actress" friends, and remembering Mama's acting career back in Central Falls, Rhode Island.

I graduated from high school in June of 1942. My father was very strict, so I had no beau to take me to our senior prom. My brother took me instead. I wasn't even allowed to wear lipstick until my graduation, a pale lipstick called Tangee.

My friend Olga came to visit soon after. It was a balmy Sunday, and we were bored staying in the house when I made a stupid mistake, suggesting we go to Coney Island just for the heck of it since she had never been there and always wanted to see Coney Island. We tried to look older than our years. Olga was fifteen, and I was seventeen. We wore my sister's makeup, and I took her high-heeled red shoes to make myself look taller. We took the subway to Coney Island, walked the boardwalk, and then sat on a bench to watch the sunbathers and the beautiful ocean. We were approached by two young sailors. It turned out they were cousins from Idaho. They were both nineteen years old, nice, and easy to talk to. We chatted and then they asked if we would be interested in going on some rides. We didn't hesitate. We said, "Yes!" We had no money for rides, but they did. We went on the Parachute Jump (what a thrill!) and the Cyclone. After the rides, we got cotton candy and the guys pitched balls at different booths to win us prizes. Olga received a bunny rabbit, and I received a teddy bear.

Unbeknownst to me, a couple of my brother's friends were sunbathing on the beach and saw me and Olga. They tattled to my brother, who in turn told Mama and Papa. We needed to get home before five-thirty as that was around the time my parents would be getting home from church in downtown Manhattan. We took the subway home after exchanging addresses with the sailors and got back at around five p.m., good timing, or so I thought. We removed our makeup, and I was returning my sister's red high heels to the shelf in the closet when, to my horror, I saw that one of the heels had been scraped and the leather torn. I guess this must have happened while I was walking on the boardwalk. The heel had slipped between the boards and emerged scraped! I panicked. They were her new shoes. I applied lipstick over the scraped heel and put the shoes farther back in the closet. When my parents got home, Olga and I were reading the Sunday comics in the living room, and the Monopoly board was on the table as though we had been playing all along. The next morning, after Olga and I finished breakfast, my father called me and said he wanted to talk to me. We went into the dining room, where Mama was sitting in a chair. He asked what I had done yesterday. I told him I played Monopoly with Olga. He pulled his belt from around his waist and swatted me across my legs.

"Don't lie to me," he said and struck me again and again. Olga started crying. Papa said he knew all about our trip to Coney Island and that we had been carousing with sailors! He was livid! The belt tore my nylon stockings into shreds. He shook me and said he did not want to hear of me doing anything like that again. I had some nasty welts on my legs. Poor Olga was beside herself, trying to comfort me. Funny, as I recall, Papa never struck my sister, only me and occasionally my brother. When he did strike my brother, Ted was made to lie across the arms of a rocking chair. After that incident, I was forced to attend the Ukrainian church services every Sunday with them. One Sunday, I noticed a very good-looking, suntanned soldier singing effortlessly in the choir. He had a beautiful baritone voice like Nelson Eddy. His name was Pete (later to become my beloved husband), and I was immediately smitten with him. Later, after services, we were introduced by his sister Anne, who also sang in the choir. She asked Pete whether he'd date me, and he replied: "She's wet behind the ears. Maybe when she's older!" The reverend of the church approached me and asked whether I could do him a favor. He wanted me to answer letters from servicemen and put excerpts from them in the church newspaper. I said I would be happy to do so. Now, I could correspond with a group of servicemen, which would give me a great opportunity to meet them when they came home! I enjoyed reading their letters, especially those from Pete. I answered their letters and, as a result, became more friendly with Pete. His letters from China were always so interesting. After a while, he decided to send his letters directly to my home instead of to the church.

One day, one of the tenants in our building, a lawyer, offered me a job in his law firm (there were six lawyers), saying I would be in a pool of stenographers and typists. My salary was $12.00 a week, and my hours were nine to five. It was a learning experience, and it caused me to become interested in law. I enjoyed my time there, although it was short-lived. One evening while listening to one of my favorite programs on station WOV, "The 1280 Club" with Alan Courtney, I heard him say, "Woe is me, Heathcliff, my right hand is leaving (having been drafted into the service), don't know how I'll get along without him." I got an idea: I would write him a letter asking for Heathcliff's job, and lo and behold, I got a call from the radio station to come in for an interview! I couldn't believe my good luck. I was interviewed and hired! Woweee! I was so excited. The hours were crazy: four in the afternoon to eleven in the evening, Monday to Saturday. During the day, WOV broadcast mostly Italian soap operas, and then a news commentator came on. His name was Hans Jacob, and he was brilliant. Alan Courtney broadcasts from seven-thirty to ten in the evening, Monday to Saturday. My job consisted of answering fan mail telephone calls, typing up the program schedule, and getting the records ready for Alan to play. He was innovative in many ways, always keeping his audience interested. He truly believed in racial equality and harmony. On Monday nights, he had a program called the Harlem Hit Parade and another called Tolerance through Music. He often scheduled live performances and didn't always use records. I frequently had to go to a music rental store and lug drums into the studio. He had many friends in the music industry, and they were frequent guests, among them Lena Horne, Cab Calloway, Count Basie and Glenn Wallich of Capitol Records, as well. Alan was a true supporter of Black musicians and their music.

One night as a joke, or so he thought, he said that if someone would buy a $100 war bond, his gal Friday would sing. Sure enough, several people called and pledged to buy a bond. Alan then told me to select a song, and I would be on the air. The first time I sang "Embraceable You," an RCA Victor record. When the music came on, they segued it and I sang. I wasn't even nervous; I loved it. Alan got a kick out of it and said we'd do it again. Selling war bonds was a good thing. He also played a mystery record, and if someone correctly identified it, they would receive passes to the Paramount Theater.

During the day, WOV was busy; all the offices were occupied. I had no office. I was in the Record Room with records and file cabinets and a small table with a typewriter and telephone. Alan was very patriotic. One evening, he broadcast that the USO was looking for female singers to go on tour to entertain the troops. He said he was going to hold auditions at the radio station and that anyone interested should come in for an audition. A time and date had been set, and several girls showed up and auditioned. Alan had records playing in another studio for the "1280 Club" so that he, along with a Captain

22

from the USO, could hear the auditions. Alan suggested that I too, audition, which I did. I sang, "You Made Me Love You." After my audition, the Captain said he was interested and handed me a contract called a "Hence and Thence" contract. He told Alan I had an interesting-sounding voice. Sometimes, I sang a little flat, but I was stacked, and the boys would love me! Alan was pleased and told me to consider it. I went home with the contract not yet signed. Because I was under 21, I needed my parent's consent. In the morning, I went into the kitchen to tell my parents and saw my brother-in-law Nick, who was on leave from the Seabees, sitting at the table having breakfast. I told them my good news but my dreams were shattered! Nick said, "Mom, don't let her go, she'll be a whore in no time!" That was the end of my singing career! (Thanks, Nick.)

My parents wanted me to leave my job because they were concerned about my riding the subway late at night after leaving my job at WOV. I usually got home at around midnight, and they felt I should get a job with normal hours. Because of the crazy hours, I had no social life, and I was lonely. I decided to look for another job, but WOV always held a special place in my heart. I truly enjoyed my time there and all the wisecracks from Alan. I remember one time when he called me to replace a broken record; I rushed down the hallway to the studio with the replacement record and popped in to hand it to him. The mike was open, and he said, "Here comes my Gal Friday. It must be jelly 'cause jam don't shake like that!" I, too, received fan mail. It was very flattering, the result of people pledging to buy war bonds after I sang. I felt sad but handed in my resignation and left WOV. I did not see Alan Courtney again, and he, too, left shortly after I did, going south to host a similar show in Miami, Florida.

I went to the unemployment office, where they found a job for me. I was tested for my steno-typing ability and was given a temporary replacement job with a company called Caltex (California Texas Oil Company). My position was to be secretary to the chief engineer. He had a private office, and I sat outside at a desk surrounded by other employees in a very large space. He was a kind, soft-spoken, patient man. He understood that in dictating to me, he used engineering phrases I had never heard of, and I needed to ask him to repeat his words several times until I got used to the terminology. Once I got the hang of it, there was no problem; it was fine. One day, one of the Civil Engineers asked if I liked football. I told him I did. He said he had an extra ticket to the Army and Notre Dame football game to be played that weekend at Yankee Stadium and if I would want it. Want it? Boy, oh boy, I could hardly wait to go! This was a major event for me. The day arrived, and I went to Yankee Stadium, not far from where I lived, and found my seat next to a young soldier who happened to be a family friend of my co-worker whom he wanted me to meet. We were introduced. The stadium was packed, as you can imagine. What a thrill! I was seated in the Army section, and in front of me were West Point Cadets. Wow! During the game, the soldier, Frank, engaged me in conversation. He said he loved playing football and that he had been admitted to West Point, where he would be going shortly. He had been a football player in college and was going to be on the West Point football team, as well. Frank had an engaging smile and broad shoulders and was quite good-looking. I was so happy meeting and conversing with him. Army beat Notre Dame soundly, 59-0. Notre Dame was the Army's arch-rival. Frank said he was meeting up with a West Point cadet after the game and wanted me to join them. We met Dave, the Cadet, so proud and handsome in his uniform. My co-worker suggested that we all have dinner together. We went to the Rainbow Room in Rockefeller Plaza and had a wonderful dinner. It was the first time I was introduced to oysters! After dinner, when it was time to leave, we exchanged addresses and phone numbers.

After a couple of weeks, I got a letter from Frank, who was attending a prep college where he was studying mechanical engineering. He wrote that upon completion of his courses, he would go to West Point sometime in July 1945. I thanked my co-worker for introducing me to Frank. I was so happy corresponding with Frank and Dave, as well as with others from the church. I was dismayed to learn that one correspondent, Eugene, a Canadian I had met at church, was reported missing after a flight. That was my first casualty. My last letter to Eugene was returned marked "Undeliverable-Deceased."

One evening, I got a call from West Point. It was Dave. He invited me to the Yearling Winter Ball at West Point, which he said would be formal but fun. Of course, I accepted. I asked for information about where to stay. I needed to buy a formal gown and make reservations at a local hotel near West Point. Dave told me the place everyone stayed at was the Thayer Hotel, just outside of West Point. I was so happy. This was all new to me. Hanya cut my hair. She gave me a great hairdo, as she was, after all, a beautician. We went to Loehman's (a clothing store in the Bronx), where I tried on umpteen gowns until my sister and I agreed on one. I chose an emerald green gown with a scalloped neckline, not too low, discreet, and fitted waist with cap sleeves. Hanya said it was a good choice. She gave me an evening bag and a pair of long white gloves (up to the elbow), as this was a requirement. I bought evening shoes as well. I was ecstatic! I purchased a round-trip ticket to West Point (Highland Falls) at the

Greyhound Bus Terminal and made a reservation at the Thayer Hotel and I was off!

West Point was fifty miles north of New York City. I was pleased to learn that a lot of the passengers on the bus were also dates and were staying at the Thayer Hotel. Those of us who were clueless about what to expect were thankfully briefed by a couple of "old timers" (repeat dates) about proper protocol. It was mid-afternoon when we arrived at the Thayer Hotel. Check-in was at four in the afternoon. The hotel was fortunately adjacent to the entry of West Point. Upon checking in, the clerk asked if I was going to the Hop. I told him I was. He then pointed to a woman seated at a desk talking to several girls. He said she would advise us on all we need to know about our visit. I approached the woman and introduced myself, saying that I was going to the Yearling Hop. She then handed me a leaflet and said it had all the information I needed about all the events: the banquet, reception, and formal hop. She told us a shuttle bus would transport us to the Cadet Mess Hall for the reception, which started at six o'clock. There would be a receiving line, after which the banquet would take place at seven and, finally, the Hop from nine to midnight. The shuttle bus would be parked outside of Cullum Memorial Hall to transport us back to the Thayer Hotel. She cautioned us not to be late since the last bus would leave promptly at twelve-thirty in the morning.

By the time I unpacked my bag, it was around four-thirty, ample time to shower and get ready for the shuttle bus at five forty-five. I left a message for Dave, and he returned my call and said that he would be waiting along with other cadets at the Cadet Mess Hall. I joined a group of girls in the lobby, all decked out in beautiful formal gowns where we waited for the shuttle bus to take us to the Cadet

Mess Hall for the banquet. Once I was on the bus, the smell of perfume was overpowering, and the chatter and giggles added to the excitement of an anticipated lovely evening.

When we arrived at the Cadet Mess Hall, I could not believe the large number of cadets in full-dress uniforms patiently waiting for their dates to alight from the bus. I scanned their faces, and I saw Dave. It seems he saw me at the same time and rushed forward to greet me. His face was flushed with excitement, and when he took my hand, he said, "I'm so happy to see you. You look amazing!" He said that before the banquet, there was a receiving line where we would be introduced by an usher (a cadet). We walked up to the entrance where the usher was standing, and Dave introduced me. The usher then introduced me and Dave to those on the receiving line. I smiled, shook hands, and proceeded with Dave to the reception hall to meet and mingle with the cadets and their dates. Snacks, cocktails, and other refreshments were available. After an hour, an announcement was made for us to go to our assigned table, where there were name cards and a program outlining the evening events and the toasts. You remained standing until everyone was at their table. Inside the program was a dance card called a Hop Card, which had spaces so that you would enter the name of your date and the names of anyone else who asked to dance with you.

I couldn't wait to go to the Hop. I loved dancing! I learned to dance from attending the Ukrainian socials held monthly in Manhattan. At one of the dances, one of my girlfriends brought her brother Andy to the dance specifically to meet me even though he didn't dance. Andy was in the merchant marines and was frequently in town. She felt he and I would click. Although he didn't dance, he enjoyed watching me (his date) dance with others. He was a genuinely sweet date, always a gentleman. We also went to Webster Hall for dances.

Getting back to the banquet, some of the toasts given were serious, whereas others were humorous. Finally, the time came for us to leave the banquet and head to Cullum Memorial Hall for the Hop. When we arrived at Cullum Hall, I laughed because there was yet another receiving line to go through before entering the ballroom. After all the formalities were done and over with, Dave and I had our first dance; thankfully, it was a Fox Trot. One cadet approached Dave and asked if he could dance with me. He signed my Hop Card. The music started up and it was a Lindy Hop! We really went to town! Dave clapped his hands and said we did a terrific job. After a while, Dave suggested we get some refreshments, relax and talk. The refreshments were outside the ballroom in the reception hall. I sat on a bench while Dave went to get me a soda.

When he returned, Dave said he thought it was a good time to talk. First and foremost, he wanted me to know that he thought I looked lovely and how well my green gown matched my beautiful green eyes! He said he was so glad that I accepted his invitation and was grateful that Frank had introduced us. He told me that back home in California, he was very close to a girl. He had told her about me and that she accepted that Dave and I were just friends and nothing more. He then told me that before I left on Sunday, he wanted to show me around West Point. Dave said that there was a Sunday brunch, after which we would go to the Protestant chapel for services and last, of course, to Flirtation Walk, where only cadets and their dates were allowed.

I told him that checkout time was eleven in the morning and that I would check out earlier and meet him at the mess hall around nine for brunch. Dave was pleased that I agreed and suggested that we head back to the ballroom as it was close to midnight when the Hop ended. We had two more dances, and then the orchestra played "Army Blue," which was the traditional tune indicating the end of a delightful evening. Dave escorted me outside, where the shuttle bus was waiting to take the dates back to the Thayer Hotel. We had a quick embrace and I kissed him on the cheek and said it was a lovely evening and I would see him in the morning for brunch. I boarded the bus and returned to the hotel, happy but a little tired and looking forward to a good night's sleep.

I awoke at seven-thirty the next day and, after showering, packed my bag and got dressed, this time casually with comfortable loafers instead of high heels. I checked out at eight forty-five. My luggage was stored until my return at around three in the afternoon. A shuttle bus took us to the hall where the brunch was being held. As before, the cadets were lined up, waiting for their dates. Dave was almost at the front of the line and saw me immediately.

We had a lovely brunch and then proceeded to attend services at the Protestant chapel at ten-thirty. The chapel was a beautiful example of Gothic Revival architecture. Dave mentioned that it had the largest pipe organ in the world. The cadet choir was singing a beautiful hymn when we entered. After the services were over, Dave said it was time to take a tour of Flirtation Walk, a must! He said, "Good, you're wearing comfortable shoes because the pathway is very rocky, sometimes a little steep." Dave mentioned that the walk wasn't very long, actually less than a mile. When we arrived at Flirtation Walk, there was a sign posted saying only cadets and their dates were permitted there. Dave was right. The walkway was, at times, rocky, with just a gravel path. Flirtation Walk runs alongside the Hudson

River shoreline. After walking just a short distance, we approached an area with a cliff where there were huge boulders. One boulder in particular jutted out: the famous "Kissing Rock." There was a custom that in order to continue on the path passing beneath the rock, the cadet and his date must kiss, or else the rock would fall and crush them! Dave laughed and said, "Who are we to break tradition?" and put his arms around me for the first time, soundly kissing me on my lips. It was a sweet, friendly kiss! We laughed and continued walking on the trail. Dave pointed out several monuments dedicated to major battles, like the Mexican War Battle of Santiago, etched into big rocks. I was so glad that I had chosen comfortable shoes! The path, although short, was indeed steep and rocky. We returned to Cullum Hall, where the shuttle bus from the hotel was loading for its return trip. I thanked Dave for a wonderful and memorable time. We said goodbye and promised to keep in touch.

I gathered my belongings at the hotel and boarded the bus to the Greyhound terminal in New York City. The bus was once again filled with girls chatting and comparing notes about their dates. It was clear that everyone had enjoyed themselves and said it ended too soon. When I got home, Hanya and Mama couldn't wait to hear about everything I saw and did. Monday was back to the old routine, returning to work. I met up with my co-worker and mentioned that I had a lovely time at West Point, which came about because he had so kindly given me the ticket to the football game, where I met Frank, who in turn introduced me to Dave. I said that the Hop was really special, formal but great. That date with Dave was the first and only time I went to West Point, and I will always cherish my time there.

One day, when reading the mail at home, I noticed an invitation. My dearest friend Evelyn was marrying her sweetheart Frank. She wanted me to be her maid of honor. Of course, I accepted. Luckily, I didn't need to buy a gown because Evelyn saw and liked the gown I had worn to West Point. It seemed as though a lot of my friends were getting married: Dorothy, Elaine (from high school), Olga, and now Evelyn, to their loves, who were all still in the service. Evelyn looked beautiful in her wedding gown, and Frank was so handsome in his marine uniform. They were married in the Catholic church across the street from her parents' apartment house (a six-story building). Evelyn was lucky because her parents had a one-bedroom apartment available at that time. After my sister's traumatic experience with her mother-in-law, I told myself when the time came, and I got married, I would never live with either set of parents. No way!

Finally, the war in Europe was coming to an end. The Germans were surrendering all over Europe. The war was declared officially over on May 8, 1945, but the conflict still raged on in the Pacific; the Japanese were still a serious menace. When the news came that the war was over in Europe, everyone in the office ecstatically left to join a huge crowd on Lexington Avenue to celebrate. Cars were honking their horns, and people were dancing, hugging, and kissing total strangers. It was a wonderful sight to behold.

Within a couple of weeks, I was told that the regular secretary to my boss had been discharged and was coming back to his old position at Caltex. He was a civil engineer. I would still be employed but would be transferred to the steno pool. I knew when I took this job it was temporary. I did not want to be in the steno pool, having heard many unfavorable comments from some of the girls in it. They did not care for some of the bosses. So, I left Caltex and went back to the unemployment office. This time, I was offered a permanent job at a real estate trustee firm in the Chrysler Building on Lexington Avenue and Forty-second Street, not too far from Caltex, which was also on Lexington Avenue. I was interviewed by a retired judge who was elderly, soft-spoken, and who patiently outlined my position. I was to be secretary to the office manager and my hours would be nine to five, Monday to Friday, normal work hours. The office was a large one with accountants and lawyers, all having their own private secretaries.

Now that the war was over, I was inundated with phone calls for dates from those recently discharged from the service. Papa said he was ready to disconnect the telephone because of all those calls. My friends Lou and Sammy from Norwich called, and I couldn't believe it – they both proposed! They were unemployed but said it didn't matter. We'd go to Norwich where, in time, they would get a job. I had always enjoyed their company and liked them, but not enough to consider marriage! I still corresponded with Dave and Frank, and whenever Frank was in town, we dated. I liked Frank more than anyone else, and he said the feeling was mutual, but I still had reservations about our future. Frank was going to West Point in July and was already placed on the football team roster. Frank was over six feet tall with really broad shoulders and was very handsome. He was affectionate but respectful, and I enjoyed my dates with him.

One day, Bobby (our reverend's son) called, saying he was in town awaiting discharge from the Canadian Army and wanted to see me and have dinner someplace in the Village. I took the subway to West 4th Street and met Bobby. We went to a nightclub where we turned out to be the one-hundredth couple to enter the premises and won a bottle of champagne! Well, we foolishly drank the whole bottle, never had dinner, and poor Bobby became inebriated. We should have had a snack along with the champagne. Fortunately, Bobby lived a short distance away. I hailed a taxi and took Bobby home. He lived with his parents and brothers on the top floor of the building. I watched him weaving up the staircase, but I had to scoot since I didn't want the reverend to see me. I took the subway home. I was a little woozy, but not in the state that Bobby was in. I had a really restless night and was terribly thirsty. In the morning I was awakened by my sister screaming, "Manya, you all right? Look at yourself." I sat up and glanced in the mirror on the wall opposite the bed and could not believe what I saw. I had a green mouth, chin, and neck, and my nightgown was all green in front as well. I knew what happened. In the middle of the night, I craved for a cold glass of water. I reached for the usual glass of water on the night table, but in my haste, I grabbed Hanya's bottle of green ink, which she used to write letters to Nick. Thankfully, I didn't drain the bottle, and there was still some left for her to use. I rushed to take a shower, and boy, it was rough getting the green ink off my face, but I did the best I could so I didn't get off scot-free from overindulging! I wondered how Bobby made out. I didn't see him again. He returned to Canada. I knew he'd write to me when he got back to camp. I learned from that night to be extra careful whenever the occasion arose that champagne was the main drink!

A year ago I had hardly any dates, but now I really needed to be selective. Many of the requests came from those who had corresponded with our church and to whom I had replied. They were all eager to meet me, and although they were friendly and nice, no one thrilled me.

The war in the Pacific finally ended in September 1945. Hallelujah! Hanya was thrilled when Nick was discharged from the Seabees, and as luck would have it, they were able to rent an apartment on the seventh floor of the 1939 Grand Concourse, where

Papa was still the superintendent. Nick went back to being the head hairdresser at Jungst's Beauty Salon in the Madison Hotel on 48th Street and Madison Avenue. Hanya also worked there as a beautician and manicurist. Hairdresser Nick was now known as "Mr.Richard". I was fortunate in that any time I wanted my hair done, I was able to use their services. Whenever there was a beauty convention, Nick would use me to model his hairstyles as I had naturally thick hair, which was great for innovative styles. Nick won many awards for his creativity. I loved being his model, and it actually led to future modeling jobs.

I had a date for almost every night of the week now that the war was over and the boys were home again. I still corresponded with Dave, Frank, Bobby, Lou, Pete, etc. etc.

One evening in December, I received a call from Pete. He was back home and said I was going to be his first date if that was okay. I unhesitatingly accepted. No sooner did I hang up than the phone rang again. It was Frank, who was now a West Point cadet. He invited me to the Downtown Athletic Club, where the Heisman Trophy was being presented to a fellow cadet, Doc Blanchard. Unfortunately, on the same evening, I was meant to see Pete. Doc Blanchard was the West Point Army fullback voted as the nation's Outstanding Player of the Year in 1945. Frank played tackle for the team. I said I was truly sorry that I couldn't go as I had a prior commitment. Frank was crushed. He pleaded to no avail, saying it would be a memorable event.

Although I was fond of Frank (the feeling, according to him, was mutual), I simply could not break my date with Pete. I enjoyed his letters so much that I was eager to see him. The last time we met was back in church when he commented, "I was wet behind the ears;

maybe when she's older." After work, Pete was going to meet me in the lobby at five-thirty. I freshened my makeup after leaving the office and went down to meet him. I saw him standing by the stairwell. He looked different in civilian clothes. My heart was racing. This was really so unusual for me. I blurted out, "Hi." He greeted me warmly and said it was good to see me after corresponding for such a long time. He asked if I liked Chinese food, and I replied that I did. "Good, because we're going to Chinatown for dinner," he said. We took the subway to Canal Street and walked to a restaurant that had been recommended to him. The food was comparable to what he was used to when serving in China. The waiters spoke Mandarin Chinese here instead of Cantonese, which Pete understood and could speak to some extent. The meal was delicious, but I was disappointed that he wasn't as relaxed as I thought he'd be. He asked about my work and my family, but when it came to him, he offered very little.

We left the restaurant and walked to the subway that went to the Bronx. On the ride home he apologized for being a bit withdrawn but said it was strange being home and seeing all the changes around him and the fact that he, like a lot of his friends, was unemployed and needed to find a job. He said he had received an invitation to have dinner at his best friend's home and asked me to go with him tomorrow. Joe and his wife Vera lived in Bayside, Queens. Joe was his best buddy, both having worked as house wreckers before the war demolishing the 1939 New York World's Fair exhibits. Although this first date with Pete was disappointing, I   accepted the dinner invitation. When we got home, it was still early so I invited him in to say hello to my folks, hoping Hanya would be there as well. Mama offered him some apple pie she had baked and coffee. After small talk, Pete said he'd see me Saturday at around five. I walked him to the door, and he casually kissed me goodnight. I was confused, to say

35

the least. My first date with Pete was a blah! But then he did say he needed to get used to being home. I decided I would have one more date with him, and if I did not enjoy his company, that would be it! I asked myself if I had made a mistake by going out with him instead of Frank. Well, Saturday would answer that question.

The following day, the newspapers were filled with admiration for Doc Blanchard and how worthy he was of winning the Heisman Trophy. I guess I missed a historical sports moment by going out with Pete. Oh well! Saturday, Pete picked me up at five at my house. Joe had told him to go to Bayside, Queens, by trolley. The trolley was just around the corner from my house on Tremont Avenue. We boarded the trolley and took it to its last stop by the Whitestone Bridge. From there, we took a bus over the bridge right into Bayside. I enjoyed the trolley rides more than the subway because we were able to do some sightseeing. We got off at the bus stop two blocks from their home. Passing a florist, I said that I wanted to get a bouquet of flowers. Pete thought it was a good suggestion. He had bought a bottle of champagne as a gift for them. Joe and his wife Vera greeted us cordially, and I sensed a true comradery for Pete. Vera was truly a natural beauty. She had dark, natural, wavy hair, a flawless complexion, rosy cheeks, and gorgeous sparkling blue eyes. She wore no makeup, being a real stunner. Before we had dinner and drinks, Vera fed their baby, Rodney, who was less than a year old, and put him in his cradle, after which we would have the evening all to ourselves.

We had a delightful dinner. The evening was filled with reminiscing about the good times they had with Pete before the War. Pete was in the Air Force and was shipped to California and then on to China (assigned to the Flying Tigers-General Chenault), whereas

Joe had been assigned to Europe. This was the first post-war get-together for them. Pete was so animated and full of jokes. We were all so relaxed I felt like I knew them forever. Time passed so quickly. We received a standing invitation to visit them at least once a month. We agreed and said it was our pleasure to accept. We left and walked to the bus stop and once again crossed the Whitestone Bridge, where we would take the trolley. On the trolley, I told Pete that I really liked his friends. I was glad that Pete was now more like the Pete I corresponded with: cordial, humorous, and totally relaxed. He had his arm around me, and I felt so comfortable being with him. It felt natural. We got off at our trolley stop and walked to my house but because it was after midnight, I could not invite him in as I had done the last time. Before we arrived at my door, we passed through an area where the incinerator was located. Our apartment was a step down from there. This was where Pete embraced and kissed me. This time, the kiss was not casual. It had a sensual feel to it, and my heart started racing. I felt a tingling down to my toes when we kissed, never having experienced this with Frank or any of my other beaus. I thought this meant that Pete was the one for me. We said goodnight and I entered my apartment and closed the door, flushed and giddy with truly happy feelings for Pete.

The next morning at breakfast, Mama scolded me for coming in so late. I told her about Vera and Joe and that I had a feeling I would marry Pete. She yelled at me, "What did he do to you?" I answered, "Nothing, he doesn't even know how I feel." My Mother was upset because she really liked Frank and said, "What has Pete to offer you? Nothing, no job. Frank is an engineer. Think about it."

I laughed. Just because I felt this way didn't mean that Pete felt the same way; only time would tell. I told Mama that we had so much in common, more so than any other person I dated. He was of Ukrainian descent, enjoyed the same foods, loved to dance (especially the polka), had a great sense of humor etc., etc.

During the following weeks, Pete was busy attending Delahanty Institute, studying for a civil service job that offered a steady income and future pension, good-paying jobs. Pete did not want to go back to house wrecking even though his father urged him to do so. He took two civil service tests, one for the Sanitation Department, for which over 300 applicants applied. He was in the first 100 and was hired almost immediately. The second exam was with the New York City Police Department, which he really wanted, but unfortunately, they were not hiring at the time so he accepted the sanitation job for the time being. At least he was employed.

Chapter Six:
Love And Marriage

Though we spoke on the phone regularly, I did not see Pete for a while. A friend of his was in town, so he was busy. The friend turned out to be a WAC (Women's Army Corps-just discharged) he had dated on numerous occasions. She was very attractive and apparently had feelings for Pete. I was jealous, to say the least, because even though I dated others, no one appealed to me like Pete. I truly missed him.

Sometime in mid-April, I received an evening call from my girlfriend, Anne, Andy's sister, who invited me to a welcome home party for her brother Nick. She said it was going to be a bang-up celebration to be held in their home in Newburgh. Her parents owned a bar and grill next door to their home, so the drinks and food would be plentiful. I asked who else was invited. She mentioned the group I knew from the Ukrainian Social Club. I asked if Pete was invited, and she said of course. He was coming up with the other guys. The party would be on Saturday, and anyone who wanted to could stay overnight rather than drive or take the bus back on Saturday evening. I accepted because I knew Nick and her brother Andy, who was also one of my steady dates. Andy was in the merchant marines and, unfortunately, would not join in the festivities because he was out of the country. That Saturday morning, I took the bus up to Newburgh, and it brought back memories of me going up to West Point last February as Dave's guest.

I wasn't in contact with Dave as much as in the past because his girlfriend from California moved to a new job in New York City and was, therefore, more involved with Dave. Our friendship was purely platonic. I was much closer to Frank, but now Pete was on my mind, and I felt a longing to be with him. Strange, since I really only had two dates with him, although we did speak on the phone quite frequently.

I took a cab to Anne's house and was surprised to see a number of cars already there. It was late afternoon when I arrived. I walked in and was greeted with cheers. It was a nice welcome. Anne told everyone to go next door to the bar, where we would have food and refreshments. I recognized a lot of the girls and guys who were there and felt comfortable. The juke-box was blaring away, and several couples were dancing. The bar was loaded with food on one side, and on the other side were the drinks (mostly alcoholic), but there were some sodas as well.

Red, a fellow I danced with many times at the Ukrainian Social Club, grabbed my hand and said, "What are you drinking?"

I responded, "Rum and Coke."

Okay, let's join the gang at the end of the bar."

A group was gathered at the end of the bar, and in their midst, I saw Pete. He was holding a drink, and when he saw me, he raised his glass like a toast. I joined the group, and Pete immediately came over to me and said, "Nice to see you again. I missed you."

Red came up and said, "Let's dance."

In the middle of the dance, Pete cut in. It was funny because Wally cut in shortly thereafter. Everyone was having a good time, drinking, eating, dancing, chatting, and, of course, getting a bit woozy. Anne told everyone to go back to the house since the bar closed, but there would still be drinks, etc., to be had inside. The house was spacious, with the living room and dining room adjoined, making it one huge room. The dining table was laden with cookies, tarts, and two huge coffee percolators, as well as ice, soda, vodka, gin, and rum. As a joke, someone suggested playing Spin the Bottle. The girls were in one group and the guys in another. We were like teenagers again.

At one point, Pete approached me and said he wanted to talk to me alone, so we walked outside to the porch. He was flushed and appeared nervous. He said, "I wanted to be alone with you because I have something to ask you, that is, will you marry me?"

I couldn't believe what I was hearing, and that he had proposed to me. I practically threw myself on him and said, "Pete, this is a dream come true because I have been in love with you ever since we went to Joe and Vera's house. Yes, I will marry you." We kissed, and again, I felt the tingle down to my toes. It was amazing!

Pete said, "Don't tell anyone inside, not until we get home." I walked into the kitchen where Anne and a few of my girlfriends were and told them confidentially that Pete had proposed, and I accepted. They were all thrilled and excited for me, especially since I had expressed my true feelings and opened my heart to him.

We returned to the living room and after we all had coffee, I guess Pete sobered up. He beckoned me to go to the porch again. I went with only happy thoughts, imagining that he was going to whisper sweet, loving words to me. He took my hands and, looking rather sheepishly, said, "I hope you didn't take me seriously. It was the booze that got to me. I do care for you, but I'm not ready for marriage. I'm sorry." And with that, he dropped my hands and walked back inside to join the others. My head was reeling, and I couldn't comprehend what had just happened. I told him I was in love with him; my God, what a fool I was! No one had ever made me feel the way he did. It had to be love. I was crushed! I went inside and sat on the floor next to Red, who was sitting in a chair, and when I reached up to ask him something, he jumped up and the heel of his shoe banged into the side of my head. He had been nodding off, and I startled him. Not only did I have a broken heart, but to make matters worse, I now had a black eye as well! Anne gave me an ice pack, and I went upstairs to her bedroom, where there were twin beds. I said I was retiring for the night. Meanwhile, Pete was leaving with several of the guys he drove up with. We did not even say goodnight. Some of the guests chose to stay overnight, as I did. A few of them lived locally.

I had a restless night, as one can imagine. I still could not face the fact that he had proposed and then rescinded the proposal. He must be gloating, especially as I had opened my heart to him. In the morning while having breakfast, the girls were still chatting about me and Pete. I was too embarrassed to tell them what actually transpired after the proposal. It's a good thing that I had long hair. I swept it up in a "Veronica Lake" style so that it concealed my black eye pretty well, along with some heavy makeup. Anne drove me to the bus terminal, and I boarded the bus back to New York. I felt dumb, numb, stupid, you name it, but somehow, it did not quell my feelings for Pete, although I felt it would take some time to get over him.

On Monday, I went back to work and told the girls that if Pete called to speak to me, I would be taking dictation or out of the office. I also told my parents that I was through with Pete and that I would no longer take his phone calls. They were perplexed but thrilled that my romance with him was over and done with.

One evening, about two weeks or so later, when I got home, my mother said that Pete's stepmother had called and asked what was going on. Pete had begged her to call Mama and ask her to please have me speak with him. I told Mama that I didn't want to answer his calls. One afternoon at the office, I forgot my resolution and picked up the phone. It was Pete. He begged me not to hang up and pleaded with me to meet him after work at Bryant Park on Sixth Avenue and Forty-Second Street. I reluctantly agreed, walked to Bryant Park, a short distance from work, and saw Pete sitting on a bench. I approached him and asked him what he wanted because he had effectively said it all back in Newburgh.

He said, "Damn it, I can't get you out of my mind. I can't sleep or eat. I see a girl walking down the street, and she looks like you. I call your name but it's not you. I've never felt this way before so it must prove that I am in love with you. I do want to marry you. Please forgive me for having been such a complete idiot before. I didn't realize how much I cared for you until you brushed me off."

I asked, "What about June, the WAC you spent so much time with?"

"June? Do you know that all the time I was with her, I thought about you and only you? She meant and means nothing to me. I took her sightseeing with her friends. You've no idea how much I looked forward to your letters after almost two years of correspondence. I loved the way you wrote; funny, serious at times, but most of all, down to earth. I knew you were special, and I could hardly wait . to see you again. You haven't disappointed me. With your vivaciousness, your fun-loving ways, the way you smile and giggle, and most of all, your natural warmth. No one can compare to you. I'd be the luckiest guy if someone as beautiful as you would even consider me for marriage. I love you, honestly.

I love you. Please believe me when I say I love you. You said you loved me too. I'm begging you.

Please say you'll marry me. Look, I'm down on my knees, say YES!"

My head was spinning, and I was crying and laughing at the same time. This is what I had dreamed of. I replied, "I do love you, and yes, I will marry you." We embraced, and I guess everyone passing by thought we were weird, but I couldn't have cared less. I was ecstatic with joy. Pete said he didn't have an engagement ring yet but that he would get one. "Our minister knows a jeweler I can go to, and I will," Pete suggested we go to his home to tell his parents the good news and discuss plans for our marriage.

We went to his home and found both parents there. His father was truly happy for us, but his stepmother, while congratulating us, was not visibly thrilled. Nevertheless, we had a nice dinner and a toast to our future. We went into the living room, where Pete and I discussed setting a date for our marriage. I felt we were rushing things, but Pete said, "The sooner, the better. How about a honeymoon in June? Wouldn't that be great?"

I told him I needed to talk to my parents. I knew they would be shocked, but I didn't tell Pete. We left after a while. Pete walked me to the subway, which I took to go home. On the subway, I closed my eyes. I was still in a state of shock and couldn't get over what had just occurred. I felt like I was walking on air.

When I got home, I rushed into the house and saw Mama and Papa in the kitchen. I breathlessly said, "I've got some wonderful news for you. I'm getting married."

Their jaws dropped, and Mama asked, "Who are you going to marry?"

I answered, "Pete."

"Pete?" she yelled, "Have you lost your mind? I would understand if you said Frank or even Andy, but definitely not Pete. My God, do you know last week, when I was walking down Saint Mark's Place to visit a sick parishioner, I saw Pete. He was lifting a garbage can into the back of a garbage truck. This is who you want to marry, a garbage man?" She started crying. "I dreamed you would marry Frank and have a wedding at West Point at the Protestant chapel and you would walk under the swords, a real fairy tale wedding."

Papa said, "What can we do to make you change your mind? A trip to Europe? Tell me."

I couldn't believe what I was hearing. I thought they'd be glad for me! I told them I was positive about my feelings for Pete, and whether they liked it or not, I was going full steam ahead with plans for a wedding in June.

Papa said, "We will not pay for a reception. You're on your own."

I was aghast when I heard this, especially since Mama nodded in total agreement. I ran into my bedroom, slammed the door, threw myself onto the bed, and buried my face in a pillow to mask my sobbing. I was so hurt. How would Pete feel when I told him my parents wouldn't give me a reception? We had selected Saturday, June 1 for our wedding day. Our minister would perform the ceremony at three in the afternoon. The following day, Pete met me after work, and we went to a local restaurant for dinner to discuss our forthcoming marriage. He surprised me with an engagement ring. It was very nice, a one-carat diamond center stone with two side stones set in platinum. He put the ring on my finger and said, "The next ring will be a wedding band."

I told him that my parents weren't pleased about my acceptance of his proposal and wouldn't even give me a reception. We were on our own, as the saying goes.

Pete smiled and said, "Don't worry about it. My parents have already planned to give us a reception at their church on Fourteenth Street. That is if it's okay with you because they have a lot of friends they want to invite and didn't think it would be fair for your parents to pay."

I was taken aback by their reactions and told Pete I truly appreciated their generosity and kindness and asked him to thank them for me. This was in late April, and there was still much to be done. June was just around the corner.

I would not be getting married in a wedding gown, but I still needed an outfit befitting a wedding. I told Evelyn, my best friend, that I would like her to be my maid of honor. Pete said he had already asked Joe to be his best man and that Joe accepted and was happy for us. I truly was on my own.

Even my sister sided with my parents. Though she liked Pete, she thought I was rushing into marriage much too soon and felt I ought to get to know him better to be sure. I reminded her that we had corresponded for over two years and really came to know each other's thoughts. When we finally met, it was as if we had been friends forever.

I went to Lord & Taylor and picked out a beige suit, which I felt complimented my figure, and a woven straw hat. This would be my wedding outfit. I was hurt and disappointed that no one came to help me pick out my outfit, especially my sister, who was such a snazzy dresser. At home, there was now a cold silence. We barely spoke, but I did get a few names of people Mom felt should be invited. The list amounted to only ten names. Olga's family from Norwich and a family friend from Mystic, Connecticut, and that was it! Evelyn was thrilled for me and accepted the offer of being my maid of honor.

Because Pete's parents were paying for the reception, I did not add them to our guest list. Pete was busy making arrangements for our honeymoon, which he did not reveal to me because he wanted to surprise me. My head was spinning. There was so much to do. Where were we going to live? Certainly not with either set of parents. That was for sure, not after my sister's experience with her "monster-in-law." Mama finally accepted the fact that I was getting married and once again became her sweet self. She was making me a bridal lingerie set of beautiful silk taffeta with lace and a sheer robe. She was always creative when it came to sewing.

The days seemed to fly by, and suddenly, it was my wedding day, June 1, 1946. Our reverend from the Ukrainian Protestant Church was to perform the nuptials at three o'clock. The services were being held at the Middle Collegiate Church on Second Avenue between Sixth and Seventh Streets.

Pete's sister, Anne, was going to sing the song "Because". She had a marvelous voice and often sang with the Goldman Band, which

47

held summer concerts on Saturdays in Central Park. After the ceremony, we would go to the Ukrainian Orthodox Church of Saint. Volodymyr on Fourteenth Street between First and Second Avenues for the reception. Pete's parents had also arranged for a quartet to play.

Chapter Seven:
The Wedding

The morning of June 1st was beautiful with bright sunshine, although the forecast predicted rain later in the day. I had set out my outfit the night before, and my suitcase was packed and ready to go. The doorbell rang. It was a florist with my wedding corsage and two corsages for Hanya and Mama. The wedding corsage had two beautiful white orchids to be pinned onto my suit.

The doorbell rang again, and I couldn't believe my eyes; it was Lou from Norwich, still in his marine uniform. He was holding a huge bouquet of roses, and he lunged forward to embrace me. I stepped back to evade the hug and said, "What are you doing here?"

He said he had been discharged from the Marines, and the first thing he wanted to do was to see me again and convince me to marry him. I was taken aback because this was his second proposal, and I had already refused him once before. I blurted out, "I'm getting married this afternoon to Pete" (whom he did not know).

Lou stepped into the living room and sat on the couch with his face buried in his hands. Weeping, he said, "I waited too long to tell you about my feelings. I thought you cared for me." I told him that I was fond of him and would always cherish our friendship over the years, but that was it. Lou and I had been friends since early childhood, meeting in the summer at Olga's house in Norwich. I told him I needed to get ready to go to the church.

Hanya walked in and consoled Lou. I went back to the bedroom and heard Hanya saying goodbye. I knew Lou had left. My head was spinning. What a way to begin the day!

Nick came in and took my suitcase to the trunk of his car. He said it was time to leave. Mama, Papa, Hanya, and I headed for the church. I sat in the back seat with Mama and Papa, closed my eyes, and tried to relax. I was still in a state of shock over Lou. I had never led him on. I guess Coleen's friends had a lot to do with my insecurity. I kept my dates more-or-less at arm's length, which they respected. We had our kissing sessions, but that was it. I was chaste, and that was the way I'd stay until my wedding day!

Traffic was light, and we arrived at the church rather early, at around two fifteen. I was pleasantly surprised to see so many guests already seated in the pews. Most of them were on the right side, friends of the Zaharkos, whereas on the left side, there were only Olga's family and a few friends who had been invited by my parents. Evelyn and her husband were seated in the first pew alongside Joe and Vera. Pete's parents and sister were on the opposite side, conversing with friends. There was no sign of Pete, but it was still early. The organist came over to discuss his selections and spoke to Pete's sister, Anne, who was going to be the soloist. It was getting close to three o'clock, and there was no sign of Pete!

I went to the rear of the church and stood in the vestibule with my father as he was going to walk me down the aisle. The organist started to play some music. The reverend walked up to the altar, and we waited. No, Pete! We waited and waited some more. Still no Pete! It was three fifteen, and people were buzzing and looking about. My heart started pounding. I was bewildered. Was Pete having second thoughts? I recalled his retracting his original proposal in Newburgh.

Was it happening again? When I glanced at some of the guests, they looked at me, covered their mouths, and whispered to the person next to them. To make matters worse and add to my discomfort, I was astonished to see Lou seated in a back pew engaged in conversation with Olga and her husband, Earle. It was almost three thirty, and my mother was shaking her head as if to say, "I told you not to jump into marrying Pete."

Pete's father walked over to Joe and asked him to go to the apartment to check on Pete. Why the delay? Their apartment was on Saint Mark's Place, only two blocks away.

Suddenly, Pete came in through the side door by the altar, all smiles, and started conversing with the reverend and apologized for being late. I noticed Pete was wearing a blazer instead of the new suit he had bought. Thank heavens he showed up, much to the chagrin of my parents. The organist played the Wedding March, and Papa took my arm and led me down the aisle to the altar.

Papa was crying, Mama was crying, Hanya was crying, and Lou was crying (not tears of joy, to be sure). I tried to hold back my tears, but unfortunately, they ran down my cheeks anyway.

The reverend took our hands, and we said the vows. Then we were finally pronounced man and wife. Pete had placed the wedding ring on my finger and kissed me lovingly. Anne, Pete's sister, sang the beautiful song "Because" as we walked up the aisle as man and wife. The photographer was snapping photos of us. As we approached the entrance to the church, I noticed that Lou had left, and I breathed a sigh of relief. The guests formed a line on either side of the entrance, and as we walked to our limo, they threw rice, confetti, and flowers at us.

We entered the limo with Evelyn, her husband Frank, Joe, and Vera and headed to our reception at the Fourteenth Street church. I asked Pete why he was late for our wedding, and to our amusement, he said, "I was on time, but when I stepped off the curb on Second Avenue and Saint Mark's Place, I stepped into a huge pile of horseshit which went not only onto my shoe but also my trouser leg! I couldn't go to our wedding smelling of horseshit! I had to go back to the apartment to change. I took out another pair of shoes from the suitcase and another pair of trousers and my blazer, as well."

We were all hysterical with laughter. Joe said, "You know, that's a sign of good luck."

When we arrived at the church, the photographer, Roman, the reverend's son, took us aside so that photos could be taken, which was perfect because we still needed to wait for all the guests to arrive. The quartet was setting up their instruments on the stage. It looked like it was going to be a fun-filled evening and that a good time would be had by all. The caterer did a great job setting up the main table and buffet tables. He arranged the tables in a "U" shape, adorned with beautiful floral arrangements. The buffet consisted of turkey, huge roast pork, kielbasa, stuffed cabbage, broiled sauerkraut, peraheh (pierogies), and roasted vegetables. On a separate table, there was a three-tier wedding cake with the usual bride and groom atop, coffee urns, and another samovar for tea. There was a bar setup with a bartender. I noticed that vodka bottles were already placed on several tables. I was taken aback by Pete's parents putting this all together. As predicted, it started to rain. When all the guests were seated, we took our place at the head table. The reverend said a prayer and then toasts were raised on our behalf. The quartet played polkas and other

Ukrainian dance music. Everyone was having a fine time. The old-timers raised their glasses and sang Ukrainian songs.

Pete was a great dancer. He loved to waltz and dance the polka. At one point, he thought it was time to leave because we had already cut the cake, and everyone had given us their good wishes, along with many wedding gift envelopes. It was close to eleven o'clock when Pete asked Nick for my suitcase to put into the limo still parked outside. When Nick returned I blew a kiss to my parents and left to enter the limo.

Pete held the door to the limo open, and I climbed in. He sat down after me, and the limo driver asked, "Where to?"

Pete replied, "The Saint Mark's Hotel, the best hotel on the Bowery."

The driver looked shocked and said, "Saint Mark's Hotel? That's a Bowery flop house. Are you sure?"

Pete laughed and said, "I'm only kidding! The Waldorf-Astoria, please."

I should have known better, the prankster that Pete is. The rain was coming down heavily, but I couldn't have cared less because I was with my sweetheart and we were going to the Waldorf-Astoria. When the limo pulled up to the hotel, Pete tipped the driver because he had hired the limo from four o'clock to midnight. A bellhop came out to take our suitcases. Pete looked at me, smiled, and said, "Take your corsage off. We don't want to broadcast that we're newly-weds when we check in." I took my corsage off but noticed that Pete had forgotten to remove the white carnation on his lapel as he walked up to the registration desk. The clerk had a smile on his face and inquired whether we were newly-weds. Pete glanced down and laughed, removed his carnation, and said, "Yes."

The clerk said the room originally reserved for us was not vacated due to the rain, so compliments of the management, we would be given a bridal suite. We were thrilled to hear this and followed the bellhop who carried our luggage to our unexpected gift, the bridal suite.

The bridal suite was beautiful, a living room and a spacious bedroom with a bathroom. Pete tipped the bellhop and carried our luggage into the bedroom. I asked Pete for a cigarette saying I was nervous and it would calm me. Unbeknownst to Pete, earlier, I had taken a pack of Chesterfield cigarettes from his blazer. My sister told me to do this in order to have him leave the room and buy another pack so that I could slip into my bridal negligee and surprise him when he came back.

Pete said he understood and said he'd join me and have a cigarette as well. He stuck his hand into his jacket pocket and said, "I don't understand. I thought I had a full pack. Oh well, I'll go down to the lobby and get the Sunday newspapers as well." He had barely left the room when I went to the bedroom and quickly snatched off my jacket, blouse, and skirt, now wearing only my bra and girdle. I placed my suitcase on the bed and opened it to get out of my bridal outfit when all of a sudden, the main door opened, and there stood the bellhop holding two suitcases, followed by a young man and woman and Pete, all looking at me stunned with their jaws agape! I picked my jacket up to cover myself and dove into the open closet!

I was mortified. How could this happen? Pete approached me, shaking his head in disbelief. He told me the room clerk had given us the wrong bridal suite. The one we were in had been reserved for the young couple I saw. I got dressed again and sheepishly followed Pete out of the suite. The bellhop said we were going down the hall to another bridal suite. As we walked down the hallway, he was humming the tune-"Hot time in the Town of Berlin." We stopped in front of two huge black doors with gold rings, and he said, "This is it, the Oriental Bridal Suite."

How ironic, Pete had spent so much time in China and now the Oriental Suite! I believe this truly beautiful suite led me to appreciate and love anything Oriental still to this day. Pete looked at me and mischievously said, "I'm going to the lobby. I'll be back soon with the Sunday papers and the Chesterfields."

I went into the bedroom and sat on the bed, shaking my head at the three flukey things that had happened that day. Surely, things would be normal from now on. First, Lou showed up not only at my parents' house but he even came to the church. Second, Pete was late for our wedding due to a mishap. Third, last, but most comical, getting the wrong bridal suite and getting caught in my undergarments-how funny is that? I undressed again and put on the beautiful outfit Mama had made for me. I brushed my hair, sprayed on a little perfume, and waited for Pete to return.

I heard him open the outer door as he conversed with someone, and my heart skipped a beat. Not another mistake! No, he was with a waiter who was carrying a tray that held an ice bucket with a bottle of champagne, two glasses, and caviar canapes. Pete, true to his word, was also carrying the Sunday papers. He tipped the waiter, and when I heard the door close, I opened the bedroom door and stood in the middle of the entryway. Pete's eyes widened. He sucked in his breath and said, "My God, you take my breath away. You're so beautiful.

You look like a movie star. I can't believe how lucky I am that you're my wife!"

With that said, we had a cigarette, drank champagne, and read the Sunday papers. And if you believe that's all that happened, then you must believe the earth is flat! All I can say is that, at last, my lonely days were over, as the song goes. Pete was so caring, gentle, and loving. He could not get over the fact that I was a virgin, especially since I'd had oodles of boyfriends.

After two wondrously illuminating days at the Waldorf-Astoria, it was time to check out. We were meant to take a train from Grand Central Station to Buffalo at noon where we would then travel to Niagara Falls. The train for Buffalo was delayed for quite some time, and when we boarded, we were told we might not be able to connect to the train for Niagara Falls as the last train leaves Buffalo at seven thirty p.m. If we missed the connection, the next train would be the following morning at eight o'clock according to schedule.

We finally arrived in Buffalo, and of course, having been delayed, we missed the last train to Niagara Falls and would have to spend the night in Buffalo. I called umpteen hotels but could not book a room because this was June, after all, and honeymooners were all over town. A sympathetic station master told us he knew of a place we could go to for an overnight stay. It was nothing fancy, a rooming house just on the other side of the terminal. Pete and I agreed to go since it was convenient and just overnight. We gathered our belongings and followed the station master across railroad tracks to the other side. It was dark. I was tripping over the rails with my high heels, but finally, we arrived at a dark wood-framed house with a porch. In the entryway there hung a light bulb with no cover, just an exposed bulb. The station master rang the doorbell, and a tough-

56

looking woman with a cigarette in her mouth opened the door. He said, "This is the couple I spoke to you about. The room is only for one night."

The woman grabbed Pete's arm and said, "Okay!" and as I stepped forward, she practically yelled, "Not you, no women allowed!" and slammed the door. I couldn't believe it! Pete was inside, and I was standing there.

Fortunately, he opened the door and said, "Looks like we're headed back to the bench in the terminal." We walked back across the railroad tracks to get to the terminal. The station master apologized saying he had only wanted to help. I thanked him for his kindness and happily sat on the bench. I did not sleep a wink while Pete curled up and snored away as though he were in a comfortable bed. We had breakfast in the terminal and thankfully boarded the train at seven thirty the next morning.

Fortunately, when we arrived in Niagara Falls, the hotel where we had booked our stay was within walking distance of the terminal. We were concerned that the room might have been released because we failed to appear last night, but thank heavens, it was still available. Truthfully, I couldn't have cared less about seeing the falls by that time. I sorely needed some shut-eye, having been up all night. I was cranky, but Pete lovingly comforted me and tucked me in bed to take a nap while he, having slept quite well, was going to check on our reservations for seeing the falls sometime that afternoon. Pete made all sorts of reservations before coming back to make sure we had time to go sightseeing not only on the American side of the Falls but on the Canadian side as well.

I slept soundly for several hours and awoke refreshed to hear Pete entering our room. He said, "Good, you're up because I brought lunch, hamburgers, and shakes, and then we'll head out to the boat Maid of the Mist, okay?"

The nap really energized me, and I was ready for our day of sightseeing. I recall taking the elevator down to the lower level and walking through a tunnel to the boat. Before boarding, we were handed ponchos with hoods and sandals and were told to prepare ourselves for a "wet" but great ride. The trip lasted approximately half an hour, and it was really fun. We headed to the base of the falls, where there was such a mist you could barely see. The water was a pretty blue-green. As we circled back to the dock a magnificent rainbow appeared. When we docked, we walked up to the Crow's Nest and again were given sandals and another poncho. We stood on the platform at the base of Bridal Falls called the Crow's Nest. We had been forewarned about getting "wet," and we indeed got soaked, but it was worth it. I could not get over the crowd of tourists-mainly honeymooners! We did some sight-seeing and finally returned to the hotel. The following day we took a tour bus to Toronto just for the day and had a terrific Chinese meal in the Chinatown district.

We returned to our hotel to check out as we were heading to our last honeymoon destination, Camp Sanita, just outside of Pawling, New York, for five days before returning to New York City. A summer camp nestled in the woods by Whaley Lake. Camp Sanita was the vacation resort for NYC sanitation workers. A summer camp nestled in the woods by Whaley Lake. Subway/trolley cars were converted into what they called Pullmanetts, complete with two bedrooms, a kitchenette, a bathroom, and a living area. We took the train again, and there was a shuttle bus to the station to take people to

Sanita Hills, where the camp was located. When we arrived at the main office to register, we were handed a key and a map indicating our site. We were absolutely thrilled when we saw our place and the layout. It was adorable, to say the least, overlooking the lake and separated from other Pullmanetts scattered about. Pete said he had to do something he meant to do before but didn't which was to pick me up and carry me over the threshold! I must say the time we spent there was and still is one of my favorite times. We were so happy, making our meals together and fishing. There was no swimming because it was too cold, but we didn't care.

Unfortunately, all good times come to an end. We soon returned to New York City and our jobs. Pete had made reservations at a residence hotel on Madison Avenue, where we would be staying until we found an apartment. The hotel was clean, and we had a suite, which included a living room, a bedroom, and a small kitchenette. Pete went back to work on Monday. He took the four p.m. to twelve a.m. shift, whereas I had the usual nine-to-five schedule. For the first week, I was on my own until he came home after midnight. One night, I was aware of a lot of activity in the hallway, so I peeked through my slightly opened door and saw a young woman in a sheer negligee, wearing a bra and panties, taking money from a man. I closed the door, realizing the hotel was more than a residence. It was a hotel for working girls as well! I couldn't wait to tell Pete and to get the hell out of there. Pete agreed. This was only a temporary place for us and if I was so upset, we could stay at his parents' apartment, but I immediately dismissed that. We needed to be on our own. To add insult to injury, the following day, when I was returning from work, I had just about closed the door when there was a knock. I opened the door, and a man, smiling, said, "Are you available?" I slammed the door. Enough was enough. It was time to take action. I went to my parents that evening and asked if any apartments were available. They told me that housing was tight and that there was nothing. I received a similar reply when I asked at my office, which was, after all, a real estate holding company with many properties throughout the city.

Mama then told me she had an idea. Perhaps we could share an apartment with an elderly widower who had a large apartment just three blocks away. He was Ukrainian and had a dog named Lucy. I remembered him visiting Mama and Papa a couple of times, so I was no stranger to him. I said I would love to see his apartment and decide whether it would be practical for us. Mama said she would contact him and have me come up. Well, it didn't take long for Mama to get things moving. Within two days, she called. I eagerly went with Mama to Mr. Solly's apartment. The building was on Creston Avenue, a six-story building with only five apartments per floor. He lived on the sixth floor. When we rang the doorbell, Mr. Solly greeted us cordially and invited us in to take a look around. He said that he had been waiting for a smaller apartment to become available because he had no need for two bedrooms. The apartment had an ample-sized bedroom to the right, which was Mr. Solly's, then a bathroom and a hallway with a large closet leading to a kitchen with a sit-in eating area and a table with four chairs. After this came a good-sized living room with French doors leading to the larger second bedroom. The living room furniture and bed were covered with sheets. I couldn't get over how clean and tidy the apartment was. I told Mama that it was ideal and that I really wanted to live there. I told Mr. Solly that we would pay the rent for the apartment and the utilities (including a telephone, which I would have installed) and that he would even be able to have meals with us. He clapped his hands to his face and said this was a godsend since he was struggling financially, being on a small pension and social security. We shook hands and he hugged and kissed me and said he welcomed us and promised not to be a busybody. He asked when we would move in, and I told him it would be that weekend. Mom agreed that the apartment would be ideal.

That night, I told Pete about it, and we packed our belongings and moved in that Saturday. We had a lot of work to do, thoroughly cleaning the entire place. Pete scrubbed the bathroom and I did the kitchen. We took the bed sheets off and were amazed to find a beautiful sofa and lounge chairs in perfect condition and our room as well. There was a radio/phonograph in the living room. I bought shades for the French doors, new curtains for the windows and new bedding. The place was perfect. What more could we ask for? The apartment was conveniently located near the IRT subway, which was just three blocks away on Jerome Avenue. The D-train was located on the Grand Concourse and Tremont Avenue is just four blocks away. I must say we had a little adjusting to do since we were sharing an apartment, but it really worked out well.

During our time there, Mr. Solly became a new man. He was able to go to the barber for a haircut, have his clothes dry cleaned, and most of all, he no longer needed to worry about paying bills. He gained weight because he was eating good food with us regularly. We bathed Lucy and combed out her tangles, brushed her, and found that she was so beautiful she would have won first prize at a dog show. Lucy, who always slept on the threshold of Mr. Solly's bedroom, now took it upon herself to sleep in the hallway, protecting us as well. Lucy was a very sweet, intelligent golden retriever, very loyal to Mr. Solly.

During this same period, Pete attended Delehanty Institute to prepare himself for the upcoming NYPD exam. Suddenly, there was a critical shortage of policemen, and an early appointment was most likely. Pete took the exam plus the strenuous physical and passed both

61

with flying colors. He was appointed to the force in December 1947. I was so happy for him because Mama could no longer call him a garbage man!

One evening, while riding the subway home, I saw a familiar face, that of an old favorite school chum, Dorothy. I noticed she was clutching a couple of ledgers and asked whether she was going to college and what she was studying. She told me that she was going to (of all places) Delehanty Institute, where she would shortly take the NYPD policewoman's exam. I was floored, telling her that Pete had also attended there and was now a policeman stationed at the 40th Precinct in the East Bronx. I said I was interested in taking the exam as well. Dorothy said I had better hurry and get my application in before the expiration date in no less than two weeks. She said she would give me her notes from class to study and that Pete could also brief me because he had books and study materials, as well. I laughed and told her it was fate that I saw her on the subway that day and that I would definitely apply. Wouldn't it be something if we both made it? During lunch hour, I went down to the Civil Service Bureau and got my application, which Pete helped me fill out that very evening. I mailed it by Certified Mail the very next morning. Dorothy told me I also needed to prepare to take a physical exam, which included weight lifting, running, and jumping. This would be no problem because Pete was so athletic. He would be my teacher. I took the written exam within two weeks of filing and waited to learn the results.

I was notified that I had passed the written exam. The physical exam was next on the agenda, but I had one problem: I was pregnant, which would have automatically disqualified me. I was in my second month and looked normal, not at all pregnant, so I proceeded to prepare myself, lifting weights and jumping rope in Mama's back yard. Everything seemed to be happening at the same time. I was notified by my employer that an apartment was available in the Pelham Bay section of the Bronx, a one-bedroom overlooking a schoolyard on Morrison Avenue. We were delighted but poor Mr. Solly broke down when we told him we were going to move. He said we were like family to him. He always spoke in Ukrainian to us, and I actually learned to speak and understand Ukrainian better because of him. Even though my parents spoke to one another in Ukrainian, they always spoke English to me.

We moved and found the apartment suitable, on the fifth floor of a walk-up with only four apartments per floor. This was really the first time we truly had a place of our own. It was convenient to go to work because the IRT elevated subway station was right on the corner of Westchester Avenue. Thank goodness the medical and physical exams were scheduled almost immediately after the results of the written exams were published in the Civil Service newspaper. I ranked 130 out of 350 accepted applicants. I received instructions to prepare for the upcoming physical: pull-over shirt, shorts and sneakers. The exam was to be held at the Police Academy in Lower Manhattan, on Leonard Street. I was confident that I would pass all the exams with flying colors like Pete, thanks to his help.

When I arrived at the Academy, we were placed in groups of ten alphabetically. I was happy to see that Dorothy was in my group. We first had the medical with three doctors: the chief surgeon, the acting chief Surgeon, and an honorary surgeon. Our blood pressure was taken, our heart rate was measured, and we undertook a vision test. I was worried about the vision test because I wore glasses for distance but could read the finest print. I did all sorts of eye exercises at home, hoping it would strengthen my eyes. I passed because the minimum was 20/40. What a relief!

Then came the weight-lifting. Dorothy held my ankles down while I did the maximum weight of thirty pounds. We had the choice of ten to thirty pounds, but with Pete's training, it was a cinch. There were newspaper photographers and reporters present and several took a photo of Dorothy holding my ankles down while I did the weight-lifting. The photo appeared in the New York Daily News.

I did several other arm presses, and then came the hurdle, jumping over a rope at either 2.50 feet or 3.50 feet, which I practiced in Mama's backyard with Pete. It was no problem. I passed all the tests with flying colors, thank heavens! Suddenly, out of the blue, I heard my name called to go to see the surgeons. When I approached them, the honorary surgeon, Dr. A., said, "Take your sneakers off." I didn't understand why, but I complied and stood there in my socks. He then told me to remove my socks. I was bewildered, but I stood there barefoot. He told me to walk forward a few steps, turn around, and walk back again. Dr. A. then said, "She's flat-footed. Disqualify her." I couldn't believe what I was hearing. My mouth opened in shock. The chief surgeon looked at me and said, "No way will she be disqualified, particularly since she scored almost one hundred percent on every exam." He said I should go back and join the other candidates. I had passed. What a relief! I almost broke into tears but would not give Dr. A. the satisfaction. Years later in my career, Dr. A. continued to be my nemesis. Many other police officers felt the same way. If anyone had known about my pregnancy, I would have been disqualified, but thankfully they never knew!

The policewomen's list was viable on an as-needed basis and would expire when all positions were filled. That was good news for me because I was in no position to accept a job offer. I looked forward to being a mom, now feeling totally domesticated after we had moved to our own apartment, sharing our love and future plans.

Time seemed to fly by. When I was in my ninth month, it was decided that I would move in with Mama and Papa temporarily because my obstetrician was associated with the Jewish Memorial Hospital in Washington Heights, and if I went into labor, I would never make it there from Pelham Bay in time. While I was at Mama's, Mr. Solly came to visit. I was shocked to see him. He had lost weight, looked disheveled, and bemoaned the fact he not only missed us but that Lucy had passed away shortly after we moved. She died in her sleep, probably of a broken heart, because she was so close to us. He said he was lonesome, so Mama told him to drop in anytime he felt the need for company.

On the morning of October 6, 1948, I went into labor. I called Nick and Hanya, who were still living in the same building as Mama on the seventh floor. Nick had offered to drive me to the hospital because Pete was working an eight-to-four shift. It was a cool, misty morning when we arrived at Jewish Memorial Hospital. Nick pushed me in a wheelchair to the emergency room, where the nurses took over. My doctor was present and said it would be a while, probably two hours. He was right. The labor pains came more frequently, and I was wheeled into the delivery room, but then the doctor did something I found unusual. To speed the delivery, he poured first hot and then cold water over my belly. It worked, and I delivered a healthy yowling, eight-pound and fifteen-ounce baby boy. The nurse placed me on a cot underneath an open window.

I fuzzily asked her to close the window because I was chilled and requested a blanket. They ignored me and I guess I drifted off to sleep in a state of exhaustion, only to wake several hours later to find myself in a private room on the maternity floor. I saw Pete sitting in a chair close to my bed. Pete was reaching over to kiss me when I felt the urge to cough, and when I did, I spewed a mouthful of blood all over my nightgown and bedding! Pete ran out of the room to get a nurse. I touched my forehead. I was on fire. The nurse came in and took my temperature. It was 103 degrees. She hurriedly left the room. In no time, there was a group gathered at my bedside: two doctors and two nurses. The doctor told me I needed a chest X-ray. I moaned because I had several stitches, and to sit up was agonizing. Nevertheless, I had the X-ray, which confirmed their suspicions: I had pneumonia! I was hastily removed from the maternity floor and taken to the medical floor. I was miserable. My breasts were so full of milk they really hurt. The nurse bound my chest because I couldn't breastfeed my newborn. I couldn't even see Stephen Paul, whom we had named after our fathers, until my discharge ten days later.

It was decided that until I got my strength back, I would stay at my parents' apartment. Mama did a great job with Steve. She bathed him, changed him, and lovingly fed him. I made the formula because, unfortunately, I could not breast feed him as I had planned. At the end of the month, I felt renewed energy, thanks to Mama's tender, loving care and good food, but the time had come for me to return to my own home.

Chapter Eight:
Our First Home

I must admit that Mama spoiled me while I was recovering from my bout of pneumonia, and I was at first exhausted getting up in the wee hours of the morning to feed Steve. He was a very good baby, happy and crying only when he was hungry. Pete was as thrilled as I was that we finally had a place of our own. The apartment was perfect, except it was on the fifth floor, and hoisting the baby carriage up the steps was rough, but I got used to it. One of my dear friends, Anne, from high school, whom I had helped in her plans to elope, also needed an apartment, and through my connections at my former office, I helped her find one two buildings away. She had also given birth recently to a son named Tommy. We would regularly take walks around the neighborhood, pushing our carriages. We often went to the Bronx Zoo, which was not too far away.

One day, I had an unusual experience at the zoo. We were at a black panther (puma) cage when I decided to speak to my new feline friend. But as soon as I did, he went into a rage and hissed and stood on his hind legs, growling at me. There were a number of people gathered in front of his cage and everyone was amazed at his reaction to me. I told Anne I would go to the other side of the cage to see if he would follow me. Sure enough, he did. I did not speak. I just stood there looking at him, and he looked back at me. I spoke softly and told him I wanted to be friends with him. Immediately, all hell broke out again. He spat at me and stood up on his hind legs. If he could, I believe he would have ripped me apart! A zookeeper witnessed this, approached me, and said that my voice must have reminded the panther of someone who abused him. He said he had never seen the panther react this way before. Needless to say, we visited the zoo many more times when I would see the panther, but I never spoke to him again to avoid upsetting him.

Pete had always wanted to be an architect, so he continued to study at Pratt Institute in his spare time. He had temporarily stopped while studying for the police exam but now he went to classes several times a week. We had plans to build a home of our own outside the city. Pete was so creative.

Olga often visited us after she and her husband, Earle, divorced. She was living with a cousin not far away in Pelham Bay. She had received a nice stipend as a divorce settlement, and although she was a model for Hattie Carnegie, she wanted to open her own modeling agency, which she did under the name of Sherry Carson. She had an office on Fifty-Seventh Street, opposite Carnegie Hall, and in no time had a group of models working for her. Olga suggested that to earn some extra income, I, too, should consider modeling, so I had Pete take photos of me for Olga to use. She told me to choose a name for modeling. I chose the name of Paula Stephens, planning to put whatever money I earned in a bank account for baby Stephen Paul. My first modeling gig was for a true detective magazine. They wanted someone to pose as a buyer for narcotics. Another time they had me pose as a lure for a stalker, etc., etc.

One day, Olga called and told me she wanted me to enter a contest she was promoting, Miss Coney Island, and that she would be participating in it as well. Believe it or not, a beautiful model, Betty Brosmere, came in first, Olga came in second, and I came in third! Thanks to Olga, I was frequently used for True Story and True Romance magazines, as well as for promoting products at convention centers. I was happy doing all this because I was making side money, which was great!

I once posed for a girlie magazine wearing a bikini, looking sexy (I suppose), and wore my favorite dangling earrings.

At a later date, my photo showed up in an unexpected place. It was mid-1951, and I was notified that the remainder of the women waiting for the appointment to NYPD were scheduled to be hired on October 1, 1951. My friend Dorothy had already been hired, having scored higher than me, and was working in the Juvenile Aid Bureau. She loved her job. We had fortunately moved by then to an apartment on the second floor of the 1939 Grand Concourse. It was great that Mama, Papa, Hanya, and Nick were also in the same building.

In late September, Olga called and said she had another job for me, along with several other models I knew. The New Yorker Hotel was hosting a toy trade show. Was I interested? I said yes, as this would be the last time I would be modeling. I was soon to become a New York City policewoman. Had I known what fate had in store for me, I never in a million years would have taken that assignment. I was happy because it sounded like it would be a lot of fun, and being a toy trade show, I might get some great toys for Steve.

Chapter Nine:
The Cajun Phony

When I arrived at the New Yorker Hotel, I went directly to the Exhibition Hall and was amazed to see so many exhibitors/dealers displaying not only toys but children's furniture as well. I went to the booth where I found Sherry (Olga), Joanne, Veronica, and Anna dressed in costumes replicating the "Scribble Doll" we were to demonstrate to potential buyers. Sherry gave me my outfit: a red and white polka dot sun bonnet, camisole, and short skirt with romper panties underneath. Surprisingly, the outfit was not cloth but made of plastic. The doll was named "Scribbles" because the doll, also plastic, had a blank face. The idea was that with a special pencil, you could draw/scribble a face, and then one could easily change the face by erasing it and drawing another one with the pencil. There was a photographer assigned to take photos of the activity in our booth. His name was Leroy. He was soft-spoken with a cute accent which we discovered was Cajun. He came from LaFayette, Louisiana. Pete and I became friends with Leroy because Pete was interested in photography. We even had a dark room in our apartment in which to develop pictures he had taken. The dark room was actually our bathroom, but it worked.

We invited Leroy to our home for dinner after the show closed. Leroy was grateful because he knew no one in New York City. Leroy gave Pete a few photography tips, which Pete appreciated. The last day of the show, a Sunday, was cool and rainy. I took my raincoat and arrived just in time to find Leroy photographing the models. He told me to get into my outfit because he wanted to photograph me as well.

70

Leroy took these black-and-white shots with a Polaroid camera. He also had a folio of colored shots taken of us during our demonstrations. Leroy said a very prominent legislator from Louisiana was in town for a business deal and, after completing his business, was coming to his suite in the hotel. He had a lucrative business and wanted a poster girl to advertise his product. He asked Leroy to bring the photos of us for him to look over. After viewing the photographs of Veronica, Anna, Sherry, Joanne, and myself, he would select one of us to be the poster girl for his famous alcohol-laden patent medicine, which he claimed not only had dietary supplements but also necessary minerals and vitamins. Leroy said that this Legislator was out of the ordinary when it came to promoting his business; not only was he a colorful politician, but he was also charismatic with a toothy grin and a true Cajun accent. The product had been touted by a caravan across the country consisting of famous singers, actors, etc., but now, he wanted a new, fresh face and therefore thought of having a poster girl!

We were all excited, hoping to be the one he selected. At mid-afternoon, Leroy went up to the legislator's suite armed with the photographs of us to show him. After a short time had passed, Leroy returned and said, "Paula (my professional name, Paula Stephens), he chose you." I could not believe my good fortune, or so I thought. I was going to be sworn in shortly as a probationary policewoman in NYPD, and I believed being a poster girl would provide additional income via royalties. Leroy said the Legislator was waiting for me to come to his suite to discuss the offer and set up a contract. Leroy told me to call him. He answered in a thick Cajun accent, "Come on up, darlin'. Door's open, anxious to meet you." I was ecstatic. I couldn't believe my good fortune (or so I thought). I took off my sun bonnet and put on my raincoat to conceal my costume as I was going in an elevator. When I approached his suite, I saw that the door was slightly ajar. I knocked and said, "I'm here; it's Paula," and stepped into the foyer and closed the door behind me. He answered me, saying, "I'm coming, darlin'. Look what I've got for you." He stepped into the foyer with an open bathrobe and an erect penis! I froze momentarily and turned to try to reach the door, but he tackled me and knocked me down to the floor. Suddenly, he was on top of me, one hand held against my throat, holding me down while the other quickly pulled down the side of my rompers, tearing the material. I struggled to no avail. It was difficult to talk or even breathe. I could only whimper, "Noooooooo, Noooooo!"-thankfully, it was quickly over and done with.

For a moment, I couldn't move, frozen out of sheer shock. He got off me, reached into his bathrobe pocket, threw a hand towel at me, and without a word or even a glance, walked into his bedroom and slammed the door. I took the hand towel and wiped his semen off my thigh and the inside of my raincoat. I was numb, feeling stupid, dirty, and angry for having been so trusting and gullible. I tossed the towel onto the floor. I had been conned! I swore never to be conned again. I knotted the torn side of my rompers and left.

When I returned to our booth, I slipped behind the curtain. It was at that time I started to shake and cry. Sherry and Leroy came and asked what was wrong. I told them, "That Cajun bastard raped me! He got me up there under false pretense. There was no upcoming poster girl contract, nada! He wanted to look at the photos so that he could choose the girl to rape. Unfortunately, it was me!" Sherry was in total shock. Leroy was beside himself because he considered the Legislator not only a friend but a patron and mentor as well. They asked what I was going to do. Tell Pete? Make out a police report?

What? I replied that I could never tell Pete (which I never did), not knowing what action he'd take. As far as a police report goes, I was in a bind. If I filed a complaint, it more than likely would jeopardize my future career in the NYPD because I was going to be sworn in as a probationary policewoman in a matter of days. What a dilemma! This so-called respected Legislator was getting away with rape scot-free! There was nothing I could do about it, but it taught me a lesson: be wary when things appear too good to be true!

I learned later that he had lied to Leroy, as well. He was in New York to finalize the sale of his company, so there was no need for a poster girl. He also misled the people who bought his company by overstating his product sales. Shortly after the company purchase, sales went down drastically and they were forced into bankruptcy! I also learned later that he ran unsuccessfully for governor of the state of Louisiana. Thank goodness he lost!

Over the years, Pete and I remained friendly with Leroy. Those last days of modeling were supposed to be joyful, not humiliating. When I recall what occurred, I still recoil, but as they say, life goes on, and one chapter leads to another. I could rejoice in the fact that I was appointed as a Probationary Policewoman in the New York City Police Department on October 1, 1951. I was looking forward to the new, exciting and different career which now awaited me.

Chapter Ten:
New Career-NYPD

Having moved back to the 1939 Grand Concourse was a blessing in that I didn't have to worry about nannies for Steve. Instead, he had his loving Baba ("grandmama" in Ukrainian) and my sister, Hanya, who lived on the 7th floor. How lucky I was! Whenever I had to work, I knew Steve was in good hands and treated with loving care, so I had peace of mind.

The day I was appointed, I attended a ceremony at Police Headquarters, 240 Centre Street. I learned that most of the women appointed had previously worked in the Department of Corrections and were, therefore, familiar with one another, whereas I, a newcomer, knew no one. I needed to break the ice and make friends, but believe it or not, I was rebuffed. They already had their "clique."

When I was in the gym, where we learned to physically protect ourselves with judo, I was luckily assigned Evelyn as a partner. We hit it off, and she became my lifelong friend. Through Evelyn, I met several of her other friends and, at last, didn't feel like a loner! We attended classes to learn civil and criminal law and took many written tests. We were also taught procedures to follow when making an arrest. We made mock arrests and learned to book our arrest in the precinct where it occurred. The arrest was recorded by the Commanding Officer into a ledger called the Blotter. The prisoner was fingerprinted and placed in a holding cell until transported to Headquarters for a Photo ID, then placed in a van to appear for arraignment and bail before a judge in court, and then placed in detention in the Tombs or Rikers Island awaiting his trial date. We all were novices, but this was vital instruction. We went to the gun range at Rodman's Neck in the Bronx, where we were trained to shoot at a target. It took a while for me to hit the target, but after some practice, I did quite well. We paid a visit to the Morgue at Bellevue Hospital, which was a little uncomfortable, to view a homicide victim. Some of the women were really squeamish and turned their heads to look away. We were measured for our uniform: a jacket, shirt, tie, skirt, and heavy overcoat plus the hat with your badge number on it. We were issued a 32 caliber Smith & Wesson revolver, which was fitted into a holster in a shoulder strap black purse.

Finally, the time had come when we graduated from the Academy and received our permanent assignments. Many women were sent to the Juvenile Aid Bureau, and the rest, me included, were assigned to the Policewomen's Bureau at 400 Broome Street opposite Police Headquarters. We were warmly greeted by the Director of the Policewomen's Bureau, Irene Peters. Our uniforms had arrived and were stacked in boxes with our names. Director Peters had us try on the uniform. She checked every one to see if alterations were needed. She spoke of the various duties we would be performing and told us to record our daily activities in a small memo pad. This was done by hourly calling in and giving location and time. Some of us would be assigned Matron Duty to precincts where there were holding cells for female prisoners prior to their court appearance. Another assignment was the DOA Reserve. In other words, Dead on Arrival. We would be working a four to twelve and twelve to eight shift, taking calls from all over the city. We would be stationed inside the Policewomen's Bureau, answering the phone and entering information into a Blotter. When we left for a DOA call, a car with a policeman driving would take us to the particular location.

Wouldn't you know it, my first night on DOA I received a call to search a DOA on East 13th Street in Manhattan. The driver picked me up and drove to an apartment house where the DOA was reported. I went up the stairs to the third floor and saw a policeman at the end of a long hallway standing in an open doorway. I approached him and identified myself. He told me to go into the bedroom where there were two other policemen, one by the door and the other by the bed. A sheet covered the body. As I came closer, the policeman lifted the sheet, and I saw a woman dressed only in a bra and panties with black satin on them. In addition to all the blood on the bedding, her head had been bashed in, and one eye was hanging down the side of her face. I gasped, turned around, and ran toward the policeman in the doorway. When he tried to block my exit, I reached out with my two hands and lifted him up like a toy so that I could get into the other room. Both of them laughed, and one of them said, "What have we here? An Amazon? What strength." I regained my composure and went back inside the bedroom and noted her articles of jewelry: a single white metal band on her left hand, two white/metal/glass earrings, and a white metal chain with a white metal cross on her neck. I entered these items into my memo book, and the Sergeant signed it.

I left and was driven back to headquarters. I could not wait to cleanse myself, washing my hands with soap and water. I even sprayed chlorine over my hands. What an experience! I realized I should have worn rubber gloves and a mask to screen out odors. Well, next time, I would be prepared. I would also take a small vial of perfume to spray. When assigned to the four to twelve and twelve to eight shifts, it would only be for a week, thank goodness! Occasionally, we would get calls reporting a crime occurring and would re-route the call to the proper precinct, as we did not respond to these types of calls. One of the policewomen who was on reserve the previous week warned me of a persistent nuisance male caller who, at first, was courteous, then would launch into vile profane language. She entered this into the Blotter and told me his whereabouts were, unfortunately, untraceable. It was inevitable that one night, while on duty I received his call. When the phone rings, you identify yourself and ask how you can assist the caller. He answered with a giggle and said, "I've seen your pictures in the newspapers," and proceeded to launch into some really foul language, telling me what he'd do to me. For some reason, his strange giggle made me feel as though I had heard that laugh before. I reprimanded him and told him not to call again. I reminded him that this phone was for police business, not monkey business. Before I hung up, he giggled and said we'd talk again soon before hanging up. I was determined to identify that giggle, and in time I did. He called again on my last night on reserve. He seemed so familiar with our schedules and routines, as though he were also on the job. He once again launched into his revolting language, giggling the whole time. I hung up on him.

Again, the telephone rang. I needed to go to Brooklyn for another DOA. A Policeman drove me to the residence. I prepared myself this time with rubber gloves, a large man's handkerchief (my mask), and a vial of perfume. When we reached the apartment house, it appeared that some of the neighbors detected a foul odor and called the police. The apartment was on the fifth floor, and as soon as you stepped out of the elevator, a foul odor was evident. I put on my rubber gloves, sprayed my handkerchief with perfume, and entered the apartment. A Sergeant and two policemen were wearing masks over their noses and mouths. I was shocked. The body was lying on the kitchen floor and was covered with maggots. I asked the Sergeant what he wanted me to do. Search her? I said I could see she had a chain with a white metal

77

cross dangling, yellow metal ball earrings, a plain yellow gold metal wedding band, and a Timex watch. The Sergeant said, "Remove them, place them in a bag, and identify them." I could not believe what he said, but I removed the articles and then handed them to him. He smirked, said, "Good Job," and then signed my Memo book. I took off my rubber gloves and threw them in the garbage pail along with my handkerchief. My stomach was churning, but I refused to give the Sergeant the satisfaction or indication of seeing it. I was so happy to get back into the car and open the windows to breathe in some fresh air all the way back to headquarters.

I entered the information in the blotter and prayed that the rest of the tour would be uneventful, and thankfully, it was. I couldn't wait to get home, take a shower, and wash my hair. Even though I washed my face and hands at work, I still felt unclean. It took some time for me to get over the image of the maggots on the deceased's body. The poor woman died of natural causes. It was not a homicide. I was so happy my tour on the reserve was over, and I looked forward to more pleasant assignments.

The swearing-in of the new officers of the Policewomen's Endowment Association was coming up, with a dinner being served at a local restaurant. Evelyn had reserved a table for a group of women we associated with. The dinner was a traditional, delicious Italian dinner. After the swearing-in of the officers, the newly appointed President outlaid plans and issues to be looked into. While this was going on, I heard a familiar laugh, or should I say a giggle, from the table behind me. I felt a chill come over me as I recognized it. The infamous giggle belonged to a co-worker's husband! Now I understood why he would make sporadic calls to the Policewomen's Bureau. It happened when his wife was working a late tour. I waited for his wife to leave the table so I could approach him. As I stood up, he did as well and said, "Hi Mary, looking good." I told him I wanted to talk to him while I had the chance with his wife away from the table. I did not waste time. I identified him as the male caller who would call the bureau on late shifts. I informed him that sexual harassment was a crime, but I would give him a pass due to my respect for his wife, someone I often work with and considered a friend. I told him that the last time he called I recorded the conversation. No additional proof is needed. I wanted his word that he would cease calling the Bureau, but if not, I would have no choice but to report him. I told him to get some counseling. I thought he was going to faint. His face turned ashen as he stuttered, "Okay, Okay, I get it. I won't make any more calls," and with that, he walked away, mopping his brow filled with perspiration. I sat down, my heart pounding. I felt happy to think that no more investigations into the harassing calls would be necessary, although many wondered why the calls suddenly ended. I never told anyone other than Pete.

Several guests were invited and sat with the newly elected Officers. I noticed one individual getting a lot of attention. He was tall, good-looking, and had a charismatic smile. I learned later that he was the Circulation Manager of a widely circulated local newspaper and was referred to as a "Police Buff" who would often go in squad cars answering radio calls just like Walter Winchell, the reporter.

I was soon given a new assignment, that of Matron Duty, at the 19th Precinct in Manhattan. Our quarters were on the second floor which had five cells to house female prisoners before they would appear in court. Always when a woman was arrested and after her information was entered into the blotter, she would be searched by a Police Matron. Most of the women were cooperative, but occasionally, one would encounter an unruly, nasty prisoner. In one instance, I had one who spat and swore at me, trying to bite and kick me. Fortunately, the arresting officer helped me put her in the holding cell. The Lieutenant at the desk I considered a friend. He was a genuinely kind person who was not aloof like some of the other desk officers. He often sent me fresh coffee and goodies as well as sandwiches and occasionally lemonade (sometimes with gin added). He was known to secretly imbibe but never to the point of showing that he was intoxicated. He did his job and was well respected. He didn't react too kindly to the prisoner's behavior and came upstairs to admonish her. He had me open the cell, grabbed the prisoner by her hair, thrust her face into the toilet, and said, "This will wash your mouth out of obscenities. I hope you've learned your lesson now." I must say I never heard a peep out of the prisoner until she left for court. She had suddenly become very docile.

Unfortunately, a few weeks later, after finishing a late tour, the same Lieutenant, while standing on the subway platform, suddenly fell onto the tracks and was run over by an oncoming train. A witness to the incident reported that he had leaned over to see if a train was coming and seemed to have lost his balance. We were all saddened by this unfortunate accident and will miss his Irish smile, as we had all held him in high regard.

One of my most memorable experiences occurred one evening at the end of my four to twelve tour. As I was about to leave, I saw a man, a guest at the Policewomen's Endowment Association dinner, talking to the Desk Officer. There was another man with him who I recognized as Detective Harry F. from the 17th Squad, whom he regularly accompanied on radio calls and runs. The man looked at me and said, "Hi, I remember you from the dinner. Let me ask you a question. Do you like Frank Sinatra?" I laughed and said, "Who doesn't?" He then said, "How would you like to be my guest and catch his last performance of the evening at the Copacabana right now?" I replied that I would be delighted. Harry"s car was right outside the Precinct, and we drove to the nightclub. He introduced himself and asked my name. My accompanying him was probably crazy, but I didn't want to miss this unbelievable opportunity to see Frank Sinatra perform. When we walked into the Club you could see the place was jammed. Jules Podell came over, shook Ivan's hand, and said, "Come, I'll get you set up on the tier so you'll be right up front." A table and three chairs were set up by the railing in front of the stage. We were fortunate in that we arrived at intermission and just in time for his last performance of the evening. I looked around and saw women dressed to the nines and dripping with jewels. I had on a green cashmere sweater and scarf. I was, after all, just getting off from work. Who knew I would have a front-row seat at the Copa? The band started up, and Frank Sinatra came on stage. The spotlight was on him as he glanced around and started to sing "I've Got You Under My Skin." He walked straight over to me. The spotlight was on me. I couldn't believe it. With all the fancily dressed women, he chose to sing to me! Ivan said. I blushed. After finishing his song, Frank kissed my hand and then proceeded to sing another set of songs. The audience's response was ear-shattering. They loved him! Jules Podell later told Ivan that Frank chose me to sing to because I reminded him of Ava Gardner. With the show over, Ivan said his chauffeur would drop him off first and then drive me home. Fortunately, the chauffeur also lived in the Bronx. Detective Harry F. went home in his own car parked nearby. I thanked Ivan for a fabulous but unexpected evening. He laughed and said, "We'll do it again sometime." When I got home I told Pete why I was so late coming home. He laughed and said, "Glad you had an exciting time at the Copa." The next day, I was bombarded with questions: Did I really go hear Frank Sinatra at the Copa?

The Matron's Quarters were compact. There was a bathroom, a main room consisting of a desk, a leather sofa on one side, and on the other side, four steel lockers, one for personal use and the other with cleaning supplies. In the middle of the room, there was a tall window with metal guards outside and a table placed atop a radiator. One of the duties of the Matron, according to Rules and Regulations, was to be responsible for the cleanliness and orderliness of the Quarters. I took this to heart, unfortunately. It was a beautiful spring day, but one could not tell because the window was filthy with dust and grime. You could barely tell if it was daylight! I decided the window needed a good cleaning, and in the supply cabinet locker, I fetched some soap, paper towels, and a bucket, which I filled with water. I placed everything on the table. I took a chair and climbed onto the table and reached into the bucket to wet the paper towels. I raised my arm to swipe the window. I managed to make one swipe. The second time I tried, I was thrown backward in a jack-knife position, scraping my spine against the wall and locker and landing on my buttocks, pinned by the table against the metal locker. I yelled, "Help" multiple times but being on the second floor in the rear of the precinct, no one heard me. I somehow managed to free myself and went to the bathroom to have a look in the mirror at my back and was shocked to see the skin scrapped off. I was bleeding. I went down to report this accident to the Desk Officer and even lifted up my blouse so that he could see my injury. He said he was calling in a squad car to take me to St. Claire's Hospital ER immediately. He also recorded this as a "Line of Duty Injury."

The patrolman drove me to the hospital's emergency room, where I was examined and had X-rays taken. The doctor told me that I had injured my lower spinal column. The X-ray appeared to show discs bulging and a possible herniated disc. He told me I should be evaluated by an orthopedic doctor. He gave me a pill and a prescription, saying, "Tomorrow and the next few days will be rough-pain wise." He suggested bed rest and the application of an ice pack to my lower back. He told me I might need surgery sometime in the future. I was driven back to the precinct and reported as "sick." I called the Policewomen's Bureau and advised them of what occurred so that a replacement would be sent up. Fortunately, there were no prisoners in the cells. I went home in real agony, and just as the doctor said, I could barely move for a couple of days.

I was on sick leave for about two weeks and then returned to the Policewomen's Bureau for reassignment. It seems that the Bureau had received multiple complaints of men harassing women at various theaters in Times Square, and Director Peters chose me and my new partner, Jean Kenny, to patrol the various theaters. Jean and I came up with a plan: we would use a particular signal when we had evidence for an arrest. We chose the Paramount Theater as our first stop, never dreaming we would be successful on our first outing. It was mid-afternoon, and the theater wasn't crowded. We chose to sit in the middle section, three seats away from each other but close enough to observe and watch for our prearranged signal, which was to touch our hair, a normal gesture if an incident occurred. I sat five seats in from the aisle. I observed a man walking up the aisle from the first row, looking from side to side, and lo and behold; he chose to enter our row sitting in the seat next to me. He made a snorting sound when he sat, and within a few minutes, he pursed his lips and made a sound like one does when calling a dog. His elbow poked me so that

I would glance at him, which I did, and immediately saw why. He was waving an erect penis and smiling. I used our prearranged signal, and Jean stood up. She, too, saw his erect penis. I grabbed him by his collar, said he was under arrest for indecent exposure, and told him to zip up his fly. He started to yell, "Please, please, I'm begging you, don't arrest me. I'm sorry. Please, my mother's a diabetic. Don't do this to me." Jean placed the cuffs on him, and we half dragged him up the aisle but finally got him upright and waited in the manager's office for a squad car to take us to the precinct to book him. After being booked, he was transferred to a van to 240 Centre St. Police Headquarters to be fingerprinted and photographed, after which he would be sent on to Night Court for arraignment. After appearing in Night Court, bail and a trial date were set for his upcoming trial.

We made multiple arrests at various theaters, which resulted in fewer complaints. I have to laugh about one arrest that Jean made at the Capitol Theater for indecent, unwanted touching. Again, we chose mid-afternoon because we felt we could be selective in our seating. This time, Jean sat four seats from the aisle, and I sat in the same row, three seats away. We had just about sat down when we observed a man coming up the aisle with his jacket over one arm. He decided to come and sit next to Jean, leaving only two seats separating us. When he sat down, he placed his hand on Jean's shoulder and smiled. He then flung his jacket onto her lap and scooped it up, grabbing her private parts (crotch) and squeezing. Jean didn't give me the usual signal. Instead, she leaped off her seat in shock. She placed her hand on his shirt collar and said he was under arrest for indecent touching. I placed the cuffs on him, and we escorted him to the manager's office to wait for a squad car to take us to the local precinct for booking. After being booked, fingerprinted, and photographed, he was taken for an appearance in Night Court. I was taken aback upon learning that he and his wife were members of my in-laws' church! His wife heard that I was the assisting arresting officer and, in court, loudly confronted me, saying, "How could you do this? He is a sweet, gentle man, and he meant no harm." She then cursed me in Ukrainian before being escorted out of court. I had some story to tell my in-laws! It wasn't too long before I learned the couple had left the congregation.

Because complaints had dwindled, we were assigned to patrol other sites where crowds gathered, such as Rockefeller Plaza, the Central Park Zoo, etc. We made several arrests at Rockefeller Plaza, where groups of people watched the ice skaters. These degenerate arrests were mostly what we called "ass warmers." The perp would press his body against an unknown female, or someone would close in on a female and then touch her backside. We weren't particularly thrilled about these arrests but were happy to get these degenerates off the streets.

Happily, we were then assigned to the 3rd Division located in the 14th Precinct on West 30th Street in Manhattan. The 14th Precinct also had detention cells for both male and female prisoners. At a later date, I did Matron Duty there. There was also the Detective Squad located on the 2nd floor next to the female cell block. The 3rd Division was on the main floor. It was a small unit comprising an Inspector, a Lieutenant, and six patrolmen, but no women. We were the first women assigned there. Our assignment was to seek out the illegal bookmakers who inundated the garment industry. Jean and I came up with an idea on how to spot a bookmaker. We decided to go to a popular cafeteria and sit at a table sipping coffee and eating bagels while scanning the customers. We observed a man reading the Daily Racing Form and writing on a piece of paper. Once he got up, we followed him. He led us to an office building just two blocks from the precinct. We followed him into the lobby and saw him open a door leading to a stairwell, leaving the door slightly ajar. We observed him in conversation with a man holding a pad on which he was writing. He took some money from the man we followed. Once the man left, we widened the door opening and said, "You're under arrest for illegal bookmaking." The bookmaker was shaken and bewildered. "Who the hell are you?" he asked. We identified ourselves, placed cuffs on him, and gathered up some paperwork he had left on the windowsill's ledge. We walked him to the Precinct, and several police officers' jaws dropped. It appeared that our bookmaker was well known. He was called "Little Augie." After booking, he was placed in the detention cell awaiting transport for the usual fingerprinting and photo and then on to Night Court for arraignment. We were successful in making numerous bookmaking arrests using the same method of tracking the bettor.

Jean and I were also used to breaking up an escort prostitution ring by posing (dressed accordingly) as prostitutes visiting a bar known to be frequented by prostitutes. After a successful arrest, we went back to arresting bookmakers, and this led to a great find. We followed one individual from the same cafeteria to an office building. We waited for him to climb the stairs ahead of us and saw that he stopped on the third floor. The door was open and one could hear multiple voices. We glanced in and saw it was a "wire room" with wall blackboards having the names of racetracks and upcoming races written on them. There were also several telephones on a desk. We walked in and said, "Oops, wrong floor. We want the Spool and Thread Company upstairs," and closed the door. We discussed our strategy and decided I would stay behind while Jean went to the office to get assistance in making our "Wire Room" arrest. In short order, Jean returned with the Lieutenant and two policemen who went inside and declared, "This is an illegal operation, and we are closing it down with an arrest of the men placing bets on the telephone." The group of men waiting to place bets were allowed to leave.

Shortly after making this arrest, Jean and I were told we were being transferred back to the Policewomen's Bureau. I returned to doing DOA and was assigned Matron Duty in various precincts. One of my Matron Duty assignments was at the 14th Precinct. As previously mentioned, the female quarters were on the 2nd floor next to the Detective Bureau. I knew a number of officers here, having been assigned to the 3rd Division, so I felt comfortable here. The Detectives were friendly and often shared snacks and sodas with me. One night, two plainclothesmen brought in a female prisoner (a prostitute) to be searched and housed in the cell. Something about their attitude, a sort of smirking, made me cautious. I approached the female. She was wearing a jacket, which I removed and searched. I then proceeded to her blouse, which I started to unbutton, and noticed her bra was heavily padded. She had no breasts and there was hair on her chest. This was not a woman! It was a man dressed as a woman. I turned to the two plainclothesmen and said, "You're in the wrong cell block. We have only females in our cells." They pretended to be shocked but then admitted it was a prank on their part to see how long it would take me to discover the prisoner's gender. They took the prisoner to the male cell block on the first floor. What a bunch of characters! I imagine they were disappointed that I discovered their trick so quickly. I have to admit, the prisoner was very attractive. I understood how easily one could be misled.

One of the policewomen on duty discovered a mouse sharing our quarters and started to feed it. The mouse eventually became so tame that when you whistled, it appeared and came right up to you! Our

Precinct now had an official mascot, although he never achieved the fame of New York's current favorite rodent celebrity ("Pizza Rat")!

One afternoon, I received a phone call from Ivan saying that he'd like me and Harry to come to his home for dinner to meet his family. Pete, at this time was using his spare time building a home out in Bayshore, Long Island. We had purchased an acre from Winthrop Gardiner in an area called "Gardiner Estate." Pete, using the architectural skills he acquired at Pratt Institute, drew the house plans and had an architect friend add the official stamp. Pete was very creative and really enjoyed doing architectural drawing and building. I also lent a hand mixing the cement. Pete even taught me how to lay bricks. I managed to build a brick retaining wall, and to this day, I have signs of callouses on the inside of my palms.

Down at the end of our street, North Gardiner Drive, was the railroad station for Deer Park, so if not driving, one could take the train. Pete and his father, Grandpa Steve, built a temporary shack where there were bunk beds, an eating area, and an outdoor grill. There was also an outhouse. The family would come for weekends and really enjoyed themselves, especially our son Steve. There were young families on the street already so he had friends to play with. We used to go to the dock at Bayshore to fish. The beach was also close by. Pete designed a beautiful house with a stonewall fireplace, a huge living room, a dining room, three bedrooms, three baths, all tiled, and a great kitchen.

As for Ivan's dinner invite, Harry picked me up (minus Pete), and we drove to Ivan's apartment located on Park Avenue. We were warmly greeted by Vi, Ivan's wife, a vivacious redhead. We met their two sons, Robert and Ted, and their fiancees. During dinner, somehow, the conversation turned to fishing. Vi told us that although

88

they had a hunting/fishing cabin in Maine, she rarely went and asked if I liked fishing. I mentioned that I frequently went fishing in Bayshore and upstate New York and found it to be very relaxing. Ivan then said, "Okay, you, Pete, and Harry will be my guests at the cabin. Let's set up a date. I'll fly. It's about time I gave Baby Doll, named after Vi, a workout." Baby Doll was his Beechcraft. Harry agreed, and we set a date that was convenient for everyone. That evening, when Pete came home, I told him about the upcoming fishing trip and he was equally as excited about it as I was.

We told Ivan we were able to take him up on his offer about ten days later. Harry came and picked us up, and we drove to Teterboro Airport in New Jersey. We met Ivan by his plane, a Beechcraft Bonanza named Baby Doll. The plane held three passengers and a pilot. It was a beautiful plane, white, navy, light blue. Pete and Harry sat behind the Pilot (Ivan), and I sat next to Ivan. I was nervous, which Ivan noticed. "You'll relax once we're in the air. Don't worry, I'm a good pilot," he told me. Ivan was right. Once we were airborne, I got used to the engine noise and marveled at the sights we flew over. As we approached Maine, the weather took a drastic turn. Heavy rain pelted the windshield, and there was lightning and thunder, as I had never seen or heard before. I clenched my jaw and sat stiffly in my seat. Pete and Harry seemed oblivious to everything. Ivan flew the plane over the lake where the cabin was located. It looked as though he was skimming the treetops. I ground my teeth and closed my eyes. Mercifully, Ivan said, "Looks like we'll have to postpone the trip. This storm is so bad I'll have to turn around, but first, we need to refuel in Boston." We landed in Boston. The weather was clearing up, and after refueling, we headed back to Teterboro Airport. When we landed in Teterboro, I breathed a sigh of relief but felt a sharp pain in my jaw. I vowed never to fly in a small plane again. Harry dropped me and Pete off and took Ivan home.

I was experiencing terrific pain in my jaw, necessitating an emergency trip to the dentist. The dentist told me that the X-ray revealed that I had ground a gold inlay into my tooth, cracking the tooth. There was no way of saving it. The tooth would need to be extracted! I had clenched my jaw to such an extent that I did damage to the tooth. This was the first and only trip I took in Baby Doll, even though numerous offers for other trips were made. I just wasn't comfortable, regardless of the fact that Ivan was a good pilot.

One day, I received a call from Policewoman Mary Spano telling me that the Policewomen's Endowment Association was going to put on a Revue featuring female members of NYPD. She suggested that I come and join her and others I knew for the upcoming auditions. The first audition was held at Police Headquarters in the lineup room. I was surprised by the large turnout. I never would have imagined that there were so many women eager to perform. There was a dance instructor with her assistant, a piano player and a wardrobe advisor, quite a team. Mary Spano surprised and thrilled us all with her fantastic voice. She had a beautiful coloratura soprano voice and sang Ave Maria. It gave us goosebumps! One group was to be dancers, whereas I, remembering those days back at WOV, was the blues singer! After several weeks of rehearsing, I also joined the dance group.

We were ready for our Revue to be held at the Henry Hudson Hotel, where I would eventually do five performances. I joined the others in the dance group for two Revues but then decided to stick to singing, which I felt more comfortable doing. Vi recommended a friend who was a vocal coach and pianist to guide me. One of the women assisting the choreographer, Ann Fogarty, looked familiar to me. I realized she had been my gym teacher at junior high school a decade ago, Miss McGuire! When I told her that I was a former student of hers, she couldn't believe it and happily hugged me. I sprained my ankle during a dance routine, and Miss McGuire tapped my leg. A photo of her doing this was taken by a Daily News Photographer. This was the incident that convinced me that I wasn't meant to dance but sing instead!

The first song I sang was "Birth of the Blues," then "That Old Black Magic," but the one that received an outstanding ovation was "Whatever Lola Wants." I guess it was the combination of a clinging silver sequin gown and the song that went over so well. The name for the Revue was "Cops and Garters." A large photo of me appeared in the centerfold section of the New York Daily News seated on a piano bench in front of a piano which brought me an onslaught of fan mail. I loved one letter in particular. It came from a group of soldiers stationed in Korea. They wrote that if ever they got arrested, they wanted me to be the one who spent the night with them in the Tombs. Pete was assigned to the 14th Precinct, and much to his chagrin, he saw my photo posted inside some of the other locker doors. I was also the poster girl for the 19th Precinct as well as for the Detectives in the 14th Detective Squad.

My vacation time soon came due. My sister, Hanya, suggested that we take a cruise to Panama to see our brother, Ted, who was working there for the General Accounting Office (GAO), whom we had not seen for quite some time. We booked a ten-day cruise with the North German Lloyd Line on the Europa. Originally, she and Nick were supposed to go on this cruise to celebrate their thirteenth wedding anniversary, but their employer objected because he would be short two hairdressers in his salon. Hanya then suggested that I go with her. I was delighted to go on the cruise and looked forward to seeing Ted.

When we entered our cabin, the aroma of roses filled the air. They were sent by Nick to Hanya for their anniversary. Great, but unfortunately, I had an allergic reaction to them. Overnight, my eyes puffed up, and I had the sniffles, not a good way to start a vacation! Once the roses were removed, my eyes became normal, and the sniffles were gone. We had the roses placed on our table in the dining room instead. The Europa was a beautiful ship. It was smaller than most cruise ships having approximately four hundred passengers. Most cruise ships have triple that number of passengers. Our cabin was more like a stateroom, spacious with a broad view from the porthole. The crew treated everyone like royalty. We were fortunate to have chosen the Europa.

Most of the passengers were families but there was a large group of young men from a famous university going to Panama to compete in a soccer match. We sat at a table for two (with our roses) in the dining room but on either side of us were the collegians. They made our time in the dining room fun. In the evening, we would go to the lounge and join in the various games they played. Other times, when the orchestra played, we never lacked partners. One evening, the "Boys" were arm wrestling, and one of them consistently won. He was declared the "Champ." As a joke, I approached him and said I, too, was a "Champ." "I bet you that I can beat you," I ventured.

Everyone started laughing and shouted, "Champ, take her on."

He asked, "What's the bet?"

"I'll bet you $100," I said. "If I lose, you can buy me a rum and coke. Deal?"

He laughed and said, "You're on. This will be the easiest way I ever get $100." He then sprawled down on the carpet, and I did the same. We were now face to face. I put my right elbow on the floor and we clenched fists.

One of the onlookers called out when to start, giving us a one, two, three. He said, "One," but before he even said, "Two," I reached over and soundly kissed my opponent on the lips.

His arm went limp. I stood up and said, "I told you I would win!" Everyone cheered and they said I was now the new "Champ." Several of them wanted to challenge me, but I declined. It was a lot of fun. From that time on, whenever anyone saw me, they called me "Champ." I have to admit their presence added to a really fun trip.

One evening, there was a knock on the cabin door, and when I opened it, I saw the Purser standing there. He said he had a cablegram for Mary Zaharko. I told him who I was and took the cablegram a little apprehensively. Was it good news or bad news? I opened it, and to my delight, it was from Pete telling me that I had been transferred from the Policewomen's Bureau effective August 7th, 1953, to the PP&C Squad (the Pickpocket and Confidence Squad) and to report at the end of my vacation to 400 Broome Street, across from Police Headquarters. I also received a promotion to Third Grade Detective. I was overcome with joy. What a fabulous surprise! I was assigned to the most desirable and sought-after squad.

The next morning, we arrived at our first port of call, Port-Au-Prince, Haiti. We arranged for a tour of the city and its highlights. It was just for one day, but we made the most of it. When we disembarked to go to our tour bus, we were besieged by scores of peddlers touting their wares. We stopped at Notre Dame Cathedral Our Lady, known for its beautiful structure. We then went to the famous Barbancourt Rum Distillery. We walked through the facility and sampled their rum, which was delicious. I bought two bottles, one for Ted and the other for home. We then went to have lunch at the El Rancho Hotel located in Petionville (the outskirts of Porto-Au-Prince), where there were many luxurious homes and hotels. The El Rancho had an outside bar by the swimming pool where a trio played dance music. Other guests from our ship were there as well so we had familiar partners to chat and dance with. After leaving El Rancho, we headed back to the city for one last tour of Marche de Fer (Iron Market). It was huge and one could barely move in the aisles, so crowded with merchants and their wares. Everything you could imagine was for sale: art, crafts, clothes, food, etc. I purchased a painting of the Market, and Hanya bought a bongo drum! It was crudely made, painted a bright red, and over 3' high. Fortunately, there was a coarse rope around the drum so that you could put it over your shoulder and carry it easily, even though it was bulky. Hanya said that Nick would love it because he was musically inclined. We were tired and glad when the tour bus arrived at the dock. The people we met were charming and spoke Creole, a language developed in the East Indies having its origins in French. Hanya knew more French than I did and used it to bargain for the Bongo Drum!

We were now headed for our next Port, Panama! We arrived in Panama after breakfast, and because it was a layover (two nights and three days), we packed our bags accordingly. Ted had made arrangements to meet us at our hotel. When we arrived, there was Ted in the lobby waiting to greet us. We embraced and were delighted to see him. After checking in, he had a tour car waiting to take us around the city. We went to the Museum of Old Panama where there were vendors exhibiting their beautiful original jewelry. The city was founded by the Spanish seeking gold. We went into the local market and purchased several items. I bought two magnificent embroidered tablecloths with twelve napkins, one set for me and the other as a gift for Vi in appreciation for her kind invite for dinner. We then returned to the hotel and had dinner. We retreated to our room to relax and enjoy conversing with Ted. He said he had made arrangements for us to go to the Gatum Locks Observation Center, where we could watch as ships entered and exited the locks. The Panama Canal is 48 miles long from the Atlantic to the Pacific Oceans. It was fascinating to watch as the huge ships were lifted and then lowered into the next lock. What a remarkable feat of engineering! After the locks, we toured the rainforest and saw amazing wildlife, unbelievable butterflies, and magnificent orchids. We also went to Monkey Island. The monkeys were also amazing. Ted then took us to meet his co-workers where we had lunch. He said he would be returning stateside in about four months and would be happy to be home. The next day, we returned to the ship as it was leaving at 5 in the evening. We met some of the soccer players and asked how they made out in the tournament. They replied that they came in second and almost made it first. Even though they were a little disappointed, they were still pleased with the way they had played.

Finally, we were now on our way home, no more stop-overs. We encountered very nasty weather around Cape Hatteras. The crew chained much of the furniture down in the lounges. They told us we were in the midst of a nasty tropical storm, rough seas, and heavy winds. Many passengers became seasick due to the motion of the ship. Hanya and I decided to stay in the lounge with others rather than remain in the cabin, getting motion sick. We joined a group and sat on the floor playing cards until the ship seemed stable again, at which time we returned to our cabin, hoping for calm seas. We were fortunately able to get a good night's sleep once the storm had passed.

We arrived in New York City and headed straight home! Nick was waiting to pick us up. Though I really had a nice time, I missed my family and was anxious to see them. Pete set up a lovely dinner, complete with champagne, to celebrate my promotion to Third Grade Detective. My vacation was over, and I was to report to the Pickpocket Squad on Monday, August 17th, 1953, at 10:00 am, a new beginning!

Chapter Eleven:
New Horizons

After returning from vacation, on my first day back at work, I arrived at the Pickpocket and Confidence Squad ten minutes early, which was perfect as the Captain was just finishing addressing the squad members. After introducing myself, I was ushered in to Captain Campion's office. He greeted me warmly and said before meeting the members of the squad, he would briefly tell me about the various activities and duties. He told me that as Detectives, we would work all over New York City, in parks, museums, stadiums, theaters, concerts, parades, and even on loan to the District Attorney as well as to Detective Squads requiring a female Detective to aid in their investigations. We would also travel out of town to extradite female prisoners. On this particular day, most of the members were present; there were about twelve male Detectives and an equal number of women.

I really didn't know anyone, although I had seen several of the women Detectives at Policewomen's meetings. Captain Campion said he was going to team me up with a seasoned Detective for the time being. I was introduced to my new partner, Helen Faulhaber. Helen was very matronly looking, devoid of makeup, a real "Brunhilda" type. She told me she was assigned to the 14th Street area, S. Kleins, Ohrbach, and Lerners Department Stores, on the lookout not only for pickpockets but shoplifters as well. Helen was not much of a talker. She was very different from the other girls in that they wore makeup, were very chic, and were fashionably dressed. I noticed that the girls were somewhat indifferent to Helen, but that did not bother her in the least. She was my partner, and I was eager to listen and learn from her.

We went to S. Kleins, located on 14th Street across from Union Square Park. In the Security Office, I was introduced to the Manager and the four store Detectives. Helen told me that even if we observed a shoplifter in action and waited for the shoplifter to leave the store, we could not make the arrest unless a store Detective observed their actions as well. This surprised me, but she explained that the stores had to protect themselves from civil suits, so it was necessary that store Detectives always be present. Helen could really spot a pickpocket working the crowded aisles. She truly amazed me! I can honestly say that she was the best tutor. In her own quiet way, she excelled. I felt very comfortable with her as my partner, and she warmed up to me. We had a great partnership. Captain Campion was very happy with the results we produced. Helen taught me the tricks of the shoplifter's trade, which I would otherwise have never known. Unfortunately, our partnership came to an end too soon for me. Helen put her papers in for retirement, and I lost a great partner!

I was reassigned to Mid-town Manhattan and would have turns with different partners. My new partners were completely the opposite of Helen Faulhaber. Helen Bauer was a little reserved but friendly. Gertrude Palmer was a knock-out with movie star looks; very open, receptive, and friendly. She and I hit it off immediately and became lifelong friends. I was telling Gertrude about my Matron Duty at the 19th Precinct when I received a call saying I had to go uptown to Harlem to do a DOA search. The Desk Officer at the time was Captain Palmer, Gertrude's husband. He was very kind and considerate, ordering a patrol car to drive me there because it was after midnight. When I arrived at the Precinct, a very distressed Black man was in the lobby. He believed the DOA was his mother and told me she had lots of money on her person. In fact, he seemed more concerned about the money than his mother. I was taken to an area where I saw the DOA. I searched the elderly Black woman. Though slim, she wore a corset. I asked for help to turn the body over so that I could remove the corset, and behold when I did, it revealed she was also wearing a money belt. Her son was right! When I opened the belt, it was full of bills. I was shocked. The bills were all $50's and $100's. I was required to list each bill and write the Id numbers. It came to a total of $4,700.00! Everyone was amazed. The son was certainly happy. The patrolman drove me back to the 19th precinct, and I told Captain Palmer what had transpired.

Shortly after the money belt incident, and while responding to a hold-up in progress, Captain Palmer suffered a heart attack and sadly passed away. Helen and I were temporarily assigned to the 47th Precinct Detective Squad, in the Bronx, which had requested two female Detectives to assist in a case of multiple muggings in the Parkchester area occurring between 9 in the evening and 2 in the morning. When my mother heard me telling Pete about my new detail, Mama said she wanted to protect me and thought she would get a bicycle helmet and glue flowers on it to protect my head. I laughed and thanked her but said I had plenty of protection from my fellow co-workers. Parkchester was a large housing development comparable to Stuyvesant Town in Manhattan. Helen patrolled the north end, and I patrolled the south end. An unmarked car with three male Detectives would drop me off, I would walk about five blocks, and then they would pick me up and drive to another location where I patrolled again. They were amused to see several cars slow up and whistle or try to pick me up. I would tell them to get lost and move on. We remained on assignment for about ten days when, thankfully, the mugger was caught in a nearby community.

Captain Campion had me work with various teams around the city as he felt this was a good way to get acquainted with my fellow Detectives and learn from them. Helen and I then returned to our previous assignment. We covered B. Altmans and Ohrbachs, both on 34th Street, and Lord & Taylor, as well as Sterns on 42nd Street. As a trio, Helen, Gertrude, and myself were successful and took turns whenever an arrest was made, which was fair. Captain Campion decided that after twenty-five years in the Pickpocket Squad, it was time to put in his retirement papers. We were all sorry to see him go. He was such a great, dedicated boss. We had several Lieutenants as temporary replacements until Sgt. Neal Behan, who had taken the Lieutenant's exam and passed, was permanently appointed head of the Pickpocket & Confidence Squad. This was great because he was one of us! I worked in Brooklyn with Marion Bushey and Mary Ayers. Mary also became a life-long friend. She was amazing. Her background accounted for her natural charm and sharpness. Mary was an actress, singer, dancer, and comedian who played sidekick to Milton Berle and Henny Youngman. Mary also appeared in the Policewomen's Revues. She was a natural, and it brought back memories of her vaudeville days. I enjoyed working with Marion and Mary.

I was then reassigned to a male team, with Jim O'Dea and Alan Gore, to patrol Central Park. One day, I spotted a Black man seated on a bench next to a sleeping White male. He was a "lush worker," taking advantage of a sleeping drunk. I observed him going through the man's pockets. We approached him and placed him under arrest. Jim and Alan had a difficult time placing cuffs on him. He had oversized wrists! When we got to the Precinct to book him, the Desk Officer (a family friend) inquired about my son, at which point the prisoner, Ezekiel J., turned to me and said, "If I go to jail today, when I come out, look out. You ain't gonna have no son!" This was the first time I had ever felt really threatened. A shiver went up my spine. However, a short time later, Ezekiel was stabbed to death during an argument while still in prison. I could now breathe easily and not have to worry about looking over my shoulder, worrying about him being released.

Jim and Alan were a great team. They were supportive and also taught me a lot. I was also requested by B.O.S.S.I. (Bureau of Special Service Investigations) to assist in an ongoing investigation of a Ukrainian woman said to be not only a psychic and clairvoyant she claimed to be a Reverend, as well. She was a sharp, cunning individual and had been accused by complainants of bilking them out of large sums of money. I was selected because they needed someone who not only spoke Ukrainian but understood it as well. My partner was Detective Bill Taraska, someone I knew as Pete's friend. He was a linguist and spoke five languages. He, too, was of Ukrainian descent. He told me that a family friend had approached him about our target, having misgivings and dealings with the "Rev. Y," and how it had cost her thousands of dollars, all for nothing. Rev. Y had an apartment in a brownstone located in the Slavic area in the lower East side of Manhattan. She had one room converted into a chapel with an adjoining office, the rest being a typical dining room, kitchen, bedrooms, and bathrooms. The plan was for me to be introduced to Rev. Y. by the complainant in order to gain her confidence. When we first met, she asked that I empty my purse so she could examine its contents so that she could get a feel for me. I had my wallet showing my phony name and a telephone number, which was the Manhattan

Hotel on Broadway in upper Manhattan. I used my cousin's phone number, claiming I was in only New York City for a couple of months and had previously lived in Connecticut. She accepted what I told her and said she would call me if she needed further information. She kept our first meeting short but said she would call as to when she would set a time for a real consultation and meditation.

The following day, she called to verify my residence and told me to come in that day as she felt I was in a serious state of mind and needed her help desperately. Bill came with me. She was surprised that I brought him but said the timing was perfect. She told Bill to sit in the chapel while she escorted me to her office. She told me to sit in a chair while she got organized. I glanced around and noticed that she had a small burner on a counter with a small pan on it. She left the office and came back carrying a bowl that contained ice cubes/water, which she placed on the table next to me. I started to feel uncomfortable. What next? She turned the burner on, and when the pan got hot enough, she took a sheet of wax, crumpled it up, and waited for it to melt. Once the wax melted, she came to me and took the bowl of ice water, placed it over my head, and before I knew it, she poured the melted hot wax into the bowl to congeal! I was in shock; thankfully, the bowl did not break because if it had, I would have been disfigured for life! Boy, was I lucky! She removed the melted, now hardened wax, placing it on a hand towel to dry. It was in many pieces. Her act was not unlike what you'd experience with gypsies. She gasped and said, "Good thing your sweetheart is here today because I see major problems. First...does he know you're pregnant?" I bent my head so that she could see tears streaming down my cheeks. "Look at the wax. I see a shape like a baby and also something that looks like a dollar sign, which means money problems as well." She said she was going to bring Bill in so that she could talk to both of us. She proceeded to tell Bill what she had seen in the melted wax and the problems facing us. She told him I was pregnant. He put on a great face of shock. She told us that the problem was that he was married and had not anticipated this outcome but not to be concerned. She would guide us.

The next problem was our finances, but that would be handled by Bill because he was a CPA. He was financially secure, but his money was dirty because he had evil clients. She then told us what we needed to do. First, Bill and I were to return tomorrow with $500.00 in cash from me and $1,000.00 in cash from Bill. Then, she would give me her special herbal medicine to take care of my pregnancy. Bill and I left, agreeing that she was in for a big surprise tomorrow. We would do what she asked: bring the money, allow her to incriminate herself, and be arrested.

The next day, she greeted us cordially, escorted us to her office, and had us sit while she prepared for a ritual. First, she asked for the money. She brought out a white envelope and told us to place the money inside, which we did. She then turned around and asked Bill to look inside and see if the bills were clean or dirty. We looked in the envelope and saw blackened bills. She held onto the envelope and said, "See, I told you your money was evil and dirty. We must destroy that evil in order for Marusha (my familiar name in Ukrainian) to be normal again." She threw the envelope into a metal basket, lit a match, and burned the envelope and its contents. She then turned to me, handed me a bottle, and said, "Tonight, drink all of this, and within two days, your pregnancy will be gone!" Bill stood up, placed his hands on her shoulders, and said, "You're under arrest for fraud and practicing medicine without a license." She was totally in shock. She couldn't believe Bill was a policeman. Bill was not as tall as most men on the force. We had totally fooled her. We found the original envelope containing the $1500.00, all intact, hidden on her person. She was booked in the 9th Precinct, then photographed and fingerprinted and taken to the 14th Precinct to await arraignment in court.

My assignment with B.O.S.S.I ended, and I returned to the Pickpocket & Confidence Squad once again.

Lieutenant Behan decided to give me the opportunity to have permanent partners and shifted me "up-town" to Saks 5th Avenue, Best & Co., Bergdorf Goodman, and Bloomingdale's. My new partners would be Peg Kearney and, occasionally, Mary Shanley. Mary was a real character. Upon our meeting, she called me "Kid," but there was no warmth. She totally ignored me. Peg Kearney was totally the opposite, gracious and looking forward to our working together. One day, when Peg and I were in Bergdorf Goodman, we spotted a famous actor seated on a bench, apparently waiting for a purchase to be wrapped and given to him. I recognized John Hodiak. Peg said, "I understand that he's of Ukrainian descent like you. Say something in Ukrainian to him." I said I would because I was a fan of his. I walked over to him. He raised his head to look at me, and I started to speak, but instead of speaking, I was tongue-tied and blurted out, "Mr. Hodiak, blah, blah, blah." I started giggling, placed my hand over my mouth, and quickly left the area. John Hodiak had a bewildered expression and shook his head from side to side. Peg was hysterical with laughter. She said she couldn't believe that I was shell-shocked by him. This was the first time she saw me lose my composure. Over the years, Peg would tease me about my total celebrity melt-down.

We saw many famous individuals shopping in Saks and Bergdorf Goodman, but I learned my lesson and never approached any of them. I vividly remember one particular Hollywood couple. They were the most beautiful couple I had ever seen. It was Arlene Dahl and her husband, Fernando Lamas. They were absolutely gorgeous! I had a good and close relationship with Peg Kearney, and many times, Mary Shanley chose not to go with us when we went to Saks, St. Patrick's Cathedral, and Bergdorf. Instead, she stayed at the Best & Co. or Bonwit Tellers security offices and multiple times simply did a disappearing act. This was not new to Peg. she was used to it. When we made our routine calls to the office, we always included her, even when she wasn't with us.

On one occasion, Peg was off, and I was making the call into the office saying the usual "Detective Zaharko." I was surprised to hear Lieutenant Behan answer the phone.

He said, "Oh, you probably want to talk to your partner Mary. She just came from court. Here she is." I was so happy he had interrupted me before I said her name and our location.

Mary got on the phone and said, "You want to talk to me, Kid?"

I bristled and said, "Mary, I'm through covering for you. Get your fat ass up to St. Pat's, and we'll thrash this out once and for all!" She said she was on her way.

Mary showed up about forty minutes later. Her face was livid. She approached me and wagged a finger in my face. "Who the hell do you think you're talking to?" I told her if she didn't want her finger broken, then get it out of my face. I said, "If you want to go on a bender and get drunk, I don't care as long as you give me a telephone number to reach you. I'm not risking my job for your weakness."

She was taken aback by what I said, but a miracle of miracles, she said she understood, and from that day forward, everything would be by the book. I told her I knew she did not particularly care for me as a partner, but I would never turn my back on her. She told me that the reason she felt the way she did was because I always seemed to get publicity whenever I made an arrest. I mentioned that I was not responsible for reporters being in a Precinct when I came in with an arrest. After this confrontation, we buried the hatchet and got along until her retirement in November 1958. Hallelujah!! There were some arrests that occurred during this period that made the headlines, and I recall them fondly. One in particular involved Marie Aherne, a Saks Store Detective. I also worked with Store Detective Nell Souchak, who was of Ukrainian descent and became a lifelong friend. Nell's brothers were well-known athletes. Frank Souchak was an All-American Football Star, and Mike Souchak was a well-known professional PGA Golfer. Nell also excelled in golf. We were a great team in that when we observed a shoplifter or pickpocket, we would converse in Ukrainian.

One day, when Marie and I were heading back to Saks after a court hearing, we exited the 50th Street Subway Station. I saw a man leaning against the railing, looking down at the people climbing the stairs. Marie and I continued walking to Saks, but I became aware of this man approaching us a little too closely. I spoke to Marie and said, "I think this man is up to no good. Let's pause, pretend we're window shopping, and see if anything happens." Sure enough, he brushed up against me and put his hand on the clasp of her purse, which popped open. I turned, shoved him against the store window, and said, "You're under arrest for jostling," and placed handcuffs on him. Marie and I then proceeded to the Security Office at Saks, which was less than a block away. This man did not look like the average pickpocket. He was tall, very handsome, and well-groomed. When we took him to the Precinct for booking, he bemoaned the fact that his luck had run out. He said he had attended the Democratic Convention in Chicago but had no luck and decided to try New York City. He chose the Rockefeller Center area because there were lots of tourists and more affluent shoppers on Fifth Avenue. He said that never in a million years would he have believed I was a policewoman. I was very attractive and well-dressed! When we arrived at the Precinct, there was a photographer from the New York Daily News who snapped photos of him after hearing of his misadventure.

Shortly after this, I received a call from Lt. Behan to come into the office for a new assignment. Hunter College had called requesting undercover Detectives to apprehend a male who had not only indecently exposed himself on several occasions but also made crude, salacious remarks to a number of students. Lt. Behan chose me and Mary McCarthy for the task, feeling that we two were the best fit to mingle among the students and be successful. Mary and I went to Hunter College, carried books, and wore flats, short skirts, and sweaters, mimicking the students. We roamed the stairways, corridors, and classrooms for almost two months without success, wondering if he would return.

One morning, when Mary and I were walking down a hallway, we observed a man dressed in a tweed jacket carrying books and looking like a Professor. As he got close to us, he mumbled foul words. At this point, we dropped our books, and he, in turn, dropped his as well and tried to get away. Mary and I ran after him, grabbed and subdued him, and took him into an empty classroom. We asked the Dean to have the students who had made complaints come to ascertain whether he was the culprit. Eleven students identified him as having accosted them in classrooms and hallways, either indecently exposing himself or using foul language. It turned out that he often paid a visit to Hunter College on the way to work. Frank P. was a married accountant with a previous record of molesting women on subways. He was charged with trespassing because he wasn't a student or Professor, along with several counts of indecent exposure. It had taken a while before he was apprehended, but our patience paid off.

When it came to arresting individuals, not all were compliant or without incident. I have been cursed at, spat upon, kicked, and even bitten. The bite was the worst because if the skin was broken, it required medical attention, meaning multiple injections to ensure no diseases had been transmitted. One arrest comes to mind with a contusion and sprain of the ring finger on my right hand as a result of a scuffle with a pickpocket. Peg and I were monitoring St. Patrick's Cathedral during Lent. It was very crowded. I sat in one pew, and Peg sat in another. I observed a man who was in line to receive Communion, placing his hand on the woman's handbag in front of him. I motioned to Peg about the "Dip," and we collared him, arresting him for jostling. We told him not to make a scene. As we walked down the steps, he wriggled, grabbed my right hand, and bent my fourth finger backward. We had not placed cuffs on him because we apprehended him inside the church, but we were about to when he struggled and broke free, running towards 52nd Street. It had snowed rather heavily the day before, and the sidewalks had snow piles up in the gutter. I was determined to catch him come hell or high water, as they say. I ran across Fifth Avenue up 52nd Street, closing in on him. Peg was further back but was catching up. The "Dip" turned around, shocked to see how close I was. He was about to jump over a snowbank, but I was too fast for him and tackled him face down in the snow. Peg reached us and thankfully had the cuffs out. I heard people clapping and laughing. All this took place in front of the famous "21 Club." Patrons were just leaving the club as this transpired. Someone said, "Only in New York." After booking him, I had X-rays taken to make sure the finger wasn't broken. Instead, the doctor said I had what they called a "baseball finger." It was quite painful. I went on sick leave for a couple of days because I had also thrown out my back when I tackled the pickpocket and really needed time to heal.

When I returned to the Squad, Lt. Behan said that B.O.S.S.I. had requested me again to go to Alderson, West Virginia, where there was a Federal Detention Center for female prisoners. I was to assist Detective Bill Taraska in escorting a female prisoner back to New York City to stand trial in court. We were to take a train from Penn Station to Alderson on a ten-hour trip, which meant an overnight stay. Bill made arrangements to stay at the Greenbrier Resort Hotel, a half hour from Alderson. He chose Greenbrier because he knew someone in management who he said would treat us like royalty. We arrived at the Hotel shortly after nine in the evening and were greeted by his friend, who asked if we had dinner. We told him we ate on the train but took his offer up for coffee and dessert and chatted with him. He asked if we could be trusted to keep a secret. We both confirmed that we could most certainly be trusted and keep a secret. He then told us to follow him because he wanted to show us something fantastic. We had no idea what was in store for us, but we followed him to the West Wing of the resort. He paused in front of a screen and slid it aside, revealing a huge steel door with a circular lock like that on a safe, and said, this is the "Greek Island Project," a bunker created for the safety of the President and members of the Senate and House of Representatives in the event of a national crisis, like a nuclear attack. He opened the door, revealing a huge tunnel. Needless to say, our jaws dropped. We proceeded inside to discover a broadcast center, a kitchen, a hospital, and a dormitory filled with bunk beds, along with a large room he referred to as the Exhibit Hall with two adjoining rooms. The larger of the two rooms was to house members of the House of Representatives, and the other was for members of the Senate. The exhibit hall could hold joint sessions with Congress. He said many of the hotel employees were actually government workers who overlooked the maintenance of the Bunker and that it operated under a "dummy" company known as Forsythe Company based in Arlington, Virginia. The secret was kept until a reporter for the Washington Post revealed its existence in 1962, at which time it had already been decommissioned by the Government. Although the Bunker was supplied and stocked for over thirty years, it was never used. Even today, it's considered a great tourist attraction. Bill and I kept the secret, but I admit that I told Pete about it.

The next morning, we drove to Alderson to pick up the female prisoner and took the train back to Penn Station. We arrived around 10 in the evening and escorted her to the Women's House of Detention in Greenwich Village for her overnight stay. It was an interesting assignment, but the long train ride really knocked me out.

As I mentioned before, some arrests were more memorable than others as they differed from the usual shoplifting and pickpocket arrests. One shoplifting arrest involved a so-called "socialite" from California, draped in a gorgeous mink coat and with bejeweled fingers. She was arrested for loitering in Bonwit Tellers. On the way to the Security Office, she pleaded to go to the bathroom. I accompanied her but did not trust her because I had not yet made a body search. I stood on the toilet in the stall next to her and watched as she proceeded to step out of her panties, attempting to discard them by flushing them down in the toilet. I realized these were not ordinary panties and grabbed them out of her hands. They were, in fact, "shoplifting bloomers." I then placed an additional charge against her, that of possession of burglar's tools. Anything adapted from its original use to be used in a crime is classified as a burglar's tool. We learned that she was out on bail, this being her second arrest. Just two months earlier, she had been charged with lifting diamond rings from the Robert Mercadel Jewelry Shop on Park Avenue and a gem shop at the Waldorf Astoria. One would think that being out on bail would make her behave in her best way.

Soon thereafter, our office received a request from Penn Station about travelers being jostled. I was assigned with Detective Lillian Smith to patrol the area. On the second day, while seated on a bench with Lillian close by, we monitored the Terminal. It was very busy. A woman with a child in tow decided to sit next to me. I had my purse on the bench next to my left side. She proceeded to take the little girl's coat off and placed it on the bench so that part of it concealed my purse. She then placed her hand under the coat and proceeded to open the clasp of my purse and started to insert her hand inside when I grabbed her hand, telling her she was under arrest for jostling. She protested her innocence, saying she was only retrieving the coat. Upon searching her, Lillian found several wallets in her possession, all with different names, signifying she had a very lucrative day. She should have quit when she was ahead! We were not surprised to learn she had multiple arrests for jostling/pickpocketing and often used a child as a decoy.

Other interesting arrests were confidence games like The Spanish Handkerchief Swindle, which occurred when one swindler approached a woman in Rockefeller Center and was apprehended by me and Gertrude Palmer after following him via taxi to the bank with the unsuspecting victim, who was about to withdraw funds. This con man was wanted for fleeing bail for a previous swindle. This particular con game usually involved Spanish-speaking men, whereas in another con game, The Pigeon Drop, also known as the Pocketbook Drop, women were the con people. The Pocketbook/Pigeon Drop usually occurs in a department store where the con woman approaches a female shopper browsing. Detective Doris McDonald and I were at Abraham & Strauss Dept. Store when we observed one con woman approach an elderly shopper. I was close enough to hear the conversation and signaled it was the start of a con. Doris and I waited until the second con woman approached before we stepped in to arrest them both. (*See Newspaper Clippings)

Another type of con game is the Gypsy Con, which often starts with telling fortunes. If the Gypsy feels the victim is gullible enough, the con begins with the perp seeing an illness or curse on their money, which she can help remove. Members of the squad were assigned to concerts, operas, baseball stadiums, etc. I covered the World Series at Ebbets Field in Brooklyn with my partner, Detective Bob Collins where we apprehended a pickpocket.

One particular arrest always brings a smile every time I think about it. On our day off, Pete and I decided to go to the Bronx Zoo with Steve, who was nine years old at the time. After spending the day at the zoo, we were on our way home to take the bus when I spotted three pickpockets working the bus line. I went on line in the back of two of the pickpockets with Steve in tow and told him to move as soon as I indicated and to step away from me. One of the pickpockets turned to look at me, so I said to Steve, "I know you're hungry, but we'll be home soon," I guess his hearing me say this made him comfortable enough to continue. The first pickpocket blocked the entry way to the bus, preventing the male victim behind him from entering and thereby giving the second pickpocket the opportunity to get the victim's wallet and pass it on to the third pickpocket. Pete was in the front of the bus and nabbed the first pickpocket. I told Steve to move, which he did, and then grabbed the two pickpockets and cuffed them immediately, telling them they were under arrest. Pete cuffed the other pickpocket. Their arrest records revealed they had over seventy-five arrests and multiple convictions. At the Precinct, some reporters were present and took photographs. (*See Newspaper Clippings) I called my sister, who lived nearby, to pick Steve up because I knew we had a long night ahead of us. Upon searching one of the pickpockets, he asked whether I noticed marks on his back. I said I had seen them. He told me that they were a result of lashings he received from being found guilty of pickpocketing at a racetrack in Maryland. At the time of his arrest, there was a Maryland law that provided for whip-lashing if he was found guilty of pickpocketing. The whip-lashing proved to be a deterrent and actually did result in a drastic downturn of pickpocketing at their tracks. That law has since been overturned as being cruel and inhumane. The squad got a kick out of this arrest because it started out as a family outing and ended in three arrests. Steve bragged about the events to his classmates. To this day, it still brings a chuckle when we think about the arrest. Steve became interested in law and order thanks to his parents being active members of the NYPD. He became a Police Cadet, after which he became a Policeman.

Another memorable assignment was that of being a member of Nikita Khrushchev's security entourage when he, his wife, and family (a son and a daughter) visited New York City in 1959. Once again, I was assigned to B.O.S.S.I., partnering with Detective Bill Taraska and Detective Mary Fitzgerald. The Khrushchevs were staying in a suite at the Waldorf Towers. There was always a large crew of Russian security agents on hand. Whenever a meal was delivered, I noticed that one of the agents would take a spoon and sample every dish before it was brought inside for the Khruschevs to eat. I heard one of the agents speaking in Ukrainian to another, saying that of all the women present, he'd love to tumble in the hay with me. Of course, I understood what he said and replied, "Not going to happen!" He then spoke to me in English and said that he was surprised that I understood Ukrainian. At that point, Oleg Troyanovsky, the official translator for the Khrushchevs, suggested we have a toast with vodka. Bill and I raised our glasses, and I said in Russian, "Mir e drushbah e scha namerdla Ukrainia," meaning Peace and Friendship, and Ukraine still has not died."

Bill kicked my ankle and said, "After what you said in the toast, they will watch you like a hawk, thinking you might be CIA."

That afternoon, we went to the United Nations, where Khrushchev was to deliver a speech. After the speech, the Russian delegation was invited by Dag Hammarskjold, Secretary General of the United Nations, to his private quarters. I tagged along with the Russian group to the elevator when the guard at the elevator looked at me and said, "Not you."

I replied in Ukrainian: "Poostet menyah," meaning let me in, and he, believing I was part of the delegation, allowed me to enter the elevator along with Police Commissioner Kennedy. We were the only Americans there. Dag Hammarskjold was very gracious. His words were translated into Russian. I stood behind Rada (Khrushchev's daughter) and her brother Sergei, when I noticed Oleg Troyanovsky hand a note to Sergei. I glanced at it and saw that it was in Cyrillic,

114

which I could not read, but I saw West 90th Street, at which point Oleg told Sergei to put the note away, saying, "She is looking at it." Later, I mentioned this incident to a member of the CIA and asked if it had any significance. He thanked me for being alert and said he would look into it.

The following day, Nikita, his wife Nina, and Sergei went to the Empire State Building, and Rada decided on a shopping trip to Saks Fifth Avenue. Money was no object. They bought whatever pleased them. That evening, Nina and Rada went to see the Broadway Musical, "The Music Man," which they enjoyed. The next day, Ambassador Henry Cabot Lodge, who was their Host and Guide, left with the Khrushchevs for a flight to Los Angeles to further arrange their tour of the United States.

After this awesome experience, I returned to the office, but my back was bothering me, so I went to see the Honorary Orthopedic Doctor, Dr. Bosworth. Dr. Bosworth advised that I have immediate surgery because the X-rays revealed that my herniated discs had become worse and would be giving me serious problems. I realized I had no choice and had the spinal fusion surgery in December 1959 at Polyclinic Hospital in Manhattan. They removed a bone from my hip for the fusion and found three dislocated discs in my lower back. The surgery went well, except that one morning, I complained to a nurse that I had a burning sensation in my left leg. When she came to examine me, I winced in pain, saying her touch really hurt! She immediately left the room and called for the doctor. A doctor came in and said, "It's a blood clot," and immediately put me on an intravenous program. Later, I was told that I was lucky that they had caught it in time and that no harm had been done.

I did not realize at that time that my career as a Detective was in jeopardy because of the surgery and that I would lose my Detective shield and be placed on limited duty until doctors at Headquarters decided to retire me. After several months of recuperating, I returned to the squad, still retaining my shield but working only inside the office, answering the phone, filing, and taking statements from victims of con games. Lt. Behan tried to keep me in the office for as long as he could, but my nemesis, our District Surgeon, Dr. A (the same doctor who tried to disqualify me for being flatfooted when I took the policewoman's physical), was determined to place me on the light-duty squad where I would be reinstated as a Policewoman. I was heartbroken about leaving the squad and was shifted around to various departments until I was notified of my retirement, effective January 31st, 1963! I was forced to retire on a line-of-duty disability, much to Dr. A's chagrin!

I can say that I had an amazing career as a Detective and received a Meritorious Police Duty Award and two Exceptional Police Duty Commendations. When I retired, benefits were non-existent. Fortunately, I was covered by Peter's group, the Sergeants' Benevolent Association. I realize now that it actually was the best time for me to retire because, truthfully, not a day goes by without my back acting up, some days worse than others, often requiring painful epidural injections.

Several of the women Detectives on the squad organized a farewell dinner for me at a local restaurant. I was thrilled that around fifty members attended, not only members of my squad but commanding officers of places in which I had worked. I received a replica of my Detective's Gold Shield, #704, and on the back was engraved, "Presented to Detective Mary M. Zaharko from members of the P.P.&C Squad retired 1-31-63". This was and still is a most cherished evening.

Chapter Twelve:
Rejoice-Into The Future!

It was quite an adjustment for me after retiring and no longer being assigned to security details for dignitaries and presidents, going on trips out of town to pick up female prisoners, and the rush one feels at the time of an arrest. Time to move on, as the saying goes! I decided to try my hand at oil painting. I enjoyed how quickly the time flew by while painting. Mama joined me, and she amazed me! She was a natural, painting in bold strokes and loving every minute of it. She kept painting well into her later years. We painted many different subjects like flowers and animals. I was partial to doing portraits. Mama sold several of her paintings and got good money for them.

Pete and I decided to change our residence from the Bronx to Long Beach, Long Island, and then eventually Lido Beach. My sister, Hanya, and her husband, Nick, rented a summer house in Long Beach every year. We fell in love with the area so much so that we purchased an empty 100'x100' lot in Lido Beach from Bill Chickory, a family friend. The lot was the second from the dunes overlooking the ocean. Pete was still attending Pratt Institute, aiming to obtain an architectural degree. He designed a really beautiful home for us in Lido Beach. His plans were approved, and we were on our way to building our dream home. We temporarily moved into a condo on 210 Shore Road in Long Beach, a three-bedroom apartment with a balcony overlooking the boardwalk, beach, and ocean on the fifth floor.

Steve was thrilled over the move. He could now go fishing, which he loved to do. He wasn't happy attending McBourney (a private school in Manhattan) and looked forward to attending school in Long Beach, which was highly rated. He said the kids at McBourney were snooty, and he had very few friends. Life in Long Beach was a real change for the better. Steve's grades improved, and he was happy that he now had a nice group of friends with whom to share mutual interests. Pete was busy hiring contractors to build our new home in Lido Beach.

On November the 22nd, 1963, an astonishing event shook the core of the nation. We were watching the local news on TV when there was an interruption. It was a TV reporter announcing the assassination of President Kennedy in Dallas, Texas. Everyone was in shock. Fortunately, the gunman was apprehended and in custody. The lone gunman was identified as Lee Harvey Oswald. He had fired from the sixth-floor window of the Texas School Board Book Depository, where he had allegedly been or was still employed, directly into President Kennedy's open limousine. In the limo beside President Kennedy was his wife, Jackie, Governor John Connelly, and his wife. Gov. Connelly was also struck by a bullet. President Kennedy was struck twice and was mortally wounded. The motorcade rushed to Parkland Memorial Hospital but to no avail. President Kennedy was DOA. Gov. Connelly was medically treated for a non-life-threatening wound. It was hard to believe that President Kennedy was gone! Vice President Lyndon Johnson was sworn in as our new President almost immediately.

Sunday after church, Steve turned the TV on in the family room, and another unbelievably shocking incident took place. We watched as Lee Harvey Oswald was leaving the Dallas Police Headquarters in the basement, where a large group of press and security were assembled. Suddenly, out of the blue, a man named Jack Ruby lunged

119

forward and shot Oswald point blank in the stomach. Ruby was overpowered, and Oswald was rushed to Parkland Memorial Hospital. He, too, died in the same Hospital as President Kennedy. The country was turned into turmoil. What was the motive? A lengthy investigation began.

Pete was busy getting contractors and obtaining permits for our anxiously awaited "dream house." Pete was just amazing because he was still working in NYPD, but he loved working alongside the contractors and checking every detail. We moved from Long Beach to Lido Beach in January 1965. We noted the completion date by scrawling our initials on the concrete floor by the furnace. The house was now livable, needing only minor finishing touches. It truly was a "dream home."

The first floor had a bedroom (which became Steve's bedroom), a full bar with a sink, stove, and refrigerator, an open fireplace, and beautiful terrazzo floors that Frank (Evelyn's husband) put in for us, plus a bathroom. The washing machine, dryer, and sink were concealed by a folding door. Pete designed a modern open staircase with a stainless-steel banister leading to the second floor. From the ceiling over the staircase hung a beautiful Venetian chandelier.

The second floor opened to a fantastic view of the dunes and ocean. The kitchen was to the left, all modern equipment with an open area over the counter as a pass through to the dining room. We had parquet floors and another fireplace, but most striking to me were the windows covering the entire length of the living room with a sliding glass door that led to a balcony covering the width of the house, one half of which had a canopy overhead.

Most of all, I loved the redwood trapezoid ceilings, a unique touch! There was a bathroom, two bedrooms, and then, the master bedroom, complete with a private dressing room, a two-story closet, and in the bathroom, surprise, surprise, a bidet! There was nothing lacking. It was so up-to-date that no other home in the community could compare. The street was unfinished, and there was an empty lot in front of us and another across the street. We befriended our neighbors across from us, the Dowlings, an elderly couple who were thrilled that we were living there year-round rather than seasonally as many of the residents were. The Dowlings spent most of their time in St. Thomas, in the U.S. Virgin Islands, where they owned a hotel and jewelry shop called Cardows.

There was a total of ten homes on either side of the street. Our street, Luchon Street, was a dead-end street like many streets in Lido Beach. One time, when I was in the house during construction, a car with two men parked in the street, observing what was going on. Pete approached them and discovered upon questioning them that they were the security/bodyguards for a neighbor of ours on Royat Street (opposite the empty lot from us), Tommy Lucchese, a notorious Mafia figure. He lived in a modest ranch house with his wife and son. Many mornings, I saw him leaving his home accompanied by a bodyguard to go to the garment district in New York City. Fortunately, there was never any unusual activity at his home.

I became pregnant with a due date of late December or early January 1966. We were thrilled and happy to learn it would be a girl. We prepared her room with all the trimmings, but I wanted a bassinet by my bed until I felt she was old enough to be in a crib in her own room. These were such happy, sweet days. Steve had many friends in the area, so he was always occupied. Behind us were the Raffertys,

121

Marie and Dick, and their children, Mike and Jeannie, who were the best neighbors one could hope for. Marie always took me grocery shopping when Pete was working. Anytime I needed something, she was there for me. We wound up being life-long friends even after they moved to Toms River, New Jersey.

Time passed by quickly, and my due date was approaching. It was decided that after spending Christmas with Mama and Papa, I would stay with them because their apartment was closer to the Hospital, Harkness Pavillion Presbyterian Hospital in upper Manhattan. Mama still had Steve's crib. On January 12th, 1966, in the wee hours of the morning, my water broke, which meant I needed to move quickly. Pete was working, so he was unable to take me, but good old reliable Nick was on hand. I called my sister and when she picked up the phone I sang "Now is the hour." She laughed and said they'd be right down. They still lived in the same building on the seventh floor. When they came down, they had two blankets and a couple of towels. Nick and Hanya drove me to Harkness Pavillion. We arrived there in short order. Nick got a wheelchair and wheeled me into the Maternity Ward. I was then handed over to a Maternity Nurse. Dr. Byshe happened to be nearby and, after examining me, said delivery would probably be in the early afternoon, so there was no need for Hanya and Nick to stick around. The shooting pains were timed, and boy, it was rough. Finally, by a natural delivery, I had a beautiful, healthy baby girl! I was really tired and taken to my room, where Pete happily waited. We decided to name her Mary Manya Zaharko. She was a beautiful baby doll and a hungry one as well. This time, unlike with Steve, I was able to breast feed her. The hospital stay was only a few days. We returned to Mama and Papa for a week until I got a little stronger.

Mama came back to Lido with us to help me adjust, and what a blessing! As we entered the house, Duchess, my Manx cat, was standing on the landing of the staircase. I said, "Duchess, Mommy's home and look what I have with me!" She meowed and turned around, promptly defecated, and walked up the stairs to the second floor! We could not believe what happened as she had never done anything like this before. Duchess was a gentle, loving cat. She even slept with me. I guess she was showing her displeasure at my having been absent for so long.

I kept the bassinet by my bed. I would lie on my side, peer inside, and look at my sleeping beauty. Manya was a good baby. She never whined and always seemed content. She rarely cried, only when she was hungry, and always had a smile. Life was good, except that Duchess was now avoiding me and would not enter the room or sleep with me as she had done in the past.

I adjusted to being a full-time mom and discovered in July that I was once again pregnant, which meant I would need to stop breast feeding Manya. We were delighted because Manya now has a companion. Time passed so quickly. My due date was predicted to be early March. This time, it would be a boy!

One day, while doing some spring cleaning, I decided to clean the glass chandelier over the staircase, and after wiping it down with a wand, I noticed a droplet of water on one of the glass coverings and decided to remove it with my fingertip. Bad, bad decision because the chandelier was lit. I placed one hand on the stainless-steel banister for support and reached into the glass only to be frozen, stunned by a wave of electrical current. I could not free myself, and I rocked back and forth, saying, "Oh, oh, oh!" Fortunately, Pete was in the garage, listening to me and seeing me rocking. He quickly shut the switch off

123

(there was a switch at the base of the stairs.) I freed my hand from the banister and went into the living room to sit and relax. Pete comforted me and said, "Boy, it was a good thing I heard you. My God, you could have been electrocuted!" I was concerned about the effect this might have on the baby. Fortunately, I had an appointment with Dr. Byshe the following day, and when I told him what happened, he said, "Maybe your boy will be another Einstein or just normal, no harm done. Hope to see you soon."

It was now mid-March, and according to the doctor, I was overdue, so he had me come in on the 21st of March for induced labor, once again, at Harkness Pavillion. On the first day of spring, March 21st, 1967, I gave birth to our second son, Peter Zaharko, Jr., a beautiful, healthy baby. After a few days at the hospital, after Dr. Byshe's orders to recuperate after a rough time, we happily came home to Lido Beach. There were two cribs now in one bedroom. Manya was in the crib, and Peter was in a bassinet for a short while. When we came home this time, Duchess became friendly again and cuddled up to me, unlike the time I came home with Manya.

Peter was quite different from Manya. He refused to be breastfed and took to a formula. This wasn't a problem because Manya was also on a formula. Peter, like Manya, was a good boy, never whining. He enjoyed being held and smiled and cooed at. A good baby! I was so fortunate to have a loving mother who never complained about lending me a hand. Mama adored the babies. I called them my "Irish Twins," being born so close to one another. Both had platinum blonde hair and big blue eyes, and when they smiled, they showed their dimples. They were adorable, happy babies.

At around the same time, Pete was on patrol answering a possible break-in at a business and discovered the business was a stainless-steel manufacturing company making furniture for famous companies, among them Pace Stainless-Steel Furniture. Pete showed the owner some of the sketches and designs he had created for furniture for our family room. They were fantastic, original designs. The owner liked them and went ahead with making them. Among the designs were the frames for three couches, an altar table, bar stools in the shape of a "Z," an obelisk etagere with a light box to illuminate articles on the shelf, light boxes for display, beautiful mirrors and a table with a matching mirror for Nick's Beauty Salon (Richard at the Carlton House). Pete was advised that upon retiring from the New York Police Department, he should open a shop. He had such great talent. Pete truly was gifted. Not only could he draw architectural plans for homes, but he could also work alongside the contractors, paint oil paintings, and make sculptures. He won first place for a sculpture while attending Pratt Institute. I loved our stainless-steel furniture because, unlike chrome, it would always be bright, shiny, and smooth, and it would never pit!

One afternoon, our doorbell rang. When I answered it, I was greeted by a young man who had his station wagon parked in the street with the back window opened, showing off boxes of vegetables, fruit, and eggs, all for sale. He said his name was Harold, and he delivered his wares all over Lido. We became his customers. He had other goods for sale as well: merchandise like men's and women's sweaters, shirts, blouses, children's clothing, and all at a great price. He said he knew several garment distributors who gave him their "left-overs" to sell. This was great, but not all sizes were available.

One time, Harold said he noticed I had quite a few oriental objects and that he knew of a customer in Long Beach who was also a collector/dealer. She had a piece he thought I might be interested in.

He said he saw a beautiful Chinese Water Buffalo with two children on its back that I would probably like. He piqued my curiosity, so I had him give me his customer's phone number. Her name was Carol Klapper, and she was happy for me to come over because Harold had told her about me.

I went to her home in Long Beach, and when I pulled up, I saw a man on a ladder cleaning the gutters. I walked up to the door and asked whether he knew if the lady of the house was home. He got off the ladder and, to my surprise, opened the door for me and yelled, "Carol, you have someone here to see you." He turned out to be Carol's husband, Dave. Carol greeted me and led me to the dining room, where on the table sat the Rosewood Water Buffalo. It was large and beautiful. I told her that I would be interested in purchasing it, but to my dismay; she said that she had just promised it to her parents, who had really admired it. Carol's home was like a museum. Everywhere you looked, there were fantastic pieces of silver, crystal vases, statues, and art, you name it. Carol was an antique lover on every level and bought whenever an estate sale came along. I learned that Carol had also just given birth to a baby boy in February. We had a lot in common: new babies and the love of antiques. Our friendship would last our whole lives. Carol was so artistic and painted beautifully. All of her works were originals. She had an amazing feel, an eye for the unusual, and was constantly on the go with her partner accumulating objects. She even designed a glass engraved crystal block, The Roaring Lion," for Moser Art Glass, one of the most famous glass companies based in Czechoslovakia. The Roaring Lion was the first of many blocks Moser made. The blocks were limited editions; no more than five were made because the engraving took so long to do. The Corning Museum in New York bought The Roaring Lion to add to their collection of art glass.

I, too, became a collector. Pete designed a magnificent stainless steel wall unit for Carol and Dave to display their collection of blocks. The unit had electrical shelves to illuminate the crystal blocks. I often went to estate sales with Carol and became involved with antiques. At this time, I also enrolled at the Gemological Institute in New York City and took an accelerated course in gemology, which came in handy in the future. I bought a G.I.A. Microscope, a gold testing kit, a jeweler's loupe, and other necessary testing materials to have on hand.

Manya and Peter were growing up so fast. Occasionally, when Pete and I had events to attend in the evening, we needed a babysitter. If one of Steven's daughters (our neighbors) were unavailable, we would use a sweet girl named Kathryn Gambino. Yes, the granddaughter of Tommy Lucchese. Her mother, Frances, was a lovely lady and had no objection to her daughter babysitting for me.

Sadly, the Black Panthers were on the move to kill police in 1972, which was a particularly bad time. Two policemen from Pete's Precinct were murdered in cold blood as they walked on patrol. Ptl. Gregory Foster, who was Black and Ptl. Rocco Laurie, who was White, were the victims, both in their mid-twenties. Because of this tragedy, we decided that Pete would put his papers in and retire!

At the suggestion of the Dowlings, we visited St. Thomas to see whether we might relocate there. I could sell from one of their jewelry shops, having some knowledge of jewelry due to my GIA course. Our friends, Emile and Irene DuPont, had a home with a two-bedroom apartment on the lower floor, which we rented. Before we left Lido for St. Thomas, I rented our family room to Al and Grace, whom we knew from the nearby People's Church, who needed a temporary place to live until their condo was ready in approximately three months, perfect or so I thought. The only problem was that we could not take Duchess with us, and Al, the tenant, said he disliked cats. I told him that, Duchess was a sweetheart and would be upstairs with Steve. Marie Rafferty and my sister would take care of her, so not to worry. On a prior visit to St. Thomas, we had purchased a one-acre lot on Skyline Drive, overlooking Hans Lolick Island, with a beautiful view also of Morningstar Beach, thinking that in the future, we'd build a vacation or retirement home there.

The DuPonts had a dog named Pasha, their guard dog, who watched their house when they were working. Pasha was tied up in their driveway. Things became different for Pasha when we moved in. She was no longer tied up and became attached to us, being a very smart and friendly dog. One morning, I woke up to discover that Manya was not in her bed, and the front door was wide open. I went outside and called her name. When there was no answer, I panicked. I saw Pasha and said "Pasha, go get Manya." Pasha took off and, to my amazement, returned with Manya, leading her home and pulling her by her nightgown, which she had clenched in her mouth. I embraced Manya and told her never to go out like she did ever again.

St. Thomas had changed since our original visit in that the natives were being indoctrinated by The Black Liberation Movement (formerly, the Black Panthers) and were becoming quite hostile. When I walked on the sidewalk with Manya and Peter, for example, some of the locals in front of me would bend their elbows so that I had to step down into the street from the sidewalk in order to pass by them. Another time, when I came out of a grocery store pushing my cart full of purchases, I found a group lounging on the back of my car. I politely said, "Excuse me, I have to unload my groceries." They laughed and raised their arms with clenched fists and said, "When we're ready, Baby." I, in turn, did a stupid thing. I did the "Italian curse" and bent one arm with the other arm thrust into my elbow and said, "NOW!" I guess I startled them, but they understood my sign, and they took off, shaking their heads and smiling. The Black Liberation Movement had a stronghold in St. Thomas.

Angela Davis was at the University of St. Thomas at that time.

We made friends with our neighbors and also with a caretaker named Daphne, who just adored Manya and Peter and had them swim in her owner's pool daily. Daphne also took care of their dog, Ranger, a huge mastiff who befriended Manya, Peter, and Pasha. Manya used to sit on Ranger's back, and he would trot around like a pony. Whenever Daphne had a doctor to see or needed to go to town for necessities, Pete took her. Unfortunately, there were home invasions happening, and it hit home. One night, when Emile was chatting with us, Irene, who had a headache and had stayed in bed, heard a strange noise. When she opened her bedroom door, she saw two men gathering up some of her possessions: a beautiful lion rug, silverware, etc. She yelled, and they ran out into their waiting car and took off. We heard her yelling. Pete and Emile asked what had happened, and when she told them, they took off in pursuit, hoping to catch the thieves. They were unsuccessful. That event made us decide to return home. I didn't feel comfortable, unlike our previous visits, and felt it best to leave St. Thomas, but we would miss our friends and Pasha. Shortly after we left, Irene and Emile chose to also leave St. Thomas, selling their home and business.

We returned home. It was good to be back in Lido Beach again. I was shocked to learn that Duchess had been chased away repeatedly by Al and was found struck by a car on Lido Blvd. and killed! I felt guilty because she was a good cat. The timing for our return was perfect because Al and Grace's condo was now available for them, and we would have the house by ourselves. While in St. Thomas, our friends, Tom and Ruth Quetell, who owned a bar, asked Pete if he could do them a favor and find them a stove because theirs was not functioning well. Pete went to a restaurant auction and found a great stove for them, which he had shipped to St. Thomas. Tommy was a local. Ruth was originally from New Jersey. Their bar was in the French Quarters of St. Thomas, which was very popular and especially known for their spicy barbecue chicken wings. Tommy called when the stove arrived and was absolutely thrilled. It was almost new and had more features on it than his old stove. He truly appreciated Pete's good taste! We remained friends over the years.

Manya was enrolled in the local elementary school in Long Beach and always loved going to school. She was a good student. However, I noticed a change after a while. She began to say that she hated school. This was surprising. One afternoon, when she got back from school, I noticed streaks on her cheeks and asked whether she had been crying. She told me that she had been punished by her teacher and put into the clothes closet for disrupting the class by making strange sounds, which she said she did not do. I was taken aback by the teacher's actions. I asked if that was the first time she was put in the clothes closet as punishment. She told me the teacher disliked her, had used Manya as an example to others, and had put her in the closet multiple times. I was furious! The next day, I approached the teacher and told her I would not tolerate her abuse of Manya and that I would report her to the Principal. I told her that if she ever did this again to Manya or anyone else, she would have to reckon with me.

Several of Manya's friends in Lido Beach attended a private school in Oceanside, which was highly recommended. I was interviewed by the Principal, who arranged for Manya's prompt transfer to St. Andrew's Episcopal School. I was thrilled. Manya and Peter both attended St Andrews. One day, my neighbor, Bill Stevens, approached me and said he had something amusing to tell me. When he had been walking past the school bus stop, he saw Manya and Peter waiting for their school bus. He told Peter he liked his maroon jacket. He asked Peter the name of his school. Peter replied, "St. Andrews Pickles School." He could not pronounce Episcopal; after all, he was only in kindergarten.

Shortly thereafter, one of Manya's friends' female dog gave birth to four pups, and upon seeing them, Manya begged for one as a pet. I went over and chose the runt of the litter, a little female and the only pup left after the others had been adopted. We were excited as it was an interesting breed, half poodle and half cocker spaniel. The pup was brought to us when she was weaned at around two months old. We all fell in love with her and called her Booji. In Ukrainian, Booji is baby talk for kiss. Booji was so sweet and cuddly, with silky black and white fur.

We acquired another pet, a beautiful parakeet, Sammy, who came to us unexpectedly. One afternoon, while I was in the kitchen, Peter approached me and said, "Mom, come and see. There's a bird sitting on the canopy railing, and he called me pretty baby." I went outside and saw this beautiful blue parakeet, obviously well-trained. When I said, "Come pretty baby to Mommy," he immediately flew onto my outstretched hand. I told Pete to go to the garage and get our old bird Dickie's cage so that we could house the parakeet too. The parakeet flew onto a picture frame in the living room and seemed very content. I cleaned the cage, filled the container with water, and left the door open. The parakeet immediately flew inside. I closed the door while he drank some water. He was really thirsty. I chopped up some lettuce and grapes, which I would do for food until we bought the proper birdseed. He was talkative and loved flying around freely in the living room. He would often perch on Peter or Manya's shoulder and say, "Kiss, kiss."

Another neighbor, knowing how fond we were of animals, brought over an abandoned kitten, an adorable tiger-striped female that I had spayed along with Booji. Manya decided to call the cat "Gyppy" instead of "Gypsy," which, for some reason Peter mispronounced as "Gyppy," so "Gyppy" it was. Our household of pets was complete.

Sammy, the parakeet, loved Gyppy and would fly onto her back and relax. Gyppy took this in stride, whereas Booji, on the other hand, would growl at Sammy. We had to be careful when Sammy was on the loose. Booji was put outside to be safe. Sammy loved to tweak Gyppy's whiskers. We took photos of him doing this. Sammy could imitate your voice. Often I would hear Dick Rafferty's voice saying, "Come here, Dooley Ooley Boy" (Dooley was their dog), only it wasn't Dick, it was actually Sammy (the Rafftertys had taken care of Sammy while we were in St. Thomas). Very often I would hear Pete whistle to get my attention whenever he was downstairs in the garage and I was in the kitchen, only to realize it was Sammy, not Pete, calling.

One afternoon, the doorbell rang. When I answered, I saw a handsome, stocky man who introduced himself as Serge. He said he was the contractor for the people who owned the empty lot in front of us, which would not be empty for long. He had permits to bulldoze and level the property for construction. He had an engaging smile and a thick Italian accent to boot. He was very charming. He asked us when would be the best time to meet the lot owner so that I could see the house plans. I told him that whenever it was convenient for them, it was fine with me because I was usually home. We arranged for a meeting the following day, which happened to be a Saturday. Pete was home, and it was his day off (Pete had returned to the NYPD for just one year after having retired last year and was now assigned to the SWAT team).

On Saturday, Serge and the owner came by. This was our first introduction to Nathan Goodman. Nathan lived in Forest Hills Gardens, where Serge was the local caretaker and maintenance man for the community. Nathan appeared overly friendly and charming, but then, this was our first of many meetings. Serge said there was a problem for them in that, there was no water or electricity available, and he asked if we could possibly share them. Pete said that we would show our bills to them and that they would have to pay anything in excess. Nat raised his glass of scotch (we were sitting at the bar) and said, "I'll drink to that." It soon became a custom that whenever Nat came by to oversee construction, he'd be bending his elbow at our bar enjoying his scotch! The plans for the Goodman residence were a total surprise to us because it was not going to be the usual routine structure, but instead a castle, and a pink one at that! The pink bricks were from a foundry in Alabama. They were also going to have an underground garage. Nat admired our wood cabinets and asked if he could have the name of our carpenter. We gladly gave him Frank's name. Anne, Nat's wife, was sedate compared to loquacious Nat. She also had something of a germ phobia. When one of the workers used a toilet in one of their bathrooms, the next day, it was out on the sidewalk for the garbage men to pick up. So, the workers rented a Port-o-Potty placed on the sidewalk to use. Many times, Anne, Nat, and her son, Alan, had dinner with us. We were on good terms. At

Christmas, they gave Manya a beautiful ballerina doll, and Peter received a windup motorboat.

Everything was going along well until they changed their plan from an underground garage to a two-car garage on the side of their house. Then, things took a drastic turn, and everything dramatically changed. All hell broke out! The Civic Association said the garage was in violation of the property code in that it was two feet from our properties, whereas the code required a minimum of five feet to prevent overcrowding. A lawsuit was filed, and now, Nat showed his true self. He was no longer friendly but quite nasty! The lawsuit named us and the Raffertys as defendants. Nat called my brother-in-law Nick and Pete "putzes," a Jewish slur when they tried to talk to him civilly (Nick and Pete were both members of the Civic Association). Whenever any member of our family walked past his house when he was outside, he would clear his throat and spit! I was truly upset. One afternoon, I decided to speak to him and try to make peace. Nat answered the door and asked what I wanted. I told him that I wanted things to return to normal. I even facetiously said I would sell him some land for a buck if it would stop the animosity, but we both knew that it was not possible. Tears rolled down my cheeks. Having no tissues, Nat gave me his handkerchief to wipe away my tears. I told him that I did not appreciate his spitting whenever I walked by with my mother. It was so vulgar. At this point, he closed the door, and I went home. I told my neighbor Bill Stevens about my conversation with Nat. Bill told me not to speak to Nat. We all knew that my offer to sell some of my property for a buck was facetious and that it would never happen. Nat also lied, claiming that the main entrance to his residence faced the dunes and not Luchon Street. A strange thing happened one day: a man approached Anne Goodman, saying he was a Building Inspector. He said, "Tell Mr. Goodman that matter has been taken care of." I heard this exchange as I was still on good terms with Anne. The pink castle was often referred to by the locals as the "Pink Brick Shit House" and drew curiosity onlookers. Sadly, people we had been friendly with now for some reason (Nat had given them his insurance business, etc.) shied away from the Raffertys and Zaharkos.

At the same time, we were in the middle of building a home for Steve opposite the Raffertys and were constantly visited by Inspectors trying to find fault with the construction. I recognized one of the Inspectors as the one who spoke to Anne Goodman previously. Had someone been paid off?

Shortly thereafter, Manya started to develop serious allergies, requiring multiple shots to relieve her condition. The doctor told us that as long as we lived in this area, she would be affected, and she suggested that we move to either Arizona or Florida. Because we had purchased some property in Deerfield Beach, Florida, on the Kingfisher Canal, one lot off the Intracoastal Waterway, and with the hostility and turmoil because of the Goodman lawsuit, we felt that the time had come to change our residence. The situation remained the same with Nat, although Anne was still friendly and expressed her regrets about the animosity. She often would ask for recipes I made when they had dinner with us and which she had enjoyed. I loved our home on Luchon Street and truly did not want to sell it. I suggested renting it, and although we tried that, it seemed that people only wanted it for a summer rental, which was not feasible.

We ended up selling our home to a lovely Taiwanese couple with three young children, two girls and one boy. They owned a clothing line in the garment district, having purchased the fashionable and well-known Adolfo brand and changed the name to LILHI. They asked about schooling, and I recommended St Andrew's Episcopal School. They said they loved the house and would never ever sell it. Living in Lido Beach had been so special. I loved the neighborly camaraderie, except for Nat, and enjoyed the many activities available, but most of all, the view and the white sandy beach. There were special moments and special times like celebrating the holidays at either Hanya's house (my sister had also moved to Lido Beach) or mine and Mama swimming in the ocean as late as November while I happily fished.

I remember one time Pete said the water was so cold I could get arthritis of the crotch! Another sweet memory I had was of Manya when she was about four years old. I had just finished dressing her in her new Easter outfit, complete with white stockings and Mary Jane shoes, and told her to wait in the living room while I dressed Peter. We were going to see Grandpa Steve and Baba Katherine in New York City for a traditional Easter dinner. I finished dressing Peter and looked for Manya but did not see her when I heard a faint voice saying, "Mommy, come lookah dah boats." I went out to the deck and, to my horror, saw Manya sitting up on the roof alongside the chimney. Pete neglected to remove a ladder when he was doing minor roof repairs, and Manya decided to climb up to see the boats in the ocean. I called Pete, and he told Manya to wait for Daddy to come up to see the boats. He climbed the ladder and sat beside her, gathered her in his arms, came down the ladder, and handed her to me. Needless to say, we needed to change her white stockings as they were dirty from her climb to the rooftop.

I loved our beautiful home and felt remorseful, but the kids were excited about our move even though they were leaving their friends behind. They looked forward to a new beginning and change. Pete had gone down a week before the moving van came to look for a rental in Deerfield Beach until our new home was built. Believe it or not, he found a beautiful home right on the Intracoastal Waterway next to our vacant lot. What luck! We drove down with our car loaded with Sammy (in his cage), Gyppy, and, of course, Booji. We made only one stop in North Carolina before continuing to Deerfield Beach, where Pete rented a room at the Ramada Inn temporarily until the moving van arrived. When I went to see the rental house, I was pleasantly surprised by all the amenities it had. The house had also been recently remodeled, with new appliances in the kitchen, four bedrooms and three bathrooms. The biggest plus was a great swimming pool with a diving board, a dock for a boat, and a screened-in patio overlooking the Intracoastal. We were fortunate that we only stayed one night at the Inn as the moving van arrived ahead of schedule. All our furniture fits beautifully into the rooms. It looked like we had always lived there. Our neighbors were very cordial, bringing in flowers, a basket of fruit, and cookies as welcome gifts, which made us happy. Pete was busy getting building permits and contractors while I was occupied with enrolling Manya and Peter in school. I had the choice of either public school or private. I chose a private school called Zion Lutheran School rather than a public school because after visiting Zion, I felt it was similar to St. Andrew's Episcopal school, and I thought they would be more comfortable there. I was right. It afforded them a wonderful opportunity to meet and make new friends.

Pete, as usual, designed another beautiful home and supervised the construction, as well as working alongside the workers. Because we were on the waterway, the Kingfisher Canal, he insisted on a solid foundation consisting of 50 pilings for the house and 12 pilings for the 20'x40' diving pool. This was costly, but he said that if a hurricane came, our house would probably be the only house on the street not affected, so it was worth it. We had solid plaster walls, unlike most homes, which had drywalls, hurricane windows, and doors. We also had a beautiful stone fireplace in the living room and Mexican tile floors on the first floor. The first floor had a step-down living room with sliding glass doors leading to a patio. The kitchen had two pantries, a huge refrigerator, double ovens, and an electric stovetop. Off the kitchen was the dining room, which also had glass sliding doors leading to a screened-in porch overlooking the pool and canal. We had an eat-in section in the kitchen as well as a built-in desk. Pete built a bar that also overlooked the canal and pool. A guest bathroom was in the foyer.

We had a step-down family room with huge windows overlooking the yard, dock, and canal. We had a bathroom, and next to it was the laundry room. On the side of the house was a shower to use whenever you got out of the pool.

A straight staircase led to the second floor. The first bedroom was the master bedroom, complete with a porch, two huge closets, a dressing table, two sinks, a bathroom with a glass-enclosed shower, a sunken bathtub, a bidet, and a toilet. It was fantastic! In the hallway was a bathroom, after which was Peter's bedroom, two closets plus a linen closet, then Manya's bedroom, and finally, the guest bedroom, complete with another bathroom. All the rooms were large and had high ceilings with overhead fans. The floors were parquet wooden floors. Pete again outdid himself with another truly gorgeous home he could be proud of.

One of the contractors turned out to be the stone mason who had worked on our home in Lido Beach, Jerry Schulte. He lived just around the corner from us. One day, he brought his wife Margaret to visit our home and meet us. This was great because I now had a new friend. Margaret asked if I would like to join her when she went to art class. I was thrilled because I hadn't painted in a long time and had time on my hands now. The kids were in school, and Pete was busy with the new construction. We went to an art class in Ft. Lauderdale. Our teacher, Gene Register, was wonderful. He put me at ease, and I truly loved his instructions. I learned a lot from him. You were free to choose your subject matter, so I did portraits, flowers, etc.

Manya and Peter were doing well in school. Peter joined a swim club in Boca Raton and practiced daily in our 20'x40' pool. Booji also participated when Pete was swimming. Peter and Booji would line up, and I would say, "Ready, set, go!" Peter would dive in the pool, and Booji would run alongside and very often finish at the end of the pool before Peter. It was so funny to watch. Sometimes, Booji was so excited she would fall into the pool!

When the house was almost done, we decided to pay Grandpa Steve, Baba Katherine, Steve, my parents, Nick, and Hanya, for a visit to Lido. Pete stayed home with Booji and Gyppy. The children and I took Amtrak to New York City. The train ride was twenty-three hours long. We did not have sleeping berths but upright seats to sleep in. It was a little rough, but we managed it. When we got to Penn Station, we took a cab to Grandpa Steve's, and they were thrilled and happy to see us. Because we were spending a couple of days in New York City, I suggested we visit the Museum of Natural History. Both Manya and Peter were happy to go. We were in the Museum for several hours when I realized Peter was no longer with us. Manya and I called his name, but there was no response! We looked around, but he was nowhere to be seen! I located a Security Guard and asked where the Lost and Found Office was. He directed me to the office,

139

and Peter was sitting on a bench there! He said he had wandered away from us and went to the Lost and Found Office, knowing that eventually we would come and get him. I was happy we were reunited and said, "Time to go."

We took the crosstown bus to Second Avenue and took transfers for the Second Avenue Bus. While waiting for the bus, I noticed a bakery and said I wanted to get some pastries to bring to Grandpa and Grandma. I told Peter to wait at the bus stop while Manya and I went to make the purchases. When we came out, to our surprise, Peter was no longer there. We called his name, but there was no answer! We looked into the nearby stores, but still no Peter. I hailed a cab and decided to drive down Second Avenue to see if we could see him, but there was still no Peter. Manya began to cry, and I really started to become concerned. Peter did not know the city. After driving around up and down for over an hour, we decided to go to the 19th Precinct and enlist their help. The Detectives put out a missing persons report, and Steve, who was working at the time in Brooklyn, saw the teletype and immediately called Grandpa Steve to ask what was going on. The Detectives drove Manya and me to Grandpa Steve's. When we arrived at their apartment building, my heart started to pound. There was a squad car parked there. We went up to the apartment to find that Peter was inside with two policemen. Apparently, he had decided to walk to Grandpa's house, but after getting as far as 42nd Street, he was exhausted. He said he stood there to unwind and try to get his bearings when a car with a Black man pulled alongside and said, "Boy, you lost? Get in the car, and I'll help you find what you're looking for." Peter noticed a group of women chatting close by, so he turned and pretended to be with them. The car drove away, thankfully! As fate would have it, a squad car also pulled up, waiting for the light to change, when Peter went up to them and told them he was lost! He mentioned that both his parents were retired NYPD officers, his brother was also a policeman, and he was visiting his grandparents. They told him to hop in and asked Grandpa Steve's name so that they could call him and get his address. They told Grandpa Steve they were on their way. I was both happy and angry with Peter but grateful that nothing bad had happened. I thanked the policemen for their kindness and told them to please remove the teletype. Steve called again to check on us and was happy that we were all safe.

The following day, we went to Lido Beach, and Peter and his cousin, Teddy, went surfing while Manya hung out with her cousin, Marianne (these were Nick and Hanya's two children). I was glad to see our former residence on Luchon Street and to have spent some time with my parents, Steve, Hanya, and Nick. After a few days, the time had come for us to say our goodbyes and return to Florida. We took the train at Penn Station. I was happy we were going home! Manya said she was hungry, so we went to the dining car. A Black waiter approached us and pointed to a table set up for three in a corner. He left to join a party of jovial Black people who were apparently celebrating and having a good time, talking and laughing and raising their glasses. I pulled my table forward in order to sit on the cushion. When I attempted to sit, the cushion slid down, and I, too, slid down, scraping my back and landing on my buttocks. I had my hand under my buttock and felt tremendous pain. It looked as though I had broken my little finger on my left hand. Some diners rushed over to help me. The waiter just stood there looking at me and shaking his head. A conductor appeared, noted my injuries, and quickly got me a bowl filled with ice to soothe my pain. The waiter had disappeared. The conductor said he would get some food for Manya and Peter and suggested we disembark in Philadelphia and go to the emergency room of the local hospital. I told him that was not feasible as we were going straight to Florida, where I would be taken care of. After Manya and Peter finished their meal, I couldn't eat. I was in real pain when we returned to our seats. I can only say it was a miserable, pain-filled night for me. A passenger gave me two aspirins to help ease the pain. I kept my hand in the ice-filled bowl all night.

When we arrived in Deerfield Beach the next morning, Pete saw how distressed I was at the crooked little finger and swollen hand. He told me to make out an Incident Report, which I did and handed to the Station Master. It was good to be home and have Pete comforting me. Pete called an orthopedic doctor, and fortunately, I was able to see him that afternoon. An X-ray revealed a broken pinky. The doctor told me I would need to have a pin inserted in order to straighten my finger. The following day, he placed a pin in my pinky and enclosed it in a cast. Even though I had surgery, to this day, I still have a crooked pinky. The upper part never straightened out. At the doctor's suggestion, I hired an attorney to proceed with a lawsuit against Amtrak. We went to trial, and I was awarded $85,000.00 for pain and discomfort. The attorney's fee was $25,000.00. To this day, I wake up every day with a backache. I am now used to my crooked finger.

One afternoon, I received a great phone call from one of my former NYPD partners, Mary Ayers. I was delighted to learn that she and her husband, Bill, lived in Fort Lauderdale. I couldn't wait to see her and reminisce about our times together. Mary and I became really close. We went shopping together. She even talked me into joining her sewing class. The class was an eye-opener for me. I never was one for sewing. I hemmed slacks and did some mending but my sewing was far from professional. The class turned things around for me. By the time the course was over, I had made a lounging robe, a bathing suit, panties, slip blouses, and outfits for Manya, and they all turned out really well. This surprised Pete because he could also sew, having attended Textile High School in New York City. I also couldn't resist shopping in thrift/antique shops and started collecting again as I had done in Lido with Carol Klapper.

Carol and Dave Klapper had decided to become professional antique dealers. They came down and stayed with us while they were exhibiting in the Miami Beach Shows. It was suggested that since I had quite a collection of antiques myself and had knowledge of jewelry, I might also join the circuit and become a dealer. We needed the extra income because the construction was costing more than projected. But first, we needed a name. I suggested "The Odyssey" because the objects I would sell came from all over the world. I needed some additional jewelry, so I contacted my jeweler in New York City, Max, of G. Wenz & Son. Max agreed to send me shipments of jewelry to sell. This was great because he wrote all the necessary information and the price he wanted, which was wholesale, and gave me a selling range so I could make a profit. My friends, the Dowlings, who had jewelry shops in St. Thomas, recommended their supplier as well, Bernard Nacht & Co. in New York City, which is well respected and known for the quality of their jewelry. I was so grateful and really appreciated both jewelers for having faith in and trusting me. Pete and I were excited about becoming antique/jewelry dealers. These were uncharted waters for us, but I felt the timing was good because both Manya and Peter were now teenagers in high school. We decided we would do only local shows so that we would be home every evening.

When we moved into our new home, two houses up from us, a new neighbor also moved in. I often saw her walking her dog, a miniature Poodle. I made her acquaintance while I was walking with Booji. She introduced herself as Roz Bouley, a Delta stewardess. Her husband, Paul, was a captain for Delta. We bonded immediately, which was a blessing for both of us. Whenever she and Paul were out of town on a flight, I would take care of Cinnamon, her poodle, and she, on the other hand, would keep an eye on Manya and Peter when we were doing shows. When I would go along with Booji to get Cinnamon, as soon as I opened the door and said, "Cinnamon, Booji is here, come, we're going to Mary's house," she would rush to us. She was almost blind and depended on Booji. It was adorable to see Booji nudging Cinnamon down the street to my house. Roz and I shared many dinners and cocktails and remained close, even more so when tragedy struck.

One morning at around three, the phone rang. I answered with apprehension. I heard a voice yelling, "He's dead, he's dead. What am I going to do?" and she hung up. I realized it was Roz's voice, and I told Pete we needed to go to Roz and find out what was going on. We rushed to her house in our night clothes to see all the lights on and the front door open! We ran inside and saw that Roz was packing clothes into a suitcase, looking extremely distressed. I asked what had happened. She told me that she had received a telephone call from someone at Delta (but because she was upset, she couldn't remember the person's name) who told her that Paul, who had been scheduled to fly to San Francisco, had become ill, necessitating an emergency landing in Dallas, Texas. He had been taken to a hospital. She said she was packing her bags to be by his side. I told her to let me see if I could get more information. I decided to call the Control Tower at Dallas International Airport, and after identifying myself as a neighbor, I asked which hospital Paul had been taken to. They gave me the name and telephone number of the hospital. I called the

Emergency Room and inquired about Paul's condition. I said I was calling on behalf of his wife. The nurse said, "Unfortunately, he is deceased, dead on arrival of apparent cardiac arrest!" She said there was no need for Roz to come because the law required an autopsy." She mentioned that it would probably take several days, and then he would be transported back to Florida for burial. Roz grabbed the phone and said, "He's dead, isn't he?" The nurse then repeated what she told me, and Roz hung up. I was crying, as well, but I told Roz we would help her in every way we could. She said we needed to go to Fort Lauderdale to tell his parents and first wife, who lived in Miami, with their children, Jonathan and Red. I couldn't believe Paul had died of a heart attack because he had just had an FAA Physical, which he had passed with flying colors. He was young, only forty-seven, and they had been married for only seven years.

That morning, I drove Roz to Paul's parents' home. They were completely shocked. His mother almost collapsed. It was so sad! Roz heard from the Coroner about a week later, and we made arrangements to have Paul brought to a local funeral home. He would be buried in the local cemetery in Deerfield Beach. Roz asked if I would design the headstone, which I did. I drew an airplane flying in the clouds with the sun in the background and the words "Flying Free." She loved it! The stone mason put a rush on it. We arranged to have a viewing at All Faith Funeral Home on Federal Highway in Deerfield Beach. Almost one hundred people came to pay their respects. A group of uniformed Delta personnel came, as well. After burial, guests were received at the Bouley residence. Larry, a childhood friend of Paul's, made arrangements for a caterer to come so that Roz wouldn't have to do anything. All in all, it was a fitting tribute for Paul. It took some time for Roz to adjust, but we became

145

even closer. I tried to get her interested in doing shows with us, but it wasn't a good fit.

I, on the other hand, was a natural when dealing with the customers, as Pete said, and I enjoyed it. We ordered a jewelry case, and Pete made shelving to display our collection. We soon realized that for precautionary reasons, we would need to change the layout of our booth. We learned that having people walk behind us was not a good idea, having learned the hard way. Once, when doing a show in Miami Beach, my sleeve caught onto a pair of earrings, and one fell on the floor. I, unfortunately, stepped on it and made the back screw crooked. I placed the earrings on the table next to me so that Pete could repair it. A man came to look at a Chinese vase in the back while I was showing a ring to a potential customer. I became aware of the man behind me. I looked at him, and he quickly left our booth with our earrings in tow. I yelled to Pete, "That guy just stole our earrings." I locked the jewelry case and asked the dealer next to us to watch our booth as we took off after the thief. Believe it or not, Pete caught up to him outside, shoved him against the wall, placed one hand on his neck, and said, "Give me the earrings back if you don't want to choke," and the miracle of miracles, the thief put his hand in his pocket and handed the earrings to Pete. I told him he was lucky we were letting him go but that we would always remember him. He took off running. I guess he couldn't believe we didn't turn him in. In retrospect, we should have. That night, Pete redesigned the layout of our booth. He also designed two stainless steel display cabinets and placed the order with the same manufacturer who made our bar stools, etageres, etc.

We were lucky they had relocated to Fort Lauderdale, and fortunately, we received them on time for our next show. This time, we had two jewelry cases with display cabinets on either side. We were now locked in. There were no shelves in the back, and no one could enter behind us as before. The display cases were stainless steel, which made our booth look classy and professional.

Manya and Peter didn't laze around, either. Instead, they both had part-time jobs to add to, as they called it, their "meager allowance" after school. Manya had a job on the beach at Pal's Captain Table, a popular restaurant. Manya was the pastry girl dishing out slices of cake, pie, cookies, etc., to the waiters and waitresses. One afternoon, she saw a young White man run into the rear of the kitchen waving a gun, and, lo and behold, shots were heard. He was a disturbed ex-boyfriend of a young waitress and wanted revenge. He shot her in the chin and shoulder and took off. Thank goodness, the wounds were not fatal. The shooter ran into the Cove Restaurant nearby, ordered a drink, and patiently waited for the police to arrive and arrest him! This incident really shook Manya, so she quit her job as a pastry girl. A friend of hers mentioned that a local pharmacy near the beach needed a stock girl, and Manya gladly took the job. One day, she was stacking new merchandise on the shelves when she heard someone say, "Don't nobody move. Give me your money." She peered down the aisle and saw a young Black man holding a gun, pointing it at the cashier. Manya said she must have made a sound because he turned and saw Manya. She immediately scrambled to the back door as fast as she could and jumped over the fence into the next property. She knew the holdup man saw her. She was really frightened but safely made it to the next store and told the store owner what had happened. They called the police. The thief took off with very little cash but, unfortunately, got away and was never apprehended. Manya quit her job that very day. She soon graduated high school and chose the

University of Florida st Gainsville as her college. Some of her closest friends would be attending the same University as well.

Peter worked at Publix and then at United Parcel Service in Fort Lauderdale while attending Broward Community College. Always an avid surfer, when the summer semester ended, he went surfing with a group of friends in Costa Rica. When he returned home after touting the beauty and surf in Costa Rica, he became quite ill, complaining of an earache. I took him to the ENT doctor, who prescribed medication for an ear infection. That evening, when I went to check on him, I saw that his face was flushed, and he was incoherent, saying, "Don't yell at me," when I was speaking in a normal tone of voice. He told me, "Look, the ceiling fan is falling." I immediately took his temperature which registered at 103 degrees! I knew we needed to get him to a hospital. I called our local doctor, Dr. Bessman, who, upon hearing about his high temperature, told us to go to the Emergency Room at Boca Raton Hospital immediately and said that he would meet us there. This was at about two in the morning. Pete and I drove Peter to the Emergency Room, where Dr. Bessman was waiting. He examined Peter and said he was calling in the infectious disease doctor because he felt it was something more serious than an ear infection.

The infectious disease doctor, Dr. Cardenas, took a spinal tap, which was extremely painful. The test revealed that Peter had contracted meningitis and needed to be quarantined as it was bacterial and not viral meningitis, the more serious of the two. The next twenty-four hours were critical, but thank goodness his temperature slowly dropped, and his headache wasn't that severe due to the doctor's quick attention. We had to wear hospital gowns, gloves, and masks when we came to see him. He had a lengthy three-week stay at the hospital but came home with no discernible defects, memory loss, or paralysis.

Surfing in polluted waters was probably the cause of his illness. This was a rough lesson, but Peter now knew he had to check the locations before entering unknown waters to surf.

Peter switched colleges and began attending Florida Atlantic University in Boca Raton. One of the courses he decided to take was Japanese Language! Pete and I were amused because he had barely passed Spanish in high school, and Japanese was a tougher language to learn, speak, and write. We made a bet that he'd quit the course within two months! One afternoon, I received a phone call from his Japanese Professor. I thought to myself: here we go; he has probably dropped the course. To my astonishment, she said there was a program offered similar to a student exchange where the student would be lodged with a local family and attend school for Japanese in Japan! She mentioned that Peter was her best student. I was thrilled to hear this. I agreed to let him go to Japan. Before he left, he organized a Surf Club/Team, the first of its kind at FAU. To this day, he is recognized as the president and organizer of the surf team and club.

Peter flew with several other students to Osaka, where they were greeted by their host families. Most of the students were lodged with families with children and shared their bedrooms. Peter was lucky; he went home with Mr. & Mrs. Kamikawa, who lived in Kyoto. They had no children and lived in a beautiful home, complete with a guest house that accommodated Peter during his stay in Japan. Peter attended classes locally and, in his spare time, went sightseeing. When he returned home, he said he would return to Japan again next semester to stay with the Kamikawas who welcomed him. He said he loved his time in Japan and frequently went surfing and snowboarding. He now spoke and understood Japanese and made several more trips to Japan.

Peter's Surf Team at FAU went to Huntington Beach, California, for a surfing contest, competing with other college surf teams. FAU came in first. How fantastic!

One afternoon, an incident occurred that, to this day, makes me recoil. As I pulled up onto my driveway and honked the horn for Peter to come and help me with my bundles, my neighbor's youngest daughter came running out of her house screaming at the top of her lungs, "She's dead, she's dead!" I ran up to her, gathered her in my arms, and asked, "Who's dead?" She replied hysterically, "Go see!" Another neighbor, upon hearing the commotion, came out to see what was happening. I told her and Peter to take the frightened girl into the neighbor's house while I went to investigate. I walked into the house and saw nothing unusual. I went to look inside the garage. To my disbelief and horror, I saw her sister suspended from the ceiling. She had hung herself. A step stool was overturned, lying on its side on the garage floor. I heard a gasp; I turned around and saw Peter. He had his hand over his mouth and was in shock. I told him to go back and try to console his friend while I called the police. I checked for a pulse, but there was none. I also noticed scars on her wrist. I looked at her other arm and saw the scars there as well. It told me that she had issues. I called 911 and stated that it was a suicide and that along with the police to have the Coroner come, as well. I told them I would wait inside for them. Years ago, when I was a policewoman, I was assigned to search many a dead female, which I did, and although it was tough, I got used to doing it. Seeing this young, beautiful girl who had her whole life ahead of her shook me up. I actually had difficulty going to sleep for some time. Her family was one that I was fond of; very down to earth, with no pretense, and also very loving parents. I truly felt heartsick for them. We remained friends for years. This unfortunate, terrible incident made Pete and me more protective, closer, and more loving to Manya, Peter, and Steve.

A few days later, I received a real surprise and a happy one! Roz came in with an envelope in her hand and said, "Open it." I opened the envelope and saw tickets for a ten-day cruise to the Caribbean. This was, as she said, her "Thank You" for my help during her stressful time after Paul's death. The timing was perfect. I really needed a break, and I truly appreciated it. We had a delightful time, but as usual, I was eager to get home because we had a full schedule of shows to do around the country.

Chapter Thirteen:
Memorable Antique Shows

While doing a show at the Coconut Grove Convention Center, I needed to verify a credit card purchase and went to the lobby where the telephones were located. I went to the last telephone and noticed a pouch shoved beneath the phone. I unzipped it open and saw the name Carolyn Kaplan on a receipt.

Inside the pouch, along with receipts, was loose jewelry and a huge stash of bills.

Carolyn was a jewelry dealer with a booth just up the aisle from me. After making my credit card verification, I approached Carolyn's booth. She was talking with a customer when I said, "Carolyn, I hate to interrupt, but I must talk to you." She gave me a dirty look and said, "Not now. Can't you see I'm busy?" I replied, "Okay," meanwhile dangling the pouch for her to see. She gasped and said, "Oh my God, that's mine." I gave it to her and started to walk back to my booth. She left her booth, embraced me, and thanked me over and over again. This was the beginning of a lifelong friendship.

Carolyn was a vivacious, intelligent, fun-loving person. After that incident, she no longer wanted to do shows and instead asked if I would sell her jewelry. I did not hesitate to say yes because a lot of her jewelry was from prominent socialites, mostly designer pieces. It must have been fate that Carolyn would become my friend. When we sold our home in Lido Beach, we went lot hunting with Bill Chickory (he had sold us the Lido lot). Bill now lived in Lake Worth. We found a beautiful lot in Manalapan right on a canal, but there was a drawback. At the end of the street, next to the empty lot, was a public dock to the canal. I told Pete that I would not feel comfortable seeing strangers coming and going right next to our home, and for that reason, we passed on the lot. Across the street from this lot was a lovely ranch home owned by Carolyn Kaplan! We would have been neighbors. Fate is so strange!

Another lifelong friend was Karen W., whom I originally met as a customer. On another afternoon at Coconut Grove, I saw a young lady with two shopping bags standing in the aisle scanning the area. Our eyes met, I smiled, and she walked over to my booth. She had several articles she wanted to sell and had offered them to other merchants but was not happy with their offers, too "low ball!" I asked to see what she had and was taken aback by the quality and beauty—silver candlesticks, a silver bowl, beautiful patch boxes, etc. When she quoted her asking price, I did not hesitate to say, "Sold!" as I knew there was plenty of room for me to make a profit. She was thrilled that I did not try to bargain for a better price as the other dealers did and said, "If you like these items, I have much more at home that I'd like to dispose of, as well. Here is my address and telephone number. Call me when you want to come and look-see!" I asked if we could stop in after the show closed the following day. Karen agreed and said she looked forward to seeing us again.

The following day, we packed up and proceeded to Karen's house. Her home was surprisingly close by on Biscayne Bay, a lovely ranch house with a three-car garage. When we walked in, we were taken aback. Her home was unreal! Everywhere you looked, there were antiques, furniture, paintings, and cabinets filled with treasures. Karen said she inherited many items, but she, too, had been an avid collector over the years. She said the reason she was disposing of certain items was because being not only a cat breeder (there was a kennel in the garage) but also a racehorse breeder, vet costs were becoming astronomical! We agreed that whenever she chose to sell, she would call, and we would pick up the items and display them at our antique shows. We sold beautiful ceramics, silverware, dinnerware, and some fantastic jewelry, as well. Karen remains our friend to this day. She said she knew we were honest, and she was always happy with the sales results. When she left South Florida to move to the Gulf Coast, she sold much of her household furniture. I fell in love with her beautiful dining room regency sideboard, which was not an antique but a reproduction. I still have it. She no longer breeds cats but still keeps her racehorses.

When we were doing a show at the Miami Beach Convention Center, on the very last day of the show, a couple approached our booth and selected a beautiful emerald and diamond platinum bracelet. The woman wrote out a check that only had her name on it, without any other information. As I looked at her, I saw she had a streak of mustard on her blouse, and I thought to myself, *this* must be a scam. She offered no ID. I said that I could not accept the check. The man laughed and said, "No problem, she owns the bank." The woman said she noted that I was from Deerfield Beach. She suggested meeting the following day at Pal's Captain Table for lunch, at which time she would give me cash instead of a check. I agreed and the following day went to the restaurant where she and a friend were waiting for me. After a lovely lunch, she said, "Let's go where I'm parked, and I'll take the bracelet." I thought we were going to the parking lot. Instead, she turned to the outside dock and proceeded to walk up a ramp onto a fabulous yacht named "Black Gold." We were greeted by her captain, the man I saw her with yesterday. On the deck was a beautiful German shepherd who must have been their guard dog. I asked whether I could pet him but was told he did not take to strangers. To their disbelief, when I called him, he approached, nuzzled me, and allowed me to pet him. They couldn't get over it. The dog even followed me below deck, where we made our transactions. I gave her the bracelet and receipt and thanked her for the lunch and cash. She said, "See you next year. I just love my bracelet." As I left, I reminded myself never to judge a book by its cover. She looked so disheveled when I first saw her, but today, what a different story. Months later, when doing a show in Tulsa, Oklahoma, she came and visited our booth and purchased some jewelry once again. I noted that she was wearing the bracelet at that time, which she said she loved.

We did another great show in Washington, D.C., at Mt. Vernon College (the auditorium) for Town & Country (the promoters were my best friends, Carol and Dave Klapper), which was a vetted show and heavily attended by many prominent politicians. I was surprised that those who could afford to buy were the ones who elected to pay on lay-away, but then, a sale is a sale! Our porters were young male students who were happy to be there. We had three porters helping us when the show ended. I handed each a generous tip, and one of them was so thrilled that he embraced me. He said the boys felt I was truly beautiful and should be in the movies instead of doing shows! Well, that was a nice compliment. As we drove off, I blew them a kiss, and they all laughed.

From Washington, we went to do a show in Wilmington, Delaware, once again for Town & Country. It was a huge show, and it was vetted and heavily attended. The dealers were chatting about a particular woman who was going from booth to booth, making many purchases. I saw her approach our booth, which she did not enter. She glanced at the cabinets and walked on! I was disappointed because I thought surely there was something she'd like in our booth. About an hour later, to my surprise, she returned and said she was interested in several items but had to take a break, and that's why she hadn't stopped by our booth the first time. I gave her a chair, and she sat down and pointed out the pieces she wanted to examine. There were four Tiffany & Co. silver candlesticks (they belonged to my sister, who had purchased them from a client and no longer needed them). The customer said she loved them and did not quibble over the price. She also selected some antique Chinese items and several expensive pieces of jewelry. She proceeded to write a check, and again, I noted only her name was on the check. I then asked for ID. She produced her driver's license. She told me I was the first dealer to ask for ID but understood that I needed to be cautious because a large sum of money was involved. She said the Chinese artifacts would be housed in the Winterthur Museum, but the Tiffany candlesticks would be put to good use in her home! Pete packed the items and carried them to her car. She said she was tired, but tomorrow was another day! To my surprise, the following day, she returned with a young lady and told her to choose whatever jewelry pleased her! The young lady chose several items: two rings, a bracelet, and several pairs of earrings. A check was given, and this time, I didn't ask for ID. They mentioned that I had interesting and unusual pieces of jewelry. This was our first show in Wilmington. She said she hoped we would return next year. All the dealers were pleased with their sales (many were due to her) and looked forward to another show next year.

Pete and I enjoyed doing shows, seeing new places, and having interactions with new customers. One of the most exciting moments came from a phone call from Steve. Steve was now retired from the NYPD due to a line-of-duty injury and was in England visiting friends. He was introduced to a very interesting individual who

156

happened to be a serious antique collector. After speaking with him, Steve mentioned the fact that his parents were antique dealers. It was suggested that I fly to England and be escorted by him to some antique shops to add to our collection. We had a heavy schedule of shows to do, so I was only able to stay in England for a week. I booked a flight, arrived at Heathrow Airport, and waited (and waited) for Steve to pick me up. He had no cell phone at that time, so I was unable to reach him. A man approached me and said he had come to pick me up because Steve was delayed in traffic. He introduced himself as Ray, Steve's friend. Steve was staying at their home. Ray, and wife Jean, were the managers of a popular pub in the village of Finchhempstead. Steve booked a room for me at a local inn for one night. Steve and his pal Gregory were staying with Ray and Jean. The following morning, Steve showed up, and we went to the pub for breakfast, where I met Dave (the collector), who after a discussion with his wife, told me I was most welcome to stay at their home while I went antiquing with him.

Dave was charming and smoked a pipe. We hit it off. There was no pretense. He had a great sense of humor, and he was a really down-to-earth guy! After breakfast, we drove to his home to meet his wife and daughter. His home was a beautiful Tudor dating back to the 1600s on a huge plot of land with stables for horses. I met his lovely wife and young daughter, who greeted me warmly as though we were old friends. I went on a tour of the house and noted that although some rooms had been remodeled, one needed to pass through an arched door leading to a narrow staircase with low ceilings to reach the bedrooms. There were four bedrooms, and I was supposed to stay in the one next to their daughter. I noted the bedroom door was ancient, with iron latches and casement windows reflecting bullseyes. I placed my suitcase against the wall opposite my bed and went downstairs to join the family for dinner. During dinner, the daughter casually asked me if I believed in ghosts. I said, "I really don't know; why do you ask?" She then told me that legend had it that their home was also home to a ghost. She did not, however, mention the gender of the ghost. Only she and her father had ever seen it. Dave's wife laughed and said, "Don't frighten Mary."

That night, I curled up in bed to have a good night's sleep as I was still a little tired from the flight, and the bed at the inn hadn't been very comfortable. Sometime in the early morning hours, I was awakened by the sound of my suitcase falling down, which I had placed upright. I sat up in bed, and to my disbelief, there standing at the foot of the bed was a man dressed, unlike the men of today. He was handsome, young, and had his hair swept back and tied with a black ribbon. His shirt was ruffled in the front and had billowing sleeves. He wore black knickers and white socks, and his shoes had big silver buckles on them. Oddly enough, I wasn't the least frightened. "Hi, my name is Mary, and I am very weary, having just returned from the colonies. I need my sleep," I told him. Not a word was spoken; he smiled and just faded. He seemed to glide into the casement window and disappear! He had apparently moved my suitcase, and that was what woke me up. I cuddled my pillow and fell back to sleep. The next morning, at breakfast, I was asked how I had slept. I mentioned I had a visit with a friendly ghost. Dave asked for the ghost's description. I then described my encounter, and both Dave and his daughter laughed and said I had really met their ghost!

The next few days were spent going from one antique shop to another and making wonderful purchases. Dave said I was to select whatever I wanted, and he would do the bargaining. He said that if they heard my American accent, the prices would never be lowered. I was thrilled. I bought Victorian and Edwardian jewelry, vinegarettes, patch boxes, and the beautiful Fairyland Luster Bowl, all at unbelievable prices. I knew I would make a hefty profit. The last day before returning home, Dave gave me a surprise treat. We had lunch at Wellington Arms Pub located in the Duke of Wellington Estate in the Village of Stratfield Turgis, Hampshire County. I will always remember how kind he and his family were to me, including the family ghost! I certainly had a lot to tell my family.

After looking over what I had bought, Pete said the collection was great and definitely would attract customers. We were now exhibiting outside Florida. One show I loved was in New Orleans, Louisiana. Dealers raved about this show, saying you could always count on great attendance not only from tourists but those attending conferences, as well. It was on the second day of the show when I recognized a woman from the day before approaching our booth. She was tall, buxom, a real "Brunhilde-type." She spoke with a German accent and said that she was interested in one item she had seen the day before. She mentioned she had been through the entire show, but no one had what she had seen here and truly wanted. I asked what item she was interested in. She replied, "I want your pearl necklace!" My pearl necklace was very special. It consisted of five strands of 9MM pearls. The clasp, which consisted of emeralds, rubies, and diamonds, had been made to order by Max, my jeweler. Pete gave me the first two strands on our first anniversary and, over the years, added the other three strands. I told her, "They were not for sale as they had sentimental value to me." She laughed and said, "My dear, everything's for sale. Name your price!" I turned to Pete, and to my surprise, he said, "Sell them. I'll replace them for you." Pete and I then decided on a firm price, thinking she would not accept it, but to our surprise and my dismay, she said, "Sold!" She entered our booth and lifted her shirt to remove a money belt, which she placed on the table, and proceeded to count out the price, all in $100 bills. She came up short, so I took some German marks (worth more than the US dollars). She asked me to fasten the necklace on her. She was as thrilled as we were. Our neighbors witnessed the entire transaction and said they were bowled over and happy for us. The customer said that she was attending a medical conference, became bored, and decided to visit the antique show. I must admit the pearls looked lovely on her, but I missed the feel of the pearls on my neck.

Later, a young man came to the counter questioning Pete about a Galle vase when I intervened. He said the vase was perfect for his shop and that he was delighted to have found it because a large enameled Galle is difficult to find. He didn't quibble over the price and happily left our booth swinging the bag. As he went up the aisle, he unfortunately hit a table, and I could hear the glass shatter! I told him I knew how much he liked the vase and that if I ever found a similar vase, I would let him know. He told me to visit the shop, M. S. Rau, which is long-established in the French Quarter and considered by dealers to be one of a kind, featuring fabulous antiques and art. Over the years, when I was no longer exhibiting, I would still visit shows and would stop and chat with Bill Rau. We would always have a good laugh about the memorable Galle vase incident.

While doing the New Orleans show, we got in touch with Leroy, the photographer from my modeling days, who lived in LaFayette. He and his wife surprised us by visiting the show and inviting us to stay at their home and talk about old times. After the show closed, we drove to LaFayette and stayed two delightful days with them. Leroy gave me some old photos from the trade shows, which I appreciated. Leroy was no longer a photographer. He had retired, having invested heavily in oil holdings, and was now a millionaire! We were so happy for him and his family.

Another fond memory was of a show we did in Tulsa, Oklahoma. Not only was there an antiques and collectibles show, but the 4-H Club was also exhibiting and competing. I was interested in seeing the teenage members of the 4-H Club tending their animals: cows, bulls, pigs, and sheep. I went to one stall and was amazed to see a young girl, probably fourteen years old, in a stall with a huge bull. She had a pointer and tapped his right leg, which he promptly put forward. She then tapped him again, and he returned his leg to its original normal position. She tapped his head, and he bowed. It was amazing. I walked around and saw young boys and girls brushing and washing their animals with such tenderness and pride.

We also did a show in Cincinnati, Ohio, and for the first time, we had to use union members as porters to unload our merchandise. It was a huge convention center and well-attended. A couple at our booth expressed interest in several items. The wife chose a beautiful, expensive pair of earrings. The husband was reluctant to purchase them, but his wife persisted and insisted, so a deal was reached. The following day, much to our surprise, they showed up at our booth again. I thought perhaps they were having misgivings over the earrings. I was wrong. The husband said he wanted to thank me for the more than fair-price. He had them looked over at a local jeweler who said the price was a bargain and that he would have sold them for more! They invited me and Pete to dinner at their home after the show closed. The home was an amazing Frank Lloyd Wright house, Pete's favorite architect. I still can't get over the fact that we had such nice relations with complete strangers.

161

Then, it was on to Dallas and Houston for another monumental experience! On opening day in Dallas, a young woman approached our booth and, after scanning the jewelry cases, said she was interested in numerous items, which turned out to be over a dozen pairs of earrings and several bracelets. I was in awe. Why so many? She said that they were to be Christmas presents for her female employees. She also bought several pairs of cuff-links for her male employees as well. I looked into her identity and discovered that she was a prominent realtor. There was no problem with her check. She made my day! On the third day of the show, she showed up, all smiles, and said she was so pleased with her purchases that she wanted to invite us to dinner and an overnight stay in her home! We accepted her kind invitation.

The show closed at six that evening, so we arrived at her home at around 6:30. We were warmly greeted by the customer and her husband. Her husband said that we could leave our bag containing the jewelry in a special room with vaults. He told us not to worry and that their home was literally a fortress; every room was security-wired. They had purchased the home from a leading CEO in technology, which explained the unusually heavy security. We were shown a beautiful pink bedroom that had been decorated for her niece, who had visited them from time to time. What grandeur! We then left in their Bentley to go to a restaurant, The Mansion at Turtle Creek. Our hosts were warmly greeted as we were led to a table. Next to our table sat the actress Cybil Sheppard, a U.S. Senator, and his family. The food was fabulous, and the atmosphere was terrific! We returned to their home, had a nightcap, and chatted for a while before going off to bed. In the morning, our hostess prepared breakfast before we returned to the show, as this was our last day exhibiting. We thanked them for their hospitality. They told us that they enjoyed our company as well. Before we went to the show, I stopped at a local florist and had a beautiful bouquet of flowers sent as a thank-you.

We finished the show, packed up, and were on our way to the Houston Convention Center for our next and last show in Texas. I looked forward to this particular show, this being our first time in Houston, as many dealers touted it as being a great show, well attended and with many wealthy patrons! While unpacking, a dealer we knew approached us and told us to be very cautious because, unfortunately, the Governor had decided to release hundreds of felons from prison due to overcrowding. It was bad, bad timing!

On opening day, there was a huge attendance, and we made many good sales. On the last day of the show, however, I started to get bad vibes when two men came to our booth and were eyeing our jewelry. When I asked if I could help them, they avoided looking at me. I reached over and touched one on his shoulder and said, "What are you looking for?" He backed away and shook his head, and he and his associate left. Pete agreed that they were very suspicious of their behavior.

As we packed our van, it started to rain. We headed to a McDonald's drive-through and then headed to our motel. Pete was always alert to see if anyone looked like they were tailing us, so he did a round-about before heading for the motel. Everything looked good. When we arrived at the motel, the parking space in front of our room was taken away, so we had to park away from our room. Pete chose a spot under a light pole so that we could see our van from our room.

At around midnight, we heard an alarm go off. It sounded like our vehicle, but when we looked out the window, our van under the light pole appeared secure; boy, were we ever wrong! In the morning, the rain stopped, and there was a knock on our door. We looked out and saw that it was security. The alarm had indeed been that of our van, and when we approached, we saw that the front window on the passenger's side was completely smashed. Several of our packed boxes of antiques were on the ground. We checked the boxes, and fortunately, nothing was taken or broken. It appears they took care of unloading and weren't interested in antiques. Inside the van, our two jewelry cases, which had been covered with a cloth, were now exposed and empty. I'm sure it surprised, shocked, and disappointed the thieves to find no jewelry. Little did they know we took it with us for safe-keeping in our room!

Although we needed to repair the window, we thanked our lucky stars for all the antiques that were intact! We were so glad to leave Houston and head home for a little respite. Even though we did well financially, I vowed never to do another show in Houston because of this incident. We had always been cautious but realized we needed to be even more so.

Unfortunately, when doing a show again in Coconut Grove, we were victims of a thief who noted that the door of one of our jewelry cases was slightly ajar. Pete was sitting behind the case, starting to doze off, having complained of a headache before. I was talking with a potential customer on the side, so my back was turned from the front case. Pete broke a cardinal rule in that he did not check the door of the jewelry case in front of him and got up to join me, thus giving the thief the opportunity to steal an Omega diamond dial watch (on consignment) because Pete did not close the door. This was the first and only time Pete left the case unguarded. The watch was one of many owned by the pianist Liberace and given to his friend, who in turn gave it to me with several other items for resale. Thank goodness we successfully sold the other items so that the consignor didn't feel too bad about the loss of the watch, for which we compensated him. This was our only theft. We were truly lucky.

Some of the other shows we attended made up for the unpleasant experiences at Huston and Coconut Grove. Among my favorites was the Blue Grass Trust in Lexington, Kentucky, the Children's Show in Jacksonville, Florida, Zita Waters Bell's shows in Palm Beach, Florida, and, of course, Town & Country in D.C. and Naples, Florida. I should also include New Orleans, Louisiana, Boone Blowing Rock, North Carolina.

One incident comes to mind, which occurred after a successful show in Bay St. Louis, Mississippi, which was well attended. An elderly woman made a lot of dealers happy while indulging in a spending spree. She loved our booth and purchased earrings, a bracelet, and a ring, paid by check, and offered proper ID. On the way home, we stopped at our local Post Office to pick up the mail in our P.O. box. To my surprise, there was an overnight package from Bay St. Louis. I took the package and asked the Postman if he would witness its contents because I had a bad feeling about it. Sure enough, there was a note saying, "Returning all purchases. A stop payment has been placed on the check." The bracelet and earrings were enclosed, but no ring! Fraud! We immediately went home, and I called the customer and told her that the package had been opened in the presence of a postman. She was committing mail fraud by saying all purchases had been returned when the ring was missing. She became very flustered and blamed her maid for accidentally omitting the ring. She told me she would send the ring out by overnight mail immediately! I told her I expected her to do so to avoid any criminal charges! I wondered if she scammed any other dealers. She was so sweet and charming when making the purchases. You just don't know when dealing with complete strangers; use your gut instinct and always verify their identification and note their demeanor.

I mentioned the Blue Grass Trust shows in Lexington, Kentucky, as being a favorite of ours. There was always a Preview Night complete with the traditional mint juleps, hors d'oeuvres, an orchestra, and elegantly dressed patrons. It was very impressive! My first customer was a charming woman who fell in love with a beautiful bangle bracelet and matching ring. The bracelet had a wide center, complete with pearls, diamonds, and rubies, which were then narrowed on the side. It was 18k yellow gold and made in France. The ring was a very wide band with smaller pearls, rubies, and diamonds, and it was also made of 18k yellow gold. I was thrilled over the genuine warmth of the guests who praised our booth. Many requested a lay-away for the following day on not only fine jewelry but silver pieces as well. One of the customers selected a fabulous emerald and diamond necklace (our most expensive piece of jewelry). Her husband said it was for their wedding anniversary, and whatever his wife selected was fine with him. Before trying on the necklace, she pulled a small jewelry bag from her purse, which contained a pair of diamond and emerald earrings. She wanted to see if the emeralds in the necklace were the same color as those of her earrings, and, lo and behold, and they matched perfectly as though made to order. She put the earrings on, and I fastened the necklace for her. We couldn't believe the extent to which they looked custom-made and just exquisite! The price of the necklace did not phase the customer's husband at all. He whipped out his checkbook and wrote me a check. I noticed that only his name was on the check, and there was no address or phone number. I hesitated about accepting the check because it was for a large amount. I asked for his ID, and he showed me his driver's license, which I had copied. They started to leave, but not before his wife gave him a hug and a kiss. I approached one of the sponsors and asked about the customer not having more information on the check. He laughed and said, "Are you kidding? He owns the bank. You have nothing to worry about."

The following year, when we returned, we received a warm welcome, and our sales were fabulous. My customer, Mrs. G., bought more jewelry because she was so pleased with her previous purchases. I noticed her band ring was missing some pearls and was dirty. I asked why the ring was in its condition. She told me it was because she loved gardening and didn't wear gloves to protect her hands. I asked if I could have the ring. I wanted to have it restored to its original beauty at no cost to her. She was thrilled that I offered to do this for her and gave me the ring, which I told her I'd mail back to her after restoration to enjoy with the matching bracelet. She promised that in the future, when gardening she would wear gloves to protect her ring unless she removed it beforehand.

When we got home after the show, I immediately took the ring to my favorite local jeweler, Seto. Seto was not only a restorer, but he also designed and made beautiful jewelry. I sold many of his pieces, which he gave me on consignment, and we had a wonderful relationship. His wife, Melanie, was a hairdresser, and she has been my personal hairdresser to this day. Wherever she worked, I followed her. I gave Seto a painting I did of an Orthodox Priest, which he loved and which still hangs in his son's home (Seto was Armenian). Seto called me when he finished repairing the damaged ring. I went to pick it up and was thrilled when I saw it. The ring looked exactly like it did when I sold it to Mrs. G. All the pearls were replaced, except for the rubies or diamonds, which were intact. The ring was polished, and all the dirt had been removed.

I mailed it to Mrs G. and said I'd see her at the show next year. I received a lovely thank you letter from Mrs. G., who said she looked forward to seeing us at the show again. When we returned the following year, I saw a magnificent bouquet of flowers at our booth. The flowers were from Mrs. G., along with a sweet thank you note. Mrs. G. came to greet us with all smiles and showed us her hand with the ring. It was pristine! She now removes the ring when gardening. She told us that she'd like to have us for lunch after the show is over and take us for a spin in her pride and joy, an Aston Martin Convertible. We thanked her, but unfortunately, we were due for our next booked show soon thereafter. What a sweet, genuine gesture!

Chapter Fourteen: Amazing Trips!

Being semi-retired, we decided to take a tour of Europe along with our friends, Mark Van Cleef and his partner Bob Barry (also antique dealers). We rented a car to tour Europe. Mark and Bob shared driving duties with Pete. We toured Belgium, Amsterdam, Germany (we visited the famous Meissen Museum in Dresden), Czechoslovakia, and Hungary.

While in Berlin, we had two great experiences. We went antiquing and stopped in one shop where I was amazed to see a beautiful collection of antique vinagarettes. The owner, a woman, was laughing and all of a sudden slapped my shoulder and said, "Dumkoff. I bought all of these from you at a show in Miami Beach." (Small wonder I was attracted to them.) The second experience occurred when Pete and I decided to visit the Berlin Zoo which we had been told was a must-see. We walked around and then went into the lion compound. It was lunch time for them and they eagerly awaited being fed. I stood behind the railing and a young male lion came and laid down licking his paws. I spoke to him saying "Looks like you enjoyed your lunch," when to our surprise he looked at me and started talking to me, not growling but in low sweet sounds. I kept talking to him and he kept responding to me. I walked to the other side of the cage and lo and behold, he followed me, purring as he walked. I talked to him again, everyone was amused. People began taping us. I asked Pete to do the same but unfortunately he had put his camera away. Pete said I always had a connection with animals and that's is true. I love all animals.

I should add that fairy-tale Bruge in Belgium was particularly beautiful. Amsterdam also left a great impression. We visited the Van Gogh and Anne Frank Museums. I must say, however, the Red Light District was jaw dropping. Women prostitutes framed in windows beckoning pedestrians. Some of the women were attractive but the majority were "over the hill."

In June, 1996, we took a trip to Alaska and then went on to Siberia to visit my mother-in-law's family. We had visas for the trip to Siberia, the first issued in many, many years! We had booked land tours, as well. We flew from Fort Lauderdale via Delta to Seattle and then boarded a bus to the airport to fly to Vancouver to board our ship, the MS Amsterdam, Holland, American. We had one problem however, our luggage did not board with us. We were told not to be concerned and that our bags would arrive at our next Port, Ketchikan. Meanwhile, we enjoyed cruising the Inside Passage. When we arrived in Ketchikan, sure enough, our luggage had been brought to our cabin intact! We enjoyed our tour of Ketchikan with its wooden sidewalks, rustic buildings and a Red Light District, in addition to many interesting shops and galleries.

Our next stop was Juneau, the state capitol at the base of Mt. Juneau. We toured the Governor's Mansion and a salmon hatchery where I ordered salmon to be sent home. We stayed overnight and in the morning a motor-coach took us to Yankee Cove where we boarded a helicopter for an awesome flight onto a glacier. The water beneath the glacier was crystal clear and a bright blue. I raised my arms up and said, "Mama, Papa, look, I'm on top of the world!" I scooped up a piece of the glacier and swallowed it. The pilot looked at me and said, "You didn't put a piece of the glacier ice in your mouth, did you?" I told him that I had and he shook his head and said,

"I hope you don't get a reaction to it. There are ice worms in the water." I gagged, but what's done is done, foolish me! We also took a river cruise to view a beautiful waterfall and visited the Mendenhall Glacier, as well. We stayed overnight in Skagway.

Next on our schedule was a train ride: "The White Pass and Yukon Railroad." The train ran along the famous Klondike Gold Rush Trail and then onto Whitehorse, the capitol of Canada's Yukon Territory. We stayed overnight in Beaver Creek where we were to have dinner and see a floor show. I, unfortunately had stomach problems, as predicted by the helicopter pilot, so I missed dinner and the show. Pete told me the show was entertaining and that he even participated in the Revue. Unfortunately, I was running a fever. I vomited but thank goodness in the morning, although weak, I felt almost normal. We boarded a motorcoach to Fairbanks where we made a brief stop at Tok where we would see how sled dogs were trained, but by the time we arrived, there was no longer any show so the dogs were returned to their shelter. I noticed a young boy who looked to be about twelve years old grooming a husky. I approached him and said I was very disappointed to have missed the show. The dog he was grooming brushed up against me and I petted him. The boy introduced himself as Josh Rallo. We are still friendly, exchanging Christmas Greetings every year (Josh is now a State Trooper). Josh said he would take me and Pete to the enclosure where the sled dogs were kept. We followed him and saw many dogs, mostly huskies, and whenever they saw him they ran up to him. I was surrounded by these friendly dogs. They all allowed me to pet them. I thanked Josh for taking us there and asked for his address so that I could keep in touch with him. I gave him a generous tip which surprised him. We stayed overnight in Fairbanks and in the morning a bus took us to the Chena River Landing where we boarded a Stern-Wheeler Riverboat, The Discover, for a river boat tour. After the cruise, the following day we left for Denali via The McKinley Explorer Railroad. The scenery was spectacular with lots of wildlife, grizzlies, caribou, moose, and most of all, the incomparable Mt. McKinley! Truly a great wildlife tour!

We stayed overnight at the McKinley Chalet and in the morning boarded the train for our final destination in Alaska, Anchorage, where we would receive our "Soviet Tour Vouchers." We would fly from Anchorage via Alaskan Airlines to Khabarosk, Siberia. We stayed overnight at an Intourist Hotel and a bus took us in the morning to the railway station to board the Trans-Siberian Railroad. We had an overnight stay on the train until we reached the City of Irkutsk. Upon arrival at Irkutsk, we were transported for a three night stay at another Intourist Hotel. The train was very modern and the food was good, but, the restroom had issues. Whenever you flushed the stainless-steel toilet, water seeped out from the base and leaked onto the stainless-steel floor. There was a mop leaning against the wall which one would use to mop up the floor. There was, of course, a urine odor so whenever I went to the restroom I would spray perfume to kill the odor! Upon leaving the restroom, I laughed when I heard someone say, "Quick, she just left let's go while it still smells fresh." The hotel accommodations were sparse, two cots instead of beds and in the bathroom, the towels were thin and more like dishtowels rather than bath towels.

We called our family, the Kowals, letting them know that we had arrived. In the morning after breakfast, we were greeted by my mother-in-law's brother, Ivan and his son. We went outside to his car which was interesting in that he had to crank it up to charge it. We drove to his residence in a six-story brick building. He lived on the fifth floor of a walk-up with no elevator. He carried the duffel bag we had packed with goodies for the family. Bill Taraska, my NYPD partner when we were assigned to the Khrushchev detail at the Waldorf-Astoria and also a dear friend, had made numerous trips to visit relatives in Ukraine and told me the most requested items to pack. I brought eyeglasses, makeup, razors, soap, lotion, clothing and liquor!

We were greeted by his wife, his elderly mother, his sister-in-law and her husband. They spoke Russian mainly with the exception of the mother-in-law and Ivan who fortunately spoke Ukrainian! The dining table was laden with food and drinks, very festive and inviting. After we finished dessert, they opened the duffel Bag. Peter Jr. had packed a Geoffrey Beene suit that he had worn only once for his graduation. Ivan tried it on and it looked like it was custom made for him. It fit him perfectly and he was thrilled. However, the best moment came when the mother-in-law, who had been trying on eyeglasses said, "Oh, my goodness, I can see, I can see clearly, no longer blurry-a miracle!" Before having these glasses she squinted but now she held her head high and could see perfectly. They also loved the soaps, perfume, lotions, brand new sneakers, clothing and liquor! Ivan drove us back to the hotel. Unfortunately, this was our only lengthy visit with them because they worked and we had tours to attend.

One tour was an hour's bus ride to Lake Baikal, the largest freshwater lake in the world. When we alighted from the bus, I noticed a young man coming toward us and sure enough, he headed straight toward one of our male tourists. A pickpocket! I alerted our bus driver who then immediately grabbed the pickpocket who in turn handed over the victim's wallet. Fortunately, there was a security guard close by who took over. Funny, you never lose your instinct! I just knew the guy was a dip! Pickpocketing was very prevalent, especially at tourist sites, so I was always on the alert and aware of our surroundings.

Our next trip was to a huge outdoor/indoor market where everything imaginable was being sold; fresh produce, meats, clothing, jewelry, etc. In the evening we went to a nightclub for dinner and a show. We invited Ivan and his wife to attend and we all thoroughly enjoyed it. The last day in Irkutsk was spent touring a local museum where I purchased a small sketch by a local artist exhibiting in the museum. We also went to an import/export store where I purchased several Russian lacquer boxes to add to my inventory to sell. When we returned to the hotel, Ivan and his wife were waiting for us and had a farewell gift for us, a Russian samovar! We thanked them and told them we truly enjoyed meeting them and their family.

In the morning, we flew via Aeroflot (the Russian state airline) to Khabarovsk for an overnight stay in the local Intourist Hotel. We then returned to the airport for another Aeroflot flight. The airport was jammed with would-be passengers. We boarded the plane without seat assignments. You were to select your own seats. I noticed a man seated and next to him was a dog, followed by an empty aisle seat. I asked if he would put the dog on his lap so that Pete and I could be together. He said, "No, I paid for the dog to have a seat next to me." I told Pete to take the empty aisle seat and I would take the empty aisle seat opposite him. My seat was leaning down and I could not upright it, but at least I was close to Pete.

I watched in awe and had some concern over what was being loaded in the bulkhead. I saw Jeeps, huge machinery, refrigerators, computer equipment, etc. I couldn't believe all that was permissible. I was surprised that the floor of the cabin had exposed wood and was not covered. The stewardess came down the aisle pushing a cart saying, "Cigars, cigarettes, candy, soda?" I was grateful when we finally landed in Anchorage where we would board an Alaskan Airlines plane to fly to Seattle for an overnight stay and then, our final flight would be via Delta to Ft. Lauderdale, Florida. Although we enjoyed our cruise and going to Siberia to meet Ivan and family, I was glad to be home as I had plans to celebrate our upcoming fiftieth wedding anniversary by taking a special trip with Steve, Peter and Manya.

We booked our anniversary trip to Asia for September, 1966! Our first stop would be in Hong Kong. We flew to San Francisco via Singapore Airlines, Business Class, which was more like First Class. It was a wonderful airline, the best I've ever flown. We arrived at the Peninsula Hotel, often referred to as the "Grand Dame of the Far East." The hotel offered spectacular views of Victoria Harbour. Hong Kong was known as one of the best shopping stops for tourists because it was duty free. A visit to Stanley Market was truly mind-boggling with its clothing, jewelry, watches, souvenirs, etc. We also visited "Bird Street" where beautiful bird cages were sold along with the many birds on display. We took a Peak Tram ride up to Victoria Peak for a breathtaking panoramic view of Hong Kong Island, Kowloon and the other surrounding islands.

We also made a reservation for dinner at the other famous hotel, The Mandarin Oriental, frequented by many dignitaries, and known for its luxury. Steve and Peter took off on their own in the afternoon but said they would meet up with us at the restaurant for dinner. Manya, Pete and I went to the restaurant and patiently waited at our table for the boys. After a while, we saw Steve and Peter walking in both wearing a silly grin. While exploring earlier they had found an

English pub and apparently enjoyed several brews! Our table had a beautiful floral centerpiece containing multiple flowers and miniature orchids. We had ordered some appetizers and while we waited for them to arrive, Steve helped himself to a couple of "orchid appetizers." To this day, he has a fondness for orchids and grows them although he no longer consumes them (he has a green thumb as far as growing them). The meal was superb and the atmosphere was beautiful.

We also decided to visit Portuguese Macau, the oldest European settlement in the Orient. We took a jetfoil ride to visit the "Monte Carlo" of the Far East but its casinos were disappointing in that they were so smoke-filled you choked. It was also virtually impossible to play any machines or tables because they were all taken by young and old Chinese players. We left the casino to visit the historic ruins of the Church of St. Paul, a beautiful Renaissance facade atop granite stone steps.

The next day was a free day in that no tours were planned. I unfortunately forgot about the International Date Line and thought we had to leave. I told everyone to hurry up and check out or we'd miss our plane connections to Bangkok. Peter told me I was wrong but I insisted and had the Desk Clerk arrange for our transportation to the Airport. Much to my chagrin, when I presented our airline tickets to the agent she told me that because we were a day early, we'd be charged $100 each person for changing the flight. Naturally, we returned to the hotel. I called the Desk Clerk and told him of my error and thankfully he said not to worry. We still had our rooms. Peter was right and I was too hasty and terribly wrong. Peter had another day to go surfing with his local friends, so he was happy. Steve and Manya took off while Pete and I decided to enjoy the Hotel's indoor swimming pool. To this day I remind myself not to make hasty decisions.

The following day we flew on Cathay Pacific Airlines to Bangkok International Airport. We were then transported to the Oriental Hotel, another luxurious hotel. Our first sightseeing tour was the Bangkok Grand Palace Tour. The golden domes were mind-boggling! The breathtaking wall murals and ceramic decorations added to the magnificence of the Temple of the Emerald Buddha. The Emerald Buddha is supposed to possess supernatural powers, and according to tradition and the season, it is dressed in robes by the King of Thailand himself. The Lord Buddha is sculptured from a piece of very impressive translucent jade.

We also booked a tour to see the Floating Market. When we approached the dock to board a narrow long-tailed speedboat, a photographer (there were many of them) took a photo of Manya and Peter aboard the boat. We paid about $5.00 for the photo centered in a white saucer which said, "Floating Market Thailand." We sailed past houses on stilts along the banks through the marshes to the unique market. We saw canoes laden with vegetables, meat, fruits, etc. for sale by the Thai farmers. The famous bridge known as "The Bridge Over The River Kwai," built by prisoners of the second World War, was a memorable sight nearby.

We left Bangkok for Singapore once again flying on Singapore Airlines. Upon arrival at the airport, we took a bus to the famous Raffles Hotel. Of course, one could not stay at The Raffles Hotel without imbibing their famous Singapore Sling Cocktail. The cocktail consisted of a half ounce of gin, one ounce of Benedictine, a half ounce of Grand Marnier, a quarter ounce of cherry liqueur and one ounce of pineapple, lime juice, a dash of Angostura Bitters and Club

Soda, garnished with an orange slice and cherry, costing $15.00 US dollars. Tasty, but I still prefer my Pama (pomegranate juice, vodka, tequila, orange juice and club soda)!

We took a boat ride down the Singapore River passing warehouses, the six British bridges, the Old Waterfront, and saw the beautiful skyline. Once ashore we went to the Thiam Hock Keng Temple, one of Singapore's oldest temples and the National Museum. One of my favorite stops was at the Singapore Zoological Gardens. Playful orangutans roamed freely along with other animals. The orangutans had a cute system. I noticed a tourist was feeding a pair of orangutans seated in front of him and on the side of him was a lone orangutan. In short order, the one on the side reached over and snatched his bag of peanuts and scooted away, while the other two joined him. I told everyone to be on guard when it came to feeding them.

Singapore, like Bangkok, has a rich multi-cultural heritage with Little India and Chinatown both having colorful trading districts. Our final stop was to be Bali. We took Singapore Airlines to Denpasar International Airport and went on to the fabulous Four Seasons Resort in Bali, Indonesia. Steve and Peter had their own private luxury villa complete with a "plunging pool." Pete and I shared a gorgeous two-bedroom pavilion with Manya and we also had a pool and a magnificent view of the beach and Jimbaron Bay, Denpasar, the largest city in Bali with colorful markets displaying produce. We visited the Bali Arts Center housing not only wood carvings but modern paintings as well. While purchasing a selection of wood carvings (needed as gifts), I noticed an unusual Ganesh on a shelf. I said I wanted to purchase it but the clerk said it was an antique, personal and not for sale. I then told him that I would not buy the woodcarvings. He relented and gave me the Ganesh. He told me that Ganesh is a Hindu God widely worshiped throughout Southeast Asia. His name means "Lord of the People," destroyer of evil and obstacles and is also worshiped as the God of Education, Wisdom, Wealth. He is believed to bring prosperity, success and protection. He is also known as the Patron of the Arts and Sciences. I was giving the Ganesh to Steve as a gift for his new home in the Hamlet Country Club, Delray Beach and for his upcoming birthday.

Steve, Peter and Manya were on the "go" in Bali while Pete and I decided to just relax and enjoy our fabulous surroundings. We were surprised that so many foreigners, Australians, New Zealanders, and Europeans were not only tourists but had taken up residence there. There was even a Hard Rock Café!

After a delightful stay, we were off to San Francisco to attend the wedding of Jack Sheehan, one of Steve's closest friends, and then finally, home! Jack fondly recalled the time when he was helping to build Steve's house in Lido Beach. He credited Pete for being a great teacher, going from a novice to an expert by the time the house was finished. We stayed at the San Ramon Marriott Hotel at Bishop Ranch, San Ramon, California. The wedding and reception were just beautiful, and Tara, Jack's wife, was such a lovely bride. Jack was beaming the whole time.

Finally, our fiftieth anniversary trip was over and we took Delta Airlines back to Atlanta, and then another Delta flight to Fort Lauderdale. I must say that although the trip was memorable, it was good to be back home in Deerfield Beach. Both Booji and Tiger were thrilled to see us!

Chapter Fifteen:
Changes "A-Coming"

Steve had recently sold his home in Lido Beach and decided to relocate to Florida, having left the NYPD due to a severe injury to his left leg, a torn achilles tendon requiring surgery (requiring stitches from his ankle to his knee). One day while reading real estate advertisements for homes for sale, saw one listed in Delray Beach at The Hamlet Golf and Country Club. Pete, Steve and I went to see the house. After viewing it, Steve said pending inspection he would make an offer. It seemed the owner did minor repairs on the roof, but upon inspection, we saw that a new roof was really needed. Because of this, Steve made no offer and we kept looking.

While the inspection was taking place, I decided to drive around the community and as luck would have it, I noticed a home on Cocoplum Way with overgrown grass looking sort of neglected. I parked my car to jot down the address when a man opened the front door and was placing a lock box on the front door knob. I asked if he was an agent and he replied that he was. I asked if I could see the interior of the house because I was looking to relocate. He invited me in to take a look. I walked in and as soon as I saw the interior, I said to myself *this* is the house for Steve. I took the realtor's card and said I would be in touch with him. The realtor left for an appointment elsewhere, much to my disappointment, as both Pete and Steve were nearby. I told Steve about the house and said "Your search is over. I found the perfect house for you." We made an appointment for the following day and as soon as Steve walked in, he put his hand to his mouth, his eyes widened and smiled. He said, "This is the ideal house for me!"

The home originally was owned by a horse breeder. He had a huge bar built at the end of the room, to accommodate his jockeys! This appealed to Steve. When you entered and walked into the foyer, the master bedroom ensuite was on the left, a guest bathroom was also in the foyer. You then stepped into a huge dining room/ living room/bar area. The high ceilings had fabulous wooden beams. The sliding glass doors revealed the expansive outdoor area with a huge swimming pool. There was a wall cabinet with a built-in TV and stereo, and shelving with glass doors opposite the bar. There was also a guest bedroom, a bathroom and a door leading to outside. At the other end was another bedroom and a full bathroom. The kitchen was near a separate laundry room with a screened-in patio accessible from the dining room and kitchen. It was truly the dream house for Steve. Steve purchased the house and was thrilled because he really liked all the amenities. I was happy that a family member was now residing in Florida. Manya was living in Atlanta while Peter was in San Diego.

One day not too long after returning from our trip, Pete experienced unusual chest pains which turned out to be a heart attack! He was hospitalized in North Broward Community Hospital. He received a stent and was under the care of a wonderful cardiologist, Dr. Funt. Our antique circuit was naturally put on hold until Pete felt better. We relaxed and Pete made some minor repairs to the outside deck.

Sometime in the fall of 1999, Steve went to England and stayed with his friends, the Barkers, as usual. He and Ray Barker went golfing which included the Old Course at St. Andrews which was really tough. Because he was going to be away for two weeks, I would drive up to get his mail and check out the house. The day before he returned, as I was picking up his mail, Bob Dodson, Steve's next-door neighbor, also came out to get his mail. I walked over to Bob and asked if he knew of any homes for sale in the Hamlet as we were contemplating selling our home and wanted to be near Steve.

Bob smiled and said, "How near to Steve do you want to be? Frances and I are going to put our home on the market. We just bought a condo in the Hamlet. Would you consider our home?"

I couldn't believe what he just said and I blurted out that I'd love to see his home. When he opened the front door, I saw a huge living room with a high wooden beamed ceiling. A large stonewalled fireplace with a compact side bar was on the end. Sliding glass doors revealed an outside patio with a lovely yard and pool.. There was a sliding door that led to a step-down enclosed patio. The dining room also had a sliding door leading to this patio as well. The kitchen was compact, with a sliding door and pass-through windows to the patio. The home really impressed me with its ten-foot ceilings. The master bedroom also had a sliding door leading to the enclosed patio. The master bedroom had a beautiful master bathroom with a jacuzzi tub, two sinks with a dressing table in between, a separate area for the toilet, a bidet and step-down shower. In the foyer were four closets, two walk-ins. The hallway, approximately ninety feet long, also contained an office. To the left of the living room were two bedrooms with full ensuite bathrooms. I was impressed, to say the least, because I knew what Pete with his artistic ability could do in renovating the home.

Bob and I walked into the kitchen where his wife, Frances, was sipping tea when I asked what he asking for. He mentioned a figure and I thrust out my hand and said, "Sold!" Frances dropped her cup but fortunately caught it before it smashed into the sink.

Bob said, "I can't believe I don't have to get an agent and that you're buying our house. Let's drink to that!" He got two jigger glasses, filled them with Scotch. We clinked glasses and downed the Scotch.

He told me that the kitchen was being updated in their condo so that they could not presently move. I told him not to worry and that I, too, needed to sell our home but that my lawyer would set up a date for the sale which turned out to be December 14, 1999 (my Christmas present). The Dodsons had moved and were residing in their condo at the time of the sale.

I drove home and when I walked in, Pete asked "What took you so long to come home? Are you all right? Your face is flushed and your chest and neck are red like you've been drinking."

I blurted out, "I just bought a house in the Hamlet."

Pete was shocked. "What? Without me? How could you? Are you crazy?" I told him our good fortune-the house being right next door to Steve. Pete then agreed it was perfect and said he couldn't wait to see it. Boy, was Steve surprised when we told him.

The next day we picked Steve up at the airport in Fort Lauderdale. I said, "Steve, you won't believe what your crazy mother did when I was in the Hamlet yesterday picking up your mail.

Steve decided to drive, smiled, and said, "You bought the house next to me!"

Of course, he was joking, but I said, "Who told you that I bought the Dodson house?"

He almost stopped the car in shock but recovered and said, "Good deal, when are you moving?" I told him that we had to either rent or sell our beautiful Deerfield Beach home and that the Dodsons had to wait for their kitchen to be completed before they moved. After the sale was finalized in December, we knew we needed to do interior work in the Deerfield house, painting, replacing a few chipped Mexican tiles, etc., in order to have the house in mint condition for rent or sale. I wanted to rent it but Pete insisted that we sell.

Our new home in the Hamlet, under Pete's critical eye, was also in need of renovations. He removed all the inside sliding glass doors leading to the indoor patio and raised the flooring level to that of the living room, dining room and kitchen. He also enclosed the wall in the master bedroom (removing the sliding glass door to the patio) which made the bedroom huge. All the carpeting was removed and beautiful large tiles were placed diagonally throughout the house. Where there had previously been sliding glass doors in the living room, dining room and kitchen, he made lovely arched doorways! The wall that had a sliding door leading to the master bedroom was now sealed and housed a beautiful cabinet Pete had made revealing a huge flat TV with mirrored shelving. Pete was so creative! The former stepdown now elevated patio would be our family room. The kitchen, although compact, looked bigger because with the sliding glass door removed, everything was now wide open. The area formerly used in the kitchen as a breakfast nook now became my computer center. It was perfect! We placed the four bar stools with the stainless steel bases that Pete designed at the pass-through counter. The three sofas with their beautiful stainless steel backs which Pete also designed were finally put to use in now the family room. I was so happy that Pete's furniture was on display. Now, when you walked in there was an openness and flow from room to room thanks to Pete's amazing artistic ability; a world of difference. Although we closed in December 1999, it wasn't until August, 2000 that we finally moved. Our beautiful home in Deerfield Beach was two stories and was on the Kingfisher Canal, one lot off the Intracoastal Waterway. We also had a huge swimming diving pool, 20'x40' and a dock as well. Here in Delray we were in gated community with a golf course and tennis courts. Most of the homes were one level. Our property was three quarters of an acre with a 15'x30' swimming pool. The backyard was filled with palm trees and flowering hedges. We didn't have much of a backyard in Deerfield Beach so this made a big difference. All the homes were beautifully maintained, with no trucks or vans in view, unlike Deerfield Beach.

Although I sincerely loved and missed Deerfield Beach as I did Lido Beach, this was a good move; not only were we close to Steve in case of an emergency, but shopping was a few blocks away, as well, and the banks, Delray Medical Center and doctor's offices were close by. I missed the boat activity on the Kingfisher Canal/Intracoastal but I adjusted as did Tiger (our cat). Booji had passed away the year before and was buried next to Gyppy in front of the fireplace in Deerfield Beach. I missed Roz dearly, my neighbor and dearest friend in Deerfield Beach, particularly because I knew no one here in the Hamlet (other than Steve).

Chapter Sixteen:
2001 The Year Of Shocks!

We were pleased that our new home had not only a two-car garage but a golf cart garage, as well. The golf cart garage housed our jewelry cases and boxes of antiques. The jewelry was kept in our bank's safety deposit box. We did only one show after moving in because Pete was complaining about his side bothering him.

He went to a recommended urologist in Fort Lauderdale for a colonoscopy which the doctor said was normal. The following month, in September, Pete went to his cardiologist for routine checkup when Dr. Funt said he was not pleased with the blood results. Pete mentioned that his side was still bothering him. Dr. Funt said he wanted Pete to get another colonoscopy with another doctor which Dr. Funt highly respected, Dr. Mack Harrell of Boca Raton. Pete made the appointment.

After examining Peter, Dr. Harrell said another colonoscopy was definitely needed. September 11th was the date set up for the colonoscopy at West Boca Raton Hospital. That day I sat in the waiting room with several other people watching NBC Morning News. I, like the others, awaited test results when suddenly an announcer on TV said they were interrupting the program with "Breaking News." It appeared that a commercial airline accidentally struck the North Tower of The World Trade Center and they were taking the broadcast to the site. All of us in the room were stunned- we saw the crash scene with smoke billowing out from the Tower when suddenly another plane appeared in view, heading toward the South Tower, and plowed into it! We could not believe what we saw.

The announcer then said that it appeared to be a deliberate attack, not accidental. It turned out that these two planes were part of an Al-Qaeda Islamic terrorist attack along with two other planes, one of which hit the Pentagon and the other, headed to Washington, D.C., was derailed by the heroic actions of several passengers and crashed into a field near Shanksville, Pennsylvania. We were all glued to the TV and to our horror, watched the collapse of the crippled Towers. It was horrific, an image never to be forgotten!

I heard my name called and saw Dr. Harrell in the doorway motioning me to come out into the hallway. He was holding some papers in his hand and said he wanted to show me the results of the colonoscopy. He said, "If this were my brother, or husband, I would elect for immediate surgery!"He explained that Pete had stage three cancer and that the cancer was eating into the wall of his intestines. If it went further, it would become fatal stage four cancer! He said that it appeared that the previous doctor had failed to do a complete colonoscopy as this was not an overnight condition but one that had been festering for quite a long time!

I was taken aback. I couldn't fathom that Pete had such a serious condition. Of course, we consented to immediate surgery. Dr. Harrell said that after surgery, Pete would need chemotherapy to assure that the cancer was eliminated, enabling Pete to live life normally. Boy, this was some day! To say that I was shocked is putting it mildly. Pete had the surgery which was successful, and there were multiple sessions of chemotherapy that had minor side effects: loss of hair and appetite which after a time returned to normal, thank goodness. Pete went to Abbey Delray Rehabilitation Center to recuperate and finally came home!

Even after recovering from his surgery and chemo, Pete never complained. As always he couldn't be idle for long. He built a redwood wooden deck poolside and additional shelving for the garage. We decided it best to scale down our out-of-town antique shows but did several shows locally, like West Palm Beach, Pompano Beach, Fort Lauderdale and Miami Beach. As fate would have it, I also developed side pains. I called them sympathy pains because of Pete, but when I went to the doctor, I was stunned to discover that I too had a serious condition, as well: acute diverticulitis requiring surgery. I had the surgery and recuperated at Abbey Delray Rehab Center. Everyone at Abbey mentioned that Pete had been such a wonderful, friendly, humorous patient.

Pete and I adjusted to living in the Hamlet. We had good neighbors who were not only friendly but often invited us to their social events and house parties. Life was good and was only about to get better!

Chapter Seventeen: 2004 Joyous Year!

Roz, saying she missed us in Deefield Beach, decided to move to the Hamlet. I searched the homes for sale and found one that upon her viewing it, she immediately said, "Sold." It was a corner house with two bedrooms, a den, living room, dining room, lovely kitchen, two and a half bathrooms, a screened in patio plus a two-car garage and a golf cart garage. I was thrilled my dearest friend would again be close by to share fun times and conversations. The only thing missing was a pool which she had installed.

In early 2004, Manya announced that having met the man of her dreams, she had become engaged to Donald Howson (tall, dark and handsome!). They opted to get married on May first, 2004. Manya told me she wanted her wedding to be held on a yacht on the Intracoastal. I asked her why not a traditional church wedding? She said she loved watching the yachts cruising up and down the Intracoastal when we lived in Deerfield Beach. A wedding on a yacht would be super and truly different. Most people have a wedding planner but Manya said that because I was retired, I would be the perfect wedding planner. There was so much to do, getting her wedding dress, wedding invitations, hotel reservations, prenuptial celebration at Steve's house, and last but most important, the selection of the yacht. I, like Manya recalled the yachts cruising and one in particular stood out, the Lady Windridge. I got in touch with the company, liked what they offered and signed them up. I chose to have the yacht reserved for five hours, 5 to 10 in the evening. The yacht couldn't be docked in Delray Beach as the docks there were undergoing renovations so we were docked instead at Royal Palm Yacht and Country Club. It was a wonderful facility but it meant that guests staying at the Marriott Hotel in Delray Beach required a bus to Boca Raton, which was not a big deal. The guests actually enjoyed the bus ride. The Lady Windridge was a fantastic yacht with three levels, one hundred seventy feet long, a huge dining room, two bars, and an upper deck where the wedding would take place. There was a beautiful floral arch and flowers were strewn on the carpet. I had mailed one hundred sixty-five wedding invitations and could not believe that one hundred fifty people accepted. Many guests were from out of state and looked forward to attending the wedding. They came from as far as Arkansas, Georgia, Delaware, Virginia, D.C., New York, New Jersey, Chicago and Ohio.

Pete walked Manya, who looked absolutely gorgeous in her wedding dress, down the carpeted aisle to the wedding arch where Donald was standing, so handsome and beaming. The Captain read the wedding vows but for some reason could not pronounce Manya and instead called her Mia. Manya corrected him several times to no avail. Adrienne Papa was her Matron of Honor and Dave Giordano was the Best Man. Alyson Burgess was her Bridesmaid and Donald's brother Dave, was the Groomsman.

At six in the evening a fantastic cocktail hour began with scrumptious hors d'oeuvres being served while the wedding pictures were taken. At 6:30, the DJ began the introduction of the wedding party and Manya and Donald had their first dance. Then, as tradition goes, the bride and her father danced and I danced with Donald. At seven, dinner was called. Everyone headed to the dining room and sought out their table where their seat assignments were marked with place cards. The cuisine was excellent: one had a choice of roast beef, fish, chicken, and even vegan! The service was very attentive. Champagne was served for the traditional toast and whatever anyone wanted to drink, they got it!

I had purchased silk white orchids for the tables in a lovely silver compote which one individual at each table whose number was called received as a souvenir. After dinner the guests went to the upper deck where on a table waiting to be cut was a fantastic four-tier wedding cake. Manya cut slices and Donald served the guests. A fabulous DJ took over and I assure you everyone had the time of their lives, dancing, partying, imbibing, talking, singing and taking in the beautiful view. The weather was perfect. At 10:15 that evening, we returned to the dock and as Manya and Donald disembarked, the guests blew bubbles and tossed confetti. I was thrilled that this turned out to be such an awesome and memorable wedding for everyone!

The guests boarded the bus back to the Marriott Hotel in Delray, some carrying their orchids, some giddy, but all happy to say the least. The next day, when Manya and Donald boarded a flight to Atlanta, some of the guests were on the same flight and several held up their orchid souvenirs in greeting! Finally, Manya and Donald flew off to Costa Rica on their honeymoon! I must say that for me it was a herculean task, but although exhausted, I was delighted to receive so many phone calls saying it was the best wedding they ever attended. Manya made a good choice having her wedding on such a magnificent yacht.

Many of the guests were floored by the previous evening spent at Steve's house in the Hamlet, a great catered affair, open bar and the opportunity to mingle and get to know one another. They loved his home. Now, my next task was to assemble and forward the many wedding gifts people had brought or had delivered to my home. It took a while for me and Pete to settle down and get back to a normal routine again. We did a couple of antique shows locally in West Palm Beach, Ft. Lauderdale and Miami Beach.

One day in December, I received a letter from Manya, and what a delightful surprise when I opened the envelope! She not only wrote a note but enclosed a page with two photos on it. The note mentioned she was pregnant and the photos were actually a sonogram showing a baby boy. Now, she said, you have to come up with a name for him. Pete and I were so happy she was having a family. That night, I came up with a name after going through the alphabet with various names. I chose the name Jamison Peter – I thought it sounded great with the last name Howson, but the final decision would up to Manya and Donald. The following morning, I spoke to Manya and she said she loved my choice! The baby was due in mid-June, 2005 and much needed to be done, buying a layette, baby furniture etc. My first grandchild had a beautiful baby shower given by Adrienne Papa, Manya's childhood friend, in her beautiful home in Boca Raton which was well attended and resulted in many wonderful gifts. Manya flew down to this wonderful reception. Just before her due date in June, I flew up to Atlanta to be with Manya and give her a helping hand when she came home with her new baby.

Chapter Eighteen:
Rejoice-June 22, 2005!

Jamison Peter Howson was born on Wednesday, June 22, 2005, at nine pounds ten ounces, a healthy, beautiful baby boy! I stayed in Atlanta for three weeks until Manya got her strength back. I loved bathing Jamison and cradling him. He was so sweet. He never whined and always seemed to have a smile for me. He was a real joy, lucky Manya!

Although her townhouse in Buckhead was nice enough, she and Donald felt the time had come to look for a larger home, one with a backyard and not attached to other homes like their townhouse. They found a lovely home in the Old Atlanta Club in Suwanee overlooking a golf course with a great backyard. It was a lovely community with young families close by. They moved in November, 2005 and celebrated the christening of Jamison with a gathering of friends in their new residence. Year 2005 was a banner year for Manya and Donald, having a new baby and a new home.

When we returned home to Florida, Pete and I had a serious discussion about doing future shows. Let's face it, we were getting on in years and it took a tremendous amount of energy to do the shows. I felt it was also taking a toll on Pete who was then in his late-80's and tired easily, and I was beginning to feel the brunt of it as well.

One day, when loading our van to do a show, we were loading a jewelry case up the ramp into our van. The case tilted and was about to fall over when I leaped forward to catch and balance it. I felt my right knee buckle. This injury (a torn meniscus) never healed and, to this day, is a thorn in my side. I have a crooked leg and daily pain. We gave up doing shows. A dealer we knew told us about a local antique center on Atlantic Avenue in Delray Beach, where we could display our antiques as well as our jewelry, called the Atlantic Antique Mall. After visiting the Mall, we decided it would be ideal, as they supplied tall, lighted display showcases, had security cameras everywhere, and employed attendants to assist customers. Pete was reluctant at first because we would not be there watching our wares, but other dealers assured us it was a secure place. We arranged two cabinets side by side, close to the main desk. I must confess our display was great and we had numerous sales rather quickly. It was a good decision because Pete wasn't feeling well.

Upon visiting a new urologist, we were told he had a kidney stone which was the reason for his discomfort. He once again needed surgery. This was a surprise because his former urologist had said it was a prostate problem. Pete went to West Boca Medical Center and had surgery to remove the kidney stone, and to everyone's amazement, the urologist told us it was the largest stone he had ever come across in all his years of practice: four inches long and two and one-half inches deep! He said he had tried to break it down but it was too large. He showed me the picture of the stone and it looked like a baked potato. He forwarded the photo to my cell phone, which I have to this day. Pete said he felt much better now that it had been removed.

Sometime in mid-May, I was reading the local newspaper when an article really hit home. We were approaching our sixtieth wedding anniversary on June 1 and needed a lift. The article that caught my attention was about a couple who found an old hotel receipt dated 1956 from the Waldorf-Astoria, where they had booked a room for their wedding night for the grand total of $21.00 a night. They wrote to the hotel management asking if they would honor their hotel bill for their fiftieth anniversary. The Manager responded affirmatively, so the couple flew to New York City, where they were greeted with champagne, dinner, and a lovely room. I also saved our hotel bill. Only our room rate was $12.00, and we had stayed three days. I showed the article to Pete and told him I was going to write to the Waldorf-Astoria asking if they would honor our bill for our sixtieth wedding anniversary on June 1, 2006

I wrote as follows:

Mr. Eric O. Long, General Manager

c.c. Mr. Matt Zolbe, Marketing Director

The Waldorf Astoria Hotel

301 Park Avenue

New York, N.Y. 10022

Dear Mr. Long,

The enclosed room voucher was for our "Honeymoon Stay" in June of 1946, which I recently came across in one of our files marked "Memories."

I was fortunate to return again in 1959 as a NYPD Detective and was assigned to the Soviet Union Premier Nikita and Nina Khrushchev detail. I was in awe of both suites of U.S. Ambassador Henry Cabot Lodge and Premier Nikita & Nina Khrushchev in the Waldorf Towers (those were exciting times.)

My husband, Peter, is now 88 years of age and I am still a spry 81 years old.

Come this June 1, 2006 we will be celebrating 60 years of a wonderful marriage and wondered whether you could honor the enclosed voucher for another memorable stay. Thank you for your kind consideration of this most "unusual" request. I am looking forward to hearing from you. I can be reached at my home (561) 498-5650 or E-Mail-MMManya@aol.com.

Sincerely yours,

Mary M. Zaharko

(I enclosed a copy of Voucher#1770 showing the room rate of $12.00.)

On May 17th, 2006, I received the following e-mail:

"Here is your confirmation number for your arrival on July 21, 3242405147. You will be accommodated in a 1BR Suite, and your room and tax will be complimentary. We are glad you are thrilled, and it is always a pleasure to assist you. We look forward to having you here to honor your celebration.

Please call or email me if you need additional assistance with anything prior to your arrival in July. Have a great day.

Soyra Morales,

Assistant to Matt Zolbe

Director of Sales & Marketing

The Waldorf-Astoria

212-872-4777

I called, thanked her, and confirmed the July 21ˢᵗ date. I told her we were grateful from the bottom of our hearts for this "gift" and could hardly wait. Manya, Donald, and Jamison came to visit us for the Fourth of July, at which time Manya told me she was pregnant again, expecting a baby girl sometime in January 2007! I said she would be "Goldilocks" because Jamison had dark hair and brown eyes!

I had also acquired a new cat, a three-month-old Maine coon cat named Nikko. Peter had chosen a Japanese name. Jamison adored Nikko, as did I, although I still missed Tiger, who had died. Their visit was so special. Jamison was so cute, alert, happy, and always smiling and inquisitive. I told Manya about our good fortune, that of a stay for our sixtieth wedding anniversary at the Waldorf-Astoria. She said, "Good for you, Mom. You both deserve a holiday and some fun time!"

I called Soyra Morales to tell her we were booked for a flight on July 21. We flew up to New York City on July 21ˢᵗ, and when we arrived at the Waldorf-Astoria, we were warmly greeted by Ms. Morales. The bellhop took our luggage and escorted us to a lovely suite! As soon as when we entered, we saw a huge, beautiful bouquet of flowers on the table, a bucket of champagne, and a lovely tray of hors d'oeuvres, as well as a reservation for dinner that evening at the Peacock Alley Restaurant and a note from Mr. Zolbe:

Mary and Peter Zaharko,

It is our pleasure to welcome you to New York City and the Waldorf-Astoria.

I hope you have a pleasant and memorable stay with us.

We are thrilled to have you back with us after 60 years. Congratulations! If the staff or I may do anything to make your stay more comfortable, please do not hesitate to contact me!

Sincerely,

Matt Zolbe, Director Sales & Marketing

We enjoyed a lovely meal at Peacock Alley, saving the champagne for later that evening. The following day, we were surprised to receive another bucket of champagne, plus a tray of hors d'oeuvres and a lovely note from the Waldorf-Towers:

Dear Mr. & Mrs. Peter Zaharko

Greetings! On behalf of the Room Service Department, I wish to extend the warmest of welcomes to you in your home away from home and a heartfelt welcome back! We wish you both the very best on your 60th Anniversary!

Our team of professionals prides itself on immediate responsiveness with personal and invisible service. We are at your service at a moment's notice should there be anything you may need to make your stay with us comfortable, pleasurable, and overall memorable.

Should my immediate attention be required at any moment, day or night, I am at your service. Please do not hesitate to contact me directly on my personal cellular line 937xxxxxxx

Sincerely yours,

Victor Wilson, Associate Director of Room Service

This was so unbelievable. Pete and I were truly overwhelmed, needless to say. When Pete went to pay the hotel bill, we were not charged at the old rate of 1946, nor for our current stay which was complimentary, but we did have other charges. We had dinner at the Inagiku Japanese Restaurant with my sister Hanya and my niece Mary. I wrote a thank you note to both Matt Zolbe and Victor Wilson for their kind wishes and generosity and for making our sixtieth wedding anniversary so very special. I felt like "Queen For A Day"---ahh, sweet memories! The Waldorf-Astoria is now undergoing renovations and has been sold.

On January 12, 2007, Manya's birthday, she gave birth to a gorgeous blonde, blue-eyed baby girl, who was eight pounds and two ounces, healthy and just beautiful. This was our Goldilocks! Manya and Donald were thrilled, feeling that their family was complete! I went up to Atlanta to assist Manya and stayed for two weeks. Manya was a natural at taking care of a new baby, and Donald was a great help with shopping and cooking. Jamison was in awe of his baby sister. I flew back home so pleased that we now had grandchildren and would return again for the christening.

One evening, I received a call from Helen, my sister-in-law, who asked if I could recommend an attorney in D.C., for she felt it was time that she and Ted drew up their wills. I told her that I didn't know of one, but I could call someone I knew (Misty, Carol Klapper's daughter) and get back to her when I had a name. I called Misty, who had a business dealing with court reporters and, as a result, knew many attorneys. She called and gave me the names of three firms, saying that they all excelled in Elder Law and Wills. I chose one, called Helen, and said that I did not personally know them but that they were highly recommended. Helen said she was thrilled and said,

"You know, whatever I have goes to my side of the family, and whatever Ted has goes to his side. We have always had separate accounts." She thanked me and said that she would call the attorney and make an appointment to draw the wills. Ted, at this time, was in a nursing facility because he was in poor health, and Helen said she was unable to handle him at home. He had developed gangrene of the big toe, which had to be amputated, and thus wound up in a wheelchair! I spoke to Ted daily, giving him results of the stock market, which he asked me to do as a favor to him, even though he had a TV in his room. I guess he enjoyed our conversations, which included family activities and the stock market. About one week later, when I was talking with Ted, he seemed incoherent and lost, but we conversed. He said a lovely Asian female attorney had come, and Helen was also present when his will was drawn, for which he thanked me. Helen called me later that day and said the lawyer was lovely and that she was so glad it was done and over with. She said her will was also done that day. (She lied; only Ted's Will was drawn that day; she did not draw a Will until much later.)

I missed seeing my brother, who often visited us in Florida, but Helen never once visited us. I decided that Peter and I should pay him a visit. We flew up to D.C. and checked into a hotel because Helen said the apartment was undergoing repairs, which was also not true. When we saw my brother, we were shocked. This always jovial, happy-go-lucky guy was in his bed, and when he talked to us, he pulled the bed cover up to his mouth. He was disoriented, and I realized that, like Hanya and our father, Ted was probably in the early stages of dementia. It was pitiful!

Shortly thereafter, Helen slipped and fell in the lobby of her building and broke her hip. She was hospitalized, and I was told by a nurse that Helen had asked for her assistance in calling their attorney to have someone come to draw up her will. An attorney came, and a will was drafted, as she had never done one before. She had lied when she told me she had one done at the same time as Ted's! Helen passed away on August 25th, 2008, at the age of 92. She was buried at the Ukrainian Catholic Church of the Assumption Cemetery in Perth Amboy, New Jersey. Not long after this, my brother passed away on November 7th, 2008, at the age of 90. He had developed sepsis and suffered a heart attack. Although my brother owned a burial plot in Pinelawn Cemetery in Farmingdale, Long Island, next to our parents, he, too, was interred in the Ukrainian Catholic Assumption Cemetery, Perth Amboy, New Jersey, next to Helen. This was a total surprise to us as he had been raised as a Protestant.

A few days later, I received a phone call from the attorney whom I had recommended to Helen. He offered his condolences and told me that there was only one heir in Ted's will, his niece, Joan Gadek. I told him that was incorrect and that Joan was Helen's niece and of no blood relation to Ted. He stated that we (the family) could sue but in all honestly, with going to court and battling it out, any inheritance would be exhausted in lawyer's fees. I asked what the estate amounted to. He said well over one million dollars, with savings, the stock market, and two apartments on Du Pont Circle! I was numb, hurt, shocked, and in total disbelief because I recalled that when Ted thanked me for getting the attorney, I told him I didn't need anything but to please remember Manya, Peter and Steve, Mary and Teddy, all his nieces and nephews. He had shouted, "Teddy gets zilch!" never getting over or forgetting an argument that they had years ago. It hit me that Helen, who was present while his will was being drawn, had lied to me by saying that her will was also being drawn at the same time and that whatever she had went to her family (Stella and Joan

201

Gadek) and whatever Ted had went to his side of the family, a blatant lie!

A few days later, I received a call from Joan Gadek. Her mother, Stella, with whom I always had a good relationship, was also on the phone. Stella was not like Helen. Stella had always been honest, kind, and not saccharin-sweet like Helen. Stella said she hoped I wasn't angry with her over Ted's will. I mentioned I was angry with Helen because, in my heart, I knew she was responsible for Ted ignoring his family ties. I said to Joan, "How would you feel if your mother bypassed you and left everything to Johnny's wife?" She said she understood, but she had nothing to do with Ted's will. I liked Joan and felt she would do the right thing. I felt that come Christmas, she would be generous and give each of his nephews and nieces $10,000, a drop in the bucket considering the amount she had inherited. But no, to this very day, not a word from Joan or her mother. It took some time for all of us to get over this crushing blow, but there was no point dwelling on it. I was told I was stupid not to have contested the will, but life is too short. Live each day, and move on!!

We went back to our old routine doing fewer shows after we had the Atlantic Antique Mall so close by, and both Pete and I were experiencing medical issues. It seems though I had diverticulitis surgery, I had also developed three hernias that needed prompt attention. My right knee was also bothering me, and according to the orthopedic surgeon, I needed a total knee replacement! I couldn't do both surgeries, so I opted for the hernia surgery, which was deemed more crucial. I had two surgeons, one for the hernia repair and the other, a prominent plastic surgeon, do a minor "tummy tuck" and a mesh implant. After the surgeries, I was stunned to discover that I no longer had a "belly button," which the plastic surgeon removed when doing the "tummy tuck." At a later date, when I showed my grandchildren that I had no "belly button," Jamison laughed and called me his "Alien Baba."

Delray Medical, where I had the surgery, said that I would need rehab and that I was going to Abbey Delray to further recuperate. After a few days, I was given a form to fill out to give my opinion of my care by the nurses at the hospital. I filled out the form and gave glowing compliments and good recommendations.

Unfortunately, I had an unforeseeable occurrence shortly thereafter. My favorite nurse suggested I sit in a chair by the window as she felt it would be good for me to get out of bed. Manya was here in Delray Beach and was with me most of the time (after having breakfast at home). We would then have lunch together. She had her laptop with her to stay in touch with her office. This day, however, she was not present, and it was mid-morning when the nurse put me in the chair and placed a blanket on my lap to keep me warm. I was by the window, and she said I could see all the goings on in the hall. Manya would be surprised to see me in the chair instead of in bed when she came to see me.

I was so happy being in the chair when, all of a sudden, the chair jolted, moved backward, and opened up so that there was an opening from the footrest to the seat. I was thrown down onto the floor! My buttocks slammed down hard onto the floor, and my back was scraped as I went down from the seat side of the chair! I was in a jack-knife position. I called for help, but no one heard me. The nurse had not given me the buzzer to call for assistance. Fortunately, a woman visitor glanced through the window, saw me lying on the floor, and ran to the nurse's station for help. They picked me up and put me back in bed. The nurse applied some body cream to my scraped back. I was surprised how quickly two maintenance men came into my room, accompanied by the Head Nurse, who instructed them to remove the chair and return with a replacement chair. A replacement chair was brought in at the same time Manya was walking in. I told her what had happened and showed her my back. I was fortunate that my stitches were still secure; no damage there!

To my surprise, that very afternoon, I was transferred to Abbey Delray for rehab. Upon arriving, I told the attending nurse what had occurred and showed her my sore spine. She said the report that came with me stated that I had "bed sores," no mention whatsoever of the chair incident, a real cover-up! I realized that because I had filled out a complimentary form previously, they would ignore what truly happened, perhaps fearing a lawsuit. That was the furthest thought in my mind, although there could have been a lawsuit over the malfunctioning chair. I was just so happy that there were no serious consequences. I should have asked to revise the form and include the mishap with the chair.

After a short stay at Abbey, I returned home and had home physical therapy. When I felt up to par, I went to Delray Medical and asked for a copy of my medical records, which I always do, whether for a doctor's visit, tests, or a hospital stay. I always like to have a copy of my medical records on hand. I received the records, and I could not believe what I had read. Nowhere was there any mention of the chair incident. I wrote a letter to the Hospital Administrator detailing the date and incident and asking that the records be corrected, but they would not acknowledge the mishap. I asked why the chair was removed. There was no reply. I let it go at that but felt it was not handled properly. I felt betrayed and would be reluctant to return to Delray Medical again, wondering how they would treat me.

As the old saying goes, "When it rains, it pours!"

We soon faced another serious medical issue. While my son, Peter, was having a physical exam necessary for his employment as a co-pilot, the cardiologist told him he needed surgery for a heart valve replacement! We were shocked to learn that he had been born with two instead of three valves and that his blood flow was impeded. We were all stunned. My children have always had all the necessary vaccinations and exams from earliest childhood. Not one doctor ever mentioned the valve or said that it would be a problem unless it was replaced!

Peter chose to go to Bethesda Hospital in Boynton Beach, which has a high-rated heart specialist. (Peter researched on the internet and saw his credentials.) The doctor replaced the old valve with a new one, but Peter was told he would eventually need a replacement in the future because they lasted only around eight to ten years at most. The doctor opened Peter's chest and inserted the valve. Peter made an amazing recovery. He was discharged after three days and was told he could resume normal activities, swimming, surfing, etc., within a month's time, but in moderation. He would be off work for about eight months. This was remarkable! Peter had always taken care of himself and was attentive to his health. He would not allow himself to be inactive or even gain unhealthy weight. He is truly a health advocate!

Chapter Nineteen: Mall Fiasco

We were enjoying our time at home without being on the road as we had been in the past. Sales were decent from exhibiting at the Antique Mall here in Delray Beach. One afternoon, I received a call from Beverly, the lead attendant at the Mall, expressing her regret over the theft of one of our rings, not an ordinary ring but an expensive one: a man's ring, platinum, with a sapphire center stone and two rubies on either side worth $4500! I was shocked, to say the least, because I felt our cases were secure. I asked for the details of the theft.

She told me that yesterday afternoon, a Black man, disheveled in appearance (which should have alerted security) but still treated as a potential customer, had wandered around the Mall, stopping at several cases but seemed particularly interested in an item I had and had asked to see it. He told the sales girl that he wanted to see a sterling silver card case on the bottom shelf. The sales girl forgot the cardinal rule, which was to always have the customer step away from the cabinet while she opened it once all shelves were exposed. As she bent down to pick up the card case, he stuck his hand inside the middle shelf where the ring was kept in a box and plucked it right out. He waited for her to stand up and show him the card case. He inquired about the price and said thank you but that he would pass, after which he quickly left the premises.

The clerk became aware of the theft when she went to lock the cabinet and saw the ring box toppled on its side with the ring missing! This salesgirl was new and had only been working there a short time. Naturally, she was beside herself over what had transpired. I asked

Beverly what the camera showed. Beverly said the camera was malfunctioning and did not record anything but that a police report had been filed, a full description of the thief was given and the local pawn shops had been alerted. A few days later, I was told that the police had brought in a known derelict who fit the description of the thief, but unfortunately, because the camera failed to record the incident, the salesgirl hadn't witnessed the removal of the ring, and the individual was not charged. He was released! Sadly, this wasn't the only theft. Another incident occurred shortly thereafter.

I received a phone call from Beverly, who said she was calling this time to give me some good news: a good sale! The sale was that of an antique 18kt gold Austrian cigarette box for $4000! She told me that a lovely Black woman had wanted a special gift for her mother and became excited when she saw the box, claiming that it would be the perfect gift. She presented her credit card. Beverly began to process the sale when she was informed that the card was overdrawn, so there was no sale! The woman asked to speak to the credit card clerk, and when Beverly handed the phone to her, she accidentally disconnected the credit card company (purposely) but told Beverly she would call them back, still holding the phone, to clarify they had been mistaken and that her credit card was good. She dialed the credit card company (supposedly) and got into a conversation with an individual (her co-conspirator) who approved the transaction. She then handed the phone back to Beverly. The co-conspirator reaffirmed the approval, which was fraudulent and not from an authentic credit card company. Beverly gave the box to the woman and thanked her for the sale! The next day, however, when processing the credit sales slip, she was notified "declined!"

Beverly realized that she had been scammed and filed another police report describing the woman, giving her credit card name and describing the fraudulent sale. A few days later, Beverly was asked to go to the Delray Beach Police Station to see if she could identify the thief in a line-up. The individual appeared to be well-known for credit card fraud and was, therefore, easily found and taken in for questioning. Five Black women were in the line-up, but Beverly failed to identify the right woman even though she was there! Beverly said the women she was viewing weren't as well dressed as the thief! So again, there was no arrest. The camera hadn't been repaired, so I was out of luck again.

I asked the owner to reimburse me because his employee made the error, and his insurance company would compensate him. He instead offered me two years of free cabinet rental. Stupidly, I accepted his offer, which turned out to be a big mistake because he was actually in the process of dismantling the Antique Mall. We were only in the Mall for a few months before we were advised of its closing. I felt bad because the Mall was so convenient for us to display, and up to this point, we had a good relationship with all the employees. We had no choice, however, and removed our items, contemplating our future plans.

Both Pete and I were no longer youngsters. He was in his mid 90's, and I was in my mid 80's. We were not in a position, health-wise, to travel any distance and then put hours into setting up our booth. Pete had issues with his heart, needed a pacemaker, and complained of having no energy or strength to do shows. I, on the other hand, still had issues with my right knee, which I injured years ago. Now, it had become a bone-on-bone issue with my leg jutting out to the right. I couldn't put my legs together, and the pain was more or less constant. I was advised to get a total knee replacement and have my leg straightened, but I kept postponing it because of Pete. I knew of a local show at West Palm Beach, and after talking it over with Steve, who was now retired and living next door to us, I asked him if he and I could try to do a couple of shows together. He agreed to do the shows, both of us hoping we could sell off our collection of jewelry, antiques and collectibles. I ordered two jewelry cases because Peter had given our three cases to a friend who was in need of them for his shop.

I saw on TV upcoming antique/collectible shows to be held at the South Fairgrounds West Palm Beach.

I called the promoter and booked three shows. Steve rented a U-Haul to load our contents saying it was much easier than loading the van the way we used to do. Much to my dismay, when we arrived for the first show, we were not in the main exhibition hall but rather in the back room where most of the dealers had their items for display simply placed on tables. We were the only ones with fancy display cabinets and jewelry cases. We looked so out of place, but we had no choice after booking so late, or so the promoter claimed. We did surprisingly well and were told by the promoter, who liked our display, that next time, we would be exhibiting in the main hall, which was great! We did the next two shows in February and March.

Pete stayed home while Steve and I exhibited. Steve was a good salesman on items other than jewelry, which he left up to me to identify and sell. I could not get over the fact that some dealers wanted an item and would offer me less than I paid for it, saying they had to make a profit as if I didn't! My sales were better with customers other than dealers to whom I gave a good price, wanting to diminish my stock. I found that doing the shows was grueling, and as the old saying goes, "The body is willing, but the flesh is weak." So true! Thank goodness Pete was spared the ordeal of sitting for almost eight hours and then coming home. He was comfortable in his recliner with Nikko as his companion and his newspapers and TV. He had no complaints. If I was exhausted, imagine how he'd feel! I had noticed a decline in his energy of late, even more so than before, but his mental outlook never changed. He had a happy-go-lucky attitude and was loving and communicative, always enjoying dinners on the Avenue in Delray Beach, even though he was in a wheelchair.

We all concurred that doing shows at this stage of our lives was no longer feasible, and we began to look for an alternative to dispose of our merchandise. Peter mentioned trying eBay as a possible source, and I said that I would research it.

Chapter Twenty:
Heartrending Times!

Even now, I find it difficult to bring back repressed memories of what transpired in mid-2014, but nonetheless, I will do my best and try to recall! We noticed that Pete was lethargic and not having much of an appetite, which was very unusual, but as the Doctor said this was part of "old age." Pete had checkups for his pacemaker and refused to do any physical activity, only wanting to snooze in his favorite recliner chair with Nikko at his side! We did, however, celebrate his 96th birthday, going out for dinner to 50 Ocean, a restaurant overlooking the beach.

Pete used a walker inside the house, but the wheelchair was necessary whenever we went to the doctor's office or to the VA for hearing tests as he said he was experiencing a loss of hearing not in one but both ears. He was given hearing aids, and even though they were surprisingly small and easily inserted into the ears and really not visible, he refused to wear them. (He was stubborn that way). I would help him when he showered, and one day, I was shocked to see what looked like a cluster of grapes at the base of his spine. They were actually blisters, and the entire area was inflamed. He had shingles, the last thing he needed. I asked why he never mentioned it, and he said it annoyed him but that he did not want to make an issue of it. This was typical of Pete. He was never a whiner and took everything in stride. I bought some medicated cream, which I applied frequently, and thank goodness, the shingles didn't spread. Instead, they disappeared.

One night, while reaching for the walker alongside our bed, he fell off the bed, landing on his buttocks in between the bed and the night table! I could not lift him up as he was too heavy for me, so I called Steve and Peter to come right over. It was around midnight so both were home, thank goodness, and still up. They came over, picked Pete up, and escorted him to the bathroom.

It was decided that our bed was too high for him. He would need to sleep in the back bedroom on a twin bed, which was lower and where the bathroom was even closer. I was concerned that I would not be able to hear Pete if he called for assistance, as the master bedroom was on the opposite side of the house. The ninety-foot hallway was quite a long distance, so I gave him a brass cow bell to ring whenever he needed me.

Pete fell off the bed again, unfortunately, but thank goodness, there were no injuries. We decided that the best thing to do would be to buy a hospital bed and put it back in our master bedroom so I was there for him at all times. This worked out perfectly. We were both happy to be in the same room where communication was easy, and there would be no more falls.

I could not help thinking that Pete's time was limited. How would I cope with that? He meant everything to me. After all, we just finished celebrating our sixty-eighth wedding anniversary on June 1, 2014! I wanted him to be around to celebrate more anniversaries!

As usual, the Howsons came in July. I was so glad they were able to spend time with me and Pete. Jamison and Jadyn went to the Trinity Lutheran Summer Camp for ten days, which they thoroughly enjoyed. Unfortunately, Pete suddenly developed a medical issue, had difficulty breathing, and was admitted to Delray Medical Hospital. He had a port implanted in the lower right rib cage with a tube inserted into his right lung to give access to the fluid collecting, which had to be drained. Thank goodness the Howsons returned home when this happened, as I did not want them around when he had the fluid drained.

He was discharged from Delray, and a visiting nurse was assigned to come to the house and drain his lung three times a week. Lance, the nurse, was very kind and compassionate. The first time, he removed 1.5 liters of bloody fluid. I was shocked. Pete said it didn't hurt and that he could breathe more easily. Pete never ceased to amaze me. With all the problems he had, he weathered them with no complaints and took everything in stride. Lance would come three days a week, flush the tube, and remove .5 to 1 liters of fluid. In September, Pete returned to Delray Medical for an adjustment to the port and stayed for a day instead of returning home. He was placed in the ICU (Intensive Care Unit). While in the ICU, I approached one of the doctors and asked if he would tell me what Pete's problem was. The doctor said that Pete had AML, Acute Myeloid Leukemia, a result of his having been treated in the past with chemotherapy and radiation for cancer. This caused fluid in the lungs to collect, requiring removal. I almost keeled over with shock. Never in a million years would I have suspected this. I guess Lance knew but he never discussed this with me. I asked the doctor if Pete would recover once the fluid was removed. The Doctor said Pete's time was limited and suggested that he be transferred from ICU to hospice care in the hospital. Pete and I were devastated. I told him that he would only be in the hospice ward for one night. I was determined to bring him home to be with his family, especially since the Dr. said his expectancy was a day-to-day issue!

The hospice people were wonderful. They arranged to have a hospital bed and a nurse to be in attendance twenty-four hours to attend to Pete. The hospital bed was placed in the back bedroom and the nurse saw to it that Pete was made comfortable. I called Manya and asked that she come to see Pete, explaining his situation as that of a day-to-day issue! Manya flew down the next day and I was so grateful that she was here not only to comfort Pete but me as well!

Lance no longer came as the hospice nurse was here and handled everything. Nikko would check on Pete every night, sitting in the doorway watching. Pete got a kick out of that. Nikko was always spooked by strangers and would not enter the room while the nurse was there. I would pick Nikko up and place him on Pete's bed so that Pete could pet him. Pete was on IV's which kept him bed-ridden. He slept a lot because he was taking pain medications.

I always put on a strong face, but at night, my pillow was wet with tears. I knew Pete's time was limited so I made up my mind to make him happy with a lot of affection, not only from me, but the kids, as well. I spoke loving phrases in Ukrainian to him rather than using English because the nurse was always present. On Sunday morning, October 12, 2014, I went in to greet him as usual and although he was sitting up, his eyes were closed and he did not respond to me. I talked to him and held his hand, but there was no response. I looked at the Nurse and said he seems to be "out of it." She looked at Pete and said, "He's in a coma. The end is close. Don't leave him."

I called Manya who was still in bed to come quickly and to call Steve and Peter to come immediately. We all huddled together at the foot of his bed and watched his breathing and sure enough, Pete took a deep breath and his head dropped back onto the pillow. He was gone! I glanced at my watch and noted that he drew his last breath at

9:20 that morning. Pete had requested that he be cremated and his ashes be buried in two places: the family plot in Mount Olivet Cemetery, in Maspeth, Queens, New York and the VA Cemetery in Lake Worth, Florida. I tried to accept that my soulmate, the man I loved, my confidant, someone I truly admired for his artistic abilities, an architect, furniture designer, someone with a wonderful sense of humor and a great father, was now gone! I was really blessed having him as my soulmate but I had to be strong for the family. Manya, Steve, Peter and I arranged for an obituary to be placed in the Sun Sentinel, The Palm Beach Post and the Valdosta Daily Times, Valdosta, Georgia.

"On Oct.12th, 2014, Peter Zaharko, Sr., of Delray Beach, Florida passed away at the age of 96 in his home surrounded by the love of his family and friends. Peter was born in New York City. He graduated from Textile High of New York City and later studied at the Pratt Institute of Design in Brooklyn, N.Y. Peter was married to Mary Zaharko on June 1, 1946 at the Ukrainian Protestant Church of New York City. He served as a Sergeant Major in the 68th Air Service Group, 14th Air Force China-Burma-India (CBI) theater of operations with the "Flying Tigers." Peter was in charge of all administrative duties for the Mengtze Air Base, Mengtze, China. Peter joined the New York City Police Department in 1947 and retired in 1972. His passion for building and designing allowed him to design and build homes in New York and Florida, as well as design unique, modern stainless-steel furniture under the name of Z'Orceny Designs. He and his wife, Mary, traveled the U.S. antique show circuit as the Odyssey until 2000. Peter was a lifetime member of the Grand Lodge No.776 of The Free and Accepted Masons of the State of New York. He was also a member of The Broward 1013 Association. Peter was a devoted father to Stephen, Manya and Peter. He loved his children with all his heart and always wanted the best for them. He is survived by his wife, Mary Zaharko and his sister, Anne Zaharko Roberts of Valdosta, Georgia, sons Stephen Zaharko, Peter Zaharko, Jr. and daughter Manya Zaharko Howson, son-in-law, Donald R. Howson, Jr., grandchildren, Jamison and Jadyn Howson, and niece and nephew. In lieu of Memorial Services, the family will have a Celebration of Life gathering with family and friends at a later determined date. Peter has requested that his ashes to be interred at both the VA National Cemetery, Lake Worth, Florida and Mount Olivet Cemetery, Maspeth, Queens, N.Y. Peter's wonderful sense of humor and creative spirit will be greatly missed but never forgotten."

We selected Sunday, December 21st for the Memorial Service-Celebration of Life and had the Boy's Farmer Market cater. The caterer arrived with a fabulous presentation of food, a huge cheese board, various dips, carved turkey with gravy, colossal shrimp, breaded chicken tenders, large fruit platter, and last but not least, an early 90th Birthday cake for me, chocolate mousse cake! We had sixty-five guests (friends) attend as well as a Chaplain from hospice who delivered a brief sermon. The Celebration of Life was held in Steve's house which was perfect. He even had a bartender! The interment was held on Tuesday, December 23rd at the VA National Cemetery in Lake Worth. We, the family, arrived at a Committal Shelter where the Service was to take place. A military funeral, which included the playing of "Taps," a Rifle Detail, Color Guard and the final presentation of a burial flag was given to me as well as a Presidential Memorial Certificate to honor deceased veterans. This was a most impressive and memorable service. Jamison and Jadlyn were moved, as we all were, and although tears were shed, we were all thrilled to have witnessed and been a part of this unforgettable military funeral. I handed the ashes over to the Military Guard who would then have them placed at Pete's headstone. The headstone, given by the Government to all veterans, was beautifully engraved with his name, dates of birth and death, and service in US 68th Air Force, devoted husband and loving father."

All the headstones were decorated with beautiful wreaths for the Christmas holiday. Row upon row of headstones with the wreaths made for an unforgettable image. I was thankful that Manya and her family were still staying with me until the New Year as it was strange not seeing and speaking with Peter. It would take some time for me to adjust to this void. 2015 would be a new way of life for me without Pete.

I decided to write a children's book which I called "The Mystical Computer." I got the idea after watching Jamison and Jadyn's fingers flying over their cell phones and laptops, thoroughly engrossed. I must admit writing was a tonic for me. I noticed that time flew by when I was writing. It was good therapy for me.

I paused the writing for a short time to gather paperwork for my personal income taxes. On March 3rd, with paperwork in hand, I was on my way to our accountant, Mitch Taylor, who had offices in the Sanctuary Building on Federal Highway, Boca Raton. When I arrived, I was forced to park a good distance away from where you take an elevator to the various floors in the building. There were no sidewalks. I had to walk in the roadway stepping over speed bumps in a dimly lit area. As bad luck would have it, I stepped over a speed bump which happened to be lower on one end than the other, and in so doing, I tripped and fell forward. I tried to shield my face but did not succeed. I face planted, my paperwork flying out of my hands, as I lay on the roadway bleeding profusely from my nose.

Fortunately, several people came to my aid. One man handed me his handkerchief to stop the bleeding. I was out of sorts and said, "My papers, my papers I need them for my accountant." A woman said she had collected them for me and asked for my accountant's name. I said, "Mitch Taylor." She laughed and said he was her accountant, as well, and that she'd bring the papers to him. I heard someone calling 911 for an ambulance. I asked the man if he could kindly call my son Steve to let him know about me. He said I would be going to the Boca Raton Regional Hospital and he would tell Steve to meet me in the Emergency Room.

The ambulance came soon thereafter. I was placed on a gurney while the EMTs tended to my injuries which included placing an ice pack on my nose to stop the bleeding. When I arrived at the Emergency Room, I was immediately taken for X-rays which revealed that I had broken my nose in two places, suffered two broken teeth and a cut to my lip. I was fortunate that I did not have a concussion.

After the X-rays, I was returned to the Emergency Room where Steve had since arrived. When he saw me, he put both his hands up to his face and shook his head in disbelief over the way I looked. I was admitted, at which time I discussed alternatives to reset my nose. I was able to avoid surgery by having my nosed placed in a splint (which looked like a clothespin). It was a wise decision. Anything to avoid surgery! I did have a major problem with my teeth, however. To repair them meant removal of a permanent bridge which originally cost me $12,000.

I did not want to sue so Steve and I went to the Sanctuary Office where we spoke to Barbara, the Administrator who was appalled by my appearance. I had two black eyes, the splint on my nose, the broken teeth and a split lip which still had a crust on it. She said she would speak to the owners and their insurance company to try to help me. She asked for the name of my dentist in the event the insurance company would pay for the replacement of my bridge. I thanked her and left feeling that all would go well as she was so compassionate. Within a week I was notified that the insurance company had forwarded a check to my dentist in the amount of $10,000 to pay for the necessary restoration and repairs. I realized they were only too happy because I was not going to bring a lawsuit! I gladly paid the balance of $2,000 for the restoration of my teeth and smile!

After visiting the dentist and having the repairs done, I decided that I had forgone writing for too long and went back to it again. I wrote constantly and finished my first book in July. Now, the hard part was getting the book published. I saw in the local newspaper that there was a Writer's Club held weekly at the Public Library. They were seeking potential authors. This was early August and I thought I'd go and get their advice. I went and saw a number of people gathered around a long table and I took a seat. At the head of the table sat a man who was the leader of the group. He asked if there were any newcomers. I raised my hand and he said, "Have you brought your manuscript with you?" I told him that I did and he asked what the story was about and to read a couple of paragraphs so that everyone could critique it. I mentioned that "The Mystical Computer" was a children's book. I started to read when someone interrupted me and said I did not belong here because this group was primarily for adult fiction not children. The leader then said, "What you've read is interesting but it's true that you should be in a children's writing group, not here."

I was stunned, picked up my belongings and left. I felt so mortified that when I got into my car I burst into tears. I drove home with tears still streaming down my cheeks and started to feel a bit weird. I had a heavy feeling in my chest. When I got home, I sat down and took a drink of water. I had difficulty swallowing and I started burping. The burping would not let up. It was followed by a severe pain in my upper chest going up my throat to my jaw! I realized that I was having a heart attack. What to do? I remembered that Steve had gone to West Palm Beach and called him for help. I told him I believed I was having a heart attack and told him my symptoms. He said he was on his way and to just relax until he got here. He arrived in about 15 minutes and drove me to Delray Medical Hospital which was very close by, thank goodness. I was struggling to catch my breath.

At the curb of the Emergency entrance there was a wheelchair. Steve wheeled me inside. A female nurse asked for ID and started questioning me about my symptoms. Steve became angry and said "Attend to my mother. She's having a heart attack. You can fill out your forms later." Thank goodness a male nurse came over, and taking me inside, gave me some tablets to place under my tongue. He placed me in a room and other nurses quickly came in to take my vitals. My blood work showed the enzymes were overly high indicating a heart attack! A scan of the heart showed an enlargement at the tip or base of the heart. The doctor said they could not put in a stent and that no surgery was necessary. I needed bed rest and hopefully, the problem would heal itself.

I could not believe what had happened. Was the incident at the Writer's Club responsible for my heart attack? I certainly hadn't experienced any symptoms before then that I could recall. After being in Delray Medical, I was discharged for rehab to Abbey Delray for ten days before returning home. Manya came to stay with me when I was released from Abbey.

One morning while I was listening to MSNBC Morning Joe with Mika Brzezinski, Mika mentioned that she was sponsoring a contest in five cities, Philadelphia, Washington, D.C., Boston, Chicago and Orlando, where she planned to give away $10,000 to five women. According to a press release, "The co-host of MSNBC Morning Joe and her employer NBC Universal announced that a "Grow Your Value Bonus Competition" will be part of the new "Know Your Value Conference." It called for women to upload a 60-second video explaining why they deserved a $10,000 bonus. Mika and a panel of judges would choose fifteen finalists, three in each city, to pitch their stories in front of a live audience with viewers across NBC Platforms. I told Manya that I wanted to enter, hoping that I would be selected so that I could have the funds to publish "The Mystical Computer." Manya laughed but went ahead and took a 60-Second video of me explaining why I entered the contest which she submitted to NBC, wishing me luck. I had Manya's cousin, Mary, edit the script so that it was ready for publication. I really wanted to win. I felt that I would hear from NBC soon, but time went by and nothing happened. I started to do some research on publishing a manuscript. Peter said I needed to copyright it which he did for me. I missed Pete terribly, even though I spoke to him nightly when I said my prayers, but not seeing or being with him still affected me. One night when I entered my bedroom, I saw a vision of him standing next to the TV. He was smiling and blew me a kiss, another "ghost" apparition like I had when I visited England. I'm not kidding, this really happened, the one and only time!

I still had not heard from NBC , even though they acknowledged receiving the TV clip needed to enter the contest. One day in September, I was reading the newspaper when I started to sweat profusely and could not seem to catch my breath, with pains clutching my throat and jaw. I realized I was having another heart attack! I immediately called next door. Peter answered and came over as Steve was playing golf in Boca. Peter took me to Bethesda Baptist Hospital in Boynton Beach. I asked him why there? Peter said they had given him superb care when he had his heart surgery a short time ago. While driving up there, I was gasping for air. I told him I didn't think I'd make it this time. Peter said, "Breathe through your nostrils. You'll be okay, we're almost there." He had called the Emergency Room on his cell phone, alerting them of our arrival. When we got there, a team of nurses were at the curb waiting with a wheelchair. They wheeled me inside, immediately gave me a nitroglycerin pill to place under my tongue and took my vitals. A scan of the heart was identical to the first time when I suffered the heart attack in August. The doctor told me that my condition was most likely "Takotosubo syndrome," the Japanese term for "broken-heart syndrome," brought on by grief over the loss of loved one!

Peter was correct. The care at Bethesda was phenomenal. I was in the hospital for over a week before they prescribed rehab at their site. I was lucky once again: no surgery, no stent, just the best physical therapy which I received for about a month going on into October. I had just completed my last session of physical therapy when out of the blue, I got a call from Robyn Gengras, a producer for MSNBC's "Know Your Value." She told me that she and Mika had reviewed my video and even though three contestants had already been selected for the Orlando event, they wanted me to come as a guest. I was asked to forward "The Mystical Computer" plus a current photo, a biography and if possible, a photo of me as a NYPD Detective. I was told that a limo would be picking me up for the drive to Orlando on Thursday, Nov. 19th to the Loew's Royal Pacific Resort where I would be staying for the final "Know Your Value" event to be held on Friday, Nov. 20th. You can't imagine the joy and uplift this gave me, particularly because I was just getting over a second "heart attack." I mentioned that I had a problem walking any distance and required my son, Steve, to assist me. They said it was no problem and that he was most welcome!

On Thursday, the limo picked us up and we had a very pleasant drive to Orlando. We checked into a lovely room at the hotel and had a great dinner in the dining room. I was so excited that I could hardly wait for morning to come when I would go to check in for the "Know Your Value" event. After breakfast, Steve took me in the wheelchair to the reception area, where we registered and received our ID, which said, "V.I.P. Guest, Know Your Value," and was ushered to the auditorium. We were in the first row, and our names were on two chairs marked "Reserved" directly in front of the stage. Mika was on the stage with a group of women, among them a model, an NBA coach, a top negotiator, a sports agent, Martha Stewart and Rachel Ray. They all spoke of their careers, empowering women to be successful and achieve their goals. Mika told the audience that she was going to show one submission that jumped out from the others, which proved that it's never too late to reinvent yourself, and with that, she showed my submission, which went as follows:

"Hi, Mika. My name is Mary Zaharko. I am 90 years old and am a retired NYPD Detective. I wrote a children's book which is both entertaining and educational. You know, Mika, as an author, how costly publishing a book can be. My purpose in entering this competition is two-fold: one, the book would be published, and two, a good portion of the proceeds would go to Alzheimer's research for a cure. This is close to my heart since my once animated, articulate and loving sister is afflicted with Alzheimers and now lives in the shadows. I hope you will consider me for the bonus so that these goals can be accomplished before I reach the ripe old age of 100, which I intend to do. Thank You!"

The audience burst into applause. Mika said they loved the submission so much that she asked Comcast, NBC Universal if they would honor me on stage in Orlando. All had agreed and so I was invited to be here today. I was asked to come on stage and was introduced as Mary Zaharko, former NYPD Detective. They showed a huge photo of me in uniform. Mika asked, "When did you decide to put in the pitch?" I told her that when I saw what was happening to my sister and read that over five million Americans were afflicted with this insidious disease, five thousand alone in Palm Beach County, I felt compelled to do something. So I wrote a book. You'd think that being a retired NYPD Detective, I'd write a detective story. Instead, I chose to write a children's story, "The Mystical Computer."

Mika then said, "We've gone ahead and will have a one hundred book publishing run for you. Look ahead and tell me what you think of the artist's rendition for the cover of "The Mystical Computer?"I saw a poster on an easel that floored me. It was great, better than what I had been thinking of doing. Mika handed me a copy of "The Mystical Computer" and said, "Before you go what advice can you give?" I answered that I had found my new value and want to tell women who have retired and are getting on in years to use their knowledge and intellect to further a cause or be a mentor. "Remember, age is only a number," I said. "Get off that rocking chair and show your value. You can do it!" We hugged and I thanked her and returned to my seat. Talk about being queen for a day, that's how I felt. Never in my wildest dreams would I have thought I'd receive this special award and recognition. Mika then proceeded to select the finalists in this competition which completed the event. We were escorted to mingle with the guests at a celebration cocktail reception followed by a fantastic luau. I went to bed that night feeling so grateful for all that occurred.

The following morning, the limo drove us back to Delray Beach, back to normalcy. I was told someone would get in touch with me regarding the publishing of "The Mystical Computer," but because the Christmas holidays were approaching, it would be most likely after the New Year. My niece, Mary, and the Howsons came to spend Christmas with me. I adored them all! It was a treat to be with my inquisitive grandchildren who were growing up so fast. 2015 certainly was a "see-saw" year for me what with the fall, broken nose and teeth, then two heart attacks. The saving grace for me was being a surprise guest at the "Know Your Value Conference" in Orlando. I looked forward to a good New Year in 2016!

Steve and Peter thought it was about time and long overdue to bury Pete's ashes in Mount Olivet Cemetery, Rego Park, Queens, N.Y., in his family's plot. In May, we booked a hotel reservation and purchased plane tickets to New York to finally inter Pete's ashes. I called Mount Olivet ahead of time to notify them as you are required to do, and paid them in advance to open the grave when we arrived. But fate intervened again. That week, I felt out of sorts. My stomach was bothering me, and I had aches similar to those when I was experiencing diverticulitis, so I thought the best thing to do would be to go on a liquid diet. I hoped that by the end of the week when we were scheduled to travel, I'd feel better. No such luck! On Saturday, May 7, 2016, I was in such agony that I had Steve drive me to Bethesda Hospital Emergency, where, once again, the staff awaited my arrival. They promptly took my vitals. I was running a temperature. It was also discovered from a CAT scan that I had an abscessed gall bladder ready to burst, necessitating immediate surgery! Wow! I never anticipated this. Dr. Breslaw said I was extremely lucky, having come just in time. Who knows what the consequences might have been otherwise? After a short stay in the hospital, I returned home and had a visiting nurse to change the bandage daily. We canceled our flight and hotel reservations, and called Mount Olivet, as well. Poor Pete! His ashes would have to wait for another time.

Meanwhile, I could not for the life of me remember where I put his ashes. I looked everywhere, but couldn't find them. I knew that they were here in the house somewhere, but where?

"The Mystical Computer" still had not been published as it required some additional editing, and illustrations were requested. A friend of the publisher was supposed to provide the illustrations, but because she was a teacher, it was put off until vacation time. This was now mid-July, and still no illustrations! I then decided to do a few sketches, which I forwarded to the publisher, who said that after minor corrections, they were acceptable, and the book could finally be published in September. I was told that the books would become available at Barnes & Noble and Amazon for $10.00 each. I was thrilled, and Manya made a post on Facebook about the book being available, which was so nice of her! The sales were slow. I guess too much time had gone by since my appearance in Orlando on November 20th, 2015, but then, even a few sales are better then none!

One day when Steve came over for his usual coffee, he said I was slurring my speech and he noticed my mouth seemed crooked. He said, "Mom, you're having a stroke," and immediately dialed 911! I argued that he was wrong, but he was right and I was wrong! The ambulance came and took me to Delray Medical where an MRI determined that I had indeed experienced a stroke. I lost a major part of hearing in my left ear and experienced a weakness in my left arm, but I felt I was fortunate to have had no major disabilities. I was discharged to Abbey Rehab where I stayed for almost a month for therapy for my weakened left arm. Abbey Delray Rehab is the place to go if you need rehab. Everyone is so dedicated and comforting.

I went home feeling normal and grateful that I was still in one piece! I no longer had the numbness in my left arm and I walked normally with no limp! I received physical therapy at home for another month into December, 2016. I was so happy Mary and the Howsons came to celebrate Christmas as they always did and I could be my old self again without any more physical therapy. I consider myself fortunate in that I still had those I held dear and could communicate with them daily, like Olga, Roz, BFF Carol Klapper and Anne Roberts, my sister-in-law.

Anne was not doing well, having had three hip surgeries and suffering the loss of her son, Rick. While she was in the hospital having hip surgery, he had fallen in her home, suffered an apparently severe blow to the head and had died as a result. It was over a week before anyone knew of his deadly injury. Anne's friend, Rosie, came to Anne's house to get some items for Anne when she discovered Rick's body. This was a real tragedy! Anne was helpless and could do nothing as she was still hospitalized. She never really got over this loss and started to decline in health thereafter. She often said she didn't want to live anymore! I asked if she would consider coming to stay with me but she said it was too late and would stay where she was and thanked me for asking. I hoped the year 2017 would be better for us all.

In February I read that the Alzheimer's Community Care organization was going to hold an Educational Conference at the Palm Beach Convention Center on March 16th, 17th, 2017 and I thought it would be a great opportunity for me to do a book signing with all the sales going to Alzheimer's Community Care. I called and spoke to Kelly Elbin, Vice President of Development, who said he would certainly welcome me to do a book signing and would give me a small booth (gratis) to exhibit my book. I was so happy to be able to have my first book signing and finally get some proceeds going to Alzheimer's Care, a cause which was so dear to me. I sold ten books the first day and fifteen the second day for a total of $250.00. Although the Conference was well attended, the crowd was mostly in the main hall where various guest speakers were giving talks. Only a sprinkling of attendees came into the booth area. I had hoped that I would sell more books, but then for the first time, twenty-five books wasn't too bad. I forwarded a check to Alzheimer's Care and in my letter asked if they would be so kind as to consider my participation for future events. Oddly, I never received an acknowledgment of my check or request! I was told by the Development Coordinator, Nicole F., to forward my check and letter to her, which I did.

A couple of weeks later, I had a delightful visit from Genny and Terry Ross, who were coming from a cruise. They lived in Canada and to see them after so many years was wonderful. I told them I would welcome them any time. (Genny's Mother was Grandpa Pete's first cousin, so there was a relationship)

The months flew by and before I knew it, New Year 2018 was fast approaching. We had the usual family visit in December which is always up-lifting! Life was routine. I still drove and would frequently have lunch with Olga. When I say life was routine, I mean that I had a daily routine taking care of my menagerie! I had my feral cats, Ginger, Coco and Blackie, as well as two ducks who would come in April and stay until June. I had named them Duke and Duchess. I also had a female fox I named Roxy and a slew of birds: blue jays, mourning doves, woodpeckers, black birds and cardinals (two that always visited I named Red and Ruby) and finally, my favorite bird, the bunting, a tiny bird with the most vivid colors, purple, yellow, red, orange, just spectacular! I also had a toad I rescued from my swimming pool who hung around and ate cat food! Roxy the Fox was initially shy but eventually would actually take food out of my hands. It was a sight to behold. With the ducks in the pool, Roxy eating her food on one side and the feral cats eating on the other side, no one had anything to fear. My sweet house cat, Nikko, would watch from inside the house, taking it all in. When Nikko decided to go outside, the feral cats would go up to him, nose to nose, and follow him as he walked off. He became their leader.

My buddy, Roz, would come over daily to feed the birds. Red and Ruby always seemed to be waiting for her to dispense their bird food. In addition to going shopping at the mall, Roz and I would go to the Seminole Casino for a relaxing afternoon. I, unlike Roz who went weekly, went every three months or so. I would only take $100 for the day, win, lose or draw, never more! She, on the other hand had no limit. One time she hit it big, $10,000! Not bad, but frequenting the Casino as often as she did, it was gone in no time!

One day while sorting the mail, I saw a letter from the Home Owners Association announcing their annual Christmas Festivity for young children at the Condo Clubhouse on Saturday, December 8th, 2018. I thought this would be a great opportunity for me to do a book signing. I called the HRA Office and they said it would be novel and great! That Saturday, I went to the Clubhouse and exhibited a photo of me with Mika on an easel. My books were ready for purchase. I was so pleased by the turnout of young families who purchased twenty-five books as Christmas gifts which I happily autographed! I sold the same amount of books at the Alzheimer's Conference the prior year. I forwarded the check and a letter to President Mary Barnes of Alzheimer's Care, who in turn, sent me a lovely acknowledgment. As usual, Manya, Donald, Jamison, Jadyn and Mary spent the Christmas holidays with me which I look forward to every year. I consider their visit as the best Christmas Gift!

Unfortunately, the saying "time heals all wounds" was not holding its water as I was still having problems which my right knee and leg which necessitated my visiting my orthopedist, Dr. Buchalter. He felt surgery was the only option to get rid of the pain once and for all. My cardiologist, on the other hand, told me not to have surgery and instead opt for cortisone injections in both knees. Now, my left leg was giving me problems because I was applying more pressure on it when walking with a cane. In late January, 2019, I had the cortisone injections which were supposed to make me pain-free and last for three months before needing another dose.

In February of the same year, Steve developed a serious condition from a scratch on his calf. It was cellulitis! His right leg swelled to twice its normal size and was so discolored (black, blue, green) he required hospitalization! He remained in the hospital for eight days and needed three weeks of intravenous treatment for the cellulitis even after returning home until all the symptoms (including the leg swelling) had disappeared. Steve loves gardening and believes a branch from a bush he had been trimming was responsible for the scratch on his calf. We were glad no other complications developed.

I was still getting injections not only in my knees but in my lower back where I had the spinal fusion, now complicated with arthritis. I can honestly say that a day does not go by when I wake without feeling back pain. Some days my knees are quiet and other days, especially at night when I'm in a deep sleep, my right knee starts throbbing like a toothache and consequently wakes me up. I often apply Salonpas (containing lidocaine) to my knee, and after a while, the pain subsides and I fall asleep again. There are nights when I cannot sleep because of the pain even after applying Salonpas so I resort to half a Tramadol to quell the pain. I am very careful not to take Tramadol too frequently as it can be addictive. I also apply a CBD salve, which helps ease the pain, and wear a knee brace as well as compression stockings. At times, I would say to myself that I should perhaps reconsider having surgery.

The year 2019 went by so fast! I socialized by attending The Church of The Palms functions, thanks to my dear neighbor and friend, Edie Kutz. I also had a number of visitors like Genny and Terry Ross who came after their cruise, and Sally Marion, Olga's darling daughter, and Nancy and Dan Ferguson, my dear friends from Texas.

In 2020, on an otherwise uneventful day, I went outside to watch Steve fill the bird feeders and as I walked onto the deck, I unfortunately tripped. I could not get up, knowing I had broken something, The pain in my left arm was so intense, it was killing me. I was lucky that Steve was close by and rushed to pick me up. I told

231

him that I believed my wrist was broken. Steve took me to Minor Urgent Care Emergency where they X-rayed my left arm and it revealed a split in the wrist bone. I was told to see an orthopedic doctor. I knew of a Dr. Meadow who was in the same office as Dr. Buchalter. Dr. Meadow specialized in ankle and wrist problems. I called and saw him immediately. He put a cast on my left arm and ordered a brace to wear once the cast was removed. I was glad it was my left wrist rather than my right which I use to do everything.

At about the same time, COVID was spreading rapidly around the country and one had to be really cautious when out shopping, etc. In mid-June, when the cast was removed, I wore the brace for support. On June 23rd, 2020, I suffered a TIA (mini-stroke) and was admitted to Delray Medial Center for three days. My neurologist then had me transferred to Pinecrest Rehabilitation Center (next to the Hospital) for necessary rehabilitation/physical therapy. I was at Pinecrest for three weeks and received the best physical therapy ever (better than Abbey, which I was fond of) every morning and afternoon. The therapists were patient and determined that when I was discharged to go home I'd feel great. The left arm weakness lessened and it didn't bother me to lift my arm up as much as it had before. The therapy really helped.

Unbeknownst to me, Steve hadn't been feeling well. The day that I was discharged and came home was the day he said he couldn't breathe. He also had a temperature so Peter decided to call 911. Steve was taken to Delray Medical and diagnosed with COVID! Steve was in the hospital for five days, insisting that he receive only traditional oxygen treatment (nasal), definitely no oxygen mask! Upon discharge from the hospital, Steve noticed that he had some after affects, namely the loss of smell and taste which was typical of COVID. This was rough on Steve because he did most of the cooking. He was our Chef! In time, he did recover his sense of smell but the taste buds were not the same. He was told it takes time for full recovery. For the first time, the Howsons did not come as they usually did for the Fourth of July. We would have to wait until December to see and enjoy the holidays with them. I looked forward to the year 2021, feeling Steve and I both had weathered unforeseen medical problems but were now healthy again!

In September, my dear friend Roz, who had been experiencing mental fog and could no longer could find her way to my house to feed the birds as she had in the past, was, on the advice of her doctor, transferred to a memory care facility, The Sheridan at Cooper City, north of Ft. Lauderdale, where she would get her medication on time, have her meals and be around people. She no longer had a telephone, having forgotten how to use her cell phone, so I relied on her cousin, Donnie Taylor (her wonderful caretaker) to keep me up-to-date. Donnie put Roz's house on the market which sold quickly. I truly miss my Roz! Our friendship had begun in Deerfield Beach in 1975, forty-five years ago! We were truly buddies, sharing good times and bad enjoying each other's company. Cooper City is over an hour's drive and with COVID still around, visiting was limited to one visitor at a time, mask mandatory! I decided that when the ban was lifted, either Steve or Manya would drive me to Cooper City to visit Roz. Donnie did on occasion call me when she was visiting Roz and would put Roz on the phone. Thankfully, she still remembered me and we would chat, which was great. The first time we spoke we both shed tears. It was really tough but she seemed well enough.

In 2021, COVID vaccines became available and Steve and I signed up to receive the multiple shots as prescribed by Moderna

233

given by Publix Pharmacy. I was still having severe pain in my right knee and saw Dr. Buchalter who, this time, injected a gel rather than the usual cortisone, hoping it would ease my pain. The gel did suppress the pain quite well. It was six weeks before I needed another gel injection. I also was fitted for a new knee brace which helped me.

Sometime in May, I noticed that Nikko was not eating his food as he usually did and was throwing up quite frequently. He had also stopped going outside to mingle with his feral feline pals and was sleeping more than before. One day I noticed that not only did he not eat his food or drink his water, he was not using his litter box. There was nothing in it. I decided to keep a close eye on Nikko. He approached me and with a soft meow and it appeared he wanted a little loving and comfort. I picked him up and cradled him. He appeared happy and stayed on my lap for the longest time before deciding to leave me. I brought his cushion-bed which I placed on the floor in front of my recliner so that I could keep a close eye on him. I noticed his breathing was laborious and I just knew he would soon be leaving this world. I decided to stay in my recliner and watch him. I called his name several times but there was no reaction or response. His breathing was becoming more shallow. I realized he was in a coma (just like Pete). Finally, he took a deep breath and that was it! My sweet Nikko was gone! He passed away on May 25th, 2021 after sixteen happy years. I adored him. He was a great companion, following me around like a dog and sleeping on my bed. He was truly a great comfort to me. I miss him terribly. I was telling everyone that after this, no more pets at this stage. Losing Nikko after all these years was like losing another family member. Steve, Peter and I said our goodbyes to Nikko the following day. He was buried next to Tiger under the palm trees in the backyard. Steve bought a memorial slab with a cat carving on which was engraved, 'Nikko, 2005-2021." The feral cats, Coco and Blackie, felt something was amiss. They would still come to the door and peek inside as though they were looking for Nikko to appear and walk with them as usual.

On June 9th, Steve received a call from one of his former co-workers who was aware of Nikko's passing and said that her neighbor had a three-year-old Balinese, neutered and healthy, who needed a home as she was going to Saudi Arabia and could not take her cat with her. The co-worker thought it would be ideal for me to have this loving cat. Steve said I did not want another pet, but out of curiosity, asked to see a photo. When she forwarded the photo, he exclaimed, "Don't offer the cat to anyone else. I'm coming over to pick him up." Steve, true to his word, left to pick up the cat to surprise me, and surprise me he did, walking into my family room carrying a pet carrier with the cat inside. When he opened the door of the carrier, the frightened cat, "Aspen" (his name), scooted out and immediately looked for a hiding place. He went behind the etagere in the dining room. I had to admit he was beautiful! He had the colors of a Siamese, but had long silky fur, a bushy tail like Nikko and bright blue eyes! He was absolutely gorgeous!

We decided to sit on the couch and let him wander about to get comfortable. I called to him: "Aspen, come to your new Mommy." Believe it or not, he approached me, smelled my extended hand and butted it. I noticed he was drooling. I knew dogs drooled but never a cat! He allowed me to pet him and then went over to Steve who also petted him.

Aspen previously lived in a townhouse and was alone much of the day until his mistress came home. He needed to adjust to an entirely different environment. I was home all the time and he had loads of great windows and glass doors which enabled him to look outside. He

235

was a house cat and had never been allowed out. Steve had taken his familiar litter box, dishes for food as well as the toys he had played with, his bed and all that he was used to having in his old home. It took about a week for him to adjust to his new quarters. He would hide behind the TV in the family room, behind the Chinese screen in the living room and on the piano as well! He was a vocal cat which we all got a kick out of especially when it came to feeding time. He came to know the Ukrainian word for food, hamu "Aspen, want to hamu?" I was so happy I had a gentle, attentive, loving cat just like Nikko. Balinese cats are also known to be non-allergic to people with pet allergies which both Donald and Jamison had. Well, time would tell. I did not coax him to jump on my bed (like Nikko used to do) but lo and behold, it seems he wanted to be close to me and began to sleep on my bed with my hand cradling his head. How sweet! I got a kick out of Aspen vocalizing when the feral cats showed up waiting for me to feed them. They were surprised when they heard and saw Aspen instead of Nikko. Aspen adjusted quickly to his new home and loved being petted by Steve and Peter whenever they came over. Having Aspen was indeed a tonic for me since I was having horrible nights because of the pain in my right knee/leg/ankle. I was comforted by reaching over and petting Aspen lying next to me. His fur was so soft and silky.

In August, I reached the point where even after the gel injections, I was so miserable that I opted for surgery. My right knee developed a baker's cyst which filled with fluid. I couldn't walk, relying on a wheelchair to get around. Dr. Buchalter removed over fifty ounces of fluid from the cyst, the most he'd ever seen. He approved surgery but wanted approval from Dr. Chaplik, my cardiologist. Dr. Chaplik had me wear a twenty-four-hour heart monitor, and pending the results, would confer with Dr. Buchalter. I had all the necessary arrangements made at Delray Medical when I received a telephone call from Dr. Buchalter saying the surgery was postponed. It appears that sometime in the early morning, my heart rate dropped to forty-two beats a minute. This was very bad, especially if this happened during surgery, so no surgery! Dr. Buchalter and I were both disappointed. I would continue with the injections and do the best I could tolerating my condition.

One evening I received a telephone call from Sally Marion, Olga's daughter, telling me she was giving Olga a 95th Birthday Celebration in October at Prime Catch in Boynton Beach and wanted me to attend. I told her I was not driving anymore and that Steve would take me. I looked forward to it. She said, "Great, I'll add him to the guest list." She mentioned that Olga was finally going to have her teeth taken care of, meaning the removal of some broken and decayed teeth in front of her mouth, so that when next we see Olga, she'll have a beautiful smile again with all the missing teeth replaced!

October is a big birthday month in our family: my father-in-law on Octoer 5th, Steve on October 6th, my mother, Nancy Ferguson and Cindy, Olga's granddaughter, on October 10th, Olga on October 15th and my sister-in-law Anne on October 21st! Anne was going to be 99! Anne was at the present time having rehab because she could not stand without collapsing and therefore needed physical therapy to regain her strength! I spoke to her daily and also received calls from Rosie Magness, Anne's friend to whom she had granted a Power of Attorney so that she could pay Anne's bills.

Olga went to the dentist and had several teeth removed. She needed to wait for the gums to heal before either implants or a bridge could be done. Unfortunately, she developed a very bad infection and was admitted to a rehab/nursing facility in Lake Worth.

On October 29th, I received a call from Rosie who appeared to be crying. She told me that Anne had passed away that morning, peacefully in her sleep! Rosie said she was going to carry out Anne's wishes to be cremated. Her ashes along with her son Rick's ashes would be strewn into the ocean off the Georgia Coast! I felt badly that I did not have a last conversation with Anne but I did call her the day before. She didn't want to speak, saying that she was so tired she only wanted to sleep and that we'd speak tomorrow when she was up to it (which of course never happened). Anne was finally at peace and now she was with her loved ones, Amen.

I was concerned about Olga who also seemed to be deteriorating rapidly. I would call her daily, but instead of being jovial, she was tense and said she felt miserable and wanted to return to her apartment. In mid-November, Sally and her daughter Cindy came to be with Olga and I had them stay with me. On Monday, November 15th, one month after her birthday, Olga passed away, also peacefully in her sleep! I wept over her loss and tried to soothe Sally and Cindy who now needed to arrange for Olga to be cremated. Sally lived in Arkansas and would have to return at a later date to inter Olga's ashes and those of her brother, Michael, alongside her Dad Leo Crawford in the family plot in Boca Raton. It was a good thing that Cindy had come with Sally. They also needed to vacate Olga's apartment at Grand Villa of West Delray on Sims Road and donate anything they didn't want to Goodwill, a difficult chore but it had to be done!

I looked forward to the Christmas visit of the Howsons and Mary for comfort. Looking back at 2021, I lost three loved ones, my sister-in-law Anne, my "cousin" Olga and my sweet pussycat, Nikko. I now had very few intimate friends left, but those I still have, I cherish. I looked forward to 2022 being a much happier year!

In January 2022, the baker's cyst reappeared behind my right knee, and I was once again unable to walk, needing to use the wheelchair until the fluid was drained. I hate being in a wheelchair and vowed it would only be temporary! Dr. Buchalter again injected gel into both knees and removed a lot of fluid, but thank heaven, I was now able to use the walker instead of the wheelchair.

In February, 2022, Steve and I attended the prestigious West Palm Beach Antique Show at the Convention Center for the purpose of obtaining cards of possible buyers for my collection of porcelain, silver and jewelry, all stored away. After I finalize my memoir, I will need to earnestly get down to business, sort and decide what to keep for the family and what to dispose of. I chatted with Billy Rau of MS. Rau of New Orleans. It was so good to see him again. We still get a chuckle out of recalling the mishap with the Galle vase when The Odyssey was exhibiting in New Orleans. I gave him a copy of "The Mystical Computer" as a token of friendship. His booth was truly amazing, just like M.S. Rau in New Orleans. I also spoke to another dealer, a lovely young lady, Bailey of Artistoric Antique Shop in Ft. Lauderdale, who expressed an interest in some of the photos I showed of my collection. She said she would call me and make an appointment to see my collection after the show was over. Around two weeks later, Bailey called and did come to my home where she viewed my collection. She bought a pair of antique Copeland candlesticks and took a Le Gras on consignment, a "French Indiana" Art Deco vase.

I did not pursue other dealers because necessary home repairs had to be taken care of. My sub-zero refrigerator wasn't cooling properly and needed repair. I was told the repair would only be temporary and that I really needed a new refrigerator. Additionally, the blinds in the family room kept falling down so they too needed replacement. Steve took me shopping for a new refrigerator, but we had a problem: the sub-zero was an oversized refrigerator, and we could not find one to fit in the space. It would have to be a special order. None of the local shops, Home Depot, Loews, or Best Buy, had the refrigerator I needed in stock. We went to The House of Appliances in Delray, and lo and behold, on display they had a Jenn-Air with the perfect dimensions, but we would have to wait until one became available, in several months possibly, but I had no choice. I was fortunate in that I had a spare refrigerator in my laundry room, particularly because my sub-zero went kaput in short order!

I also decided to take Manya's advice, get rid of the blinds, and get the newest blinds on the market, electric blinds. These blinds would roll up and down with the push of a button. The blinds were ordered and would take several weeks for delivery. I also had blinds made for the guest bedroom, which truly made a tremendous difference in shielding it from the morning sun. Sorely needed hurricane glass doors were installed in both the living room and the guest bedroom. All three repairs came at just the right time, before the arrival of the Howsons' annual Fourth of July vacation/visit. (It was perfect!)

In August, I finally gave in to Steve's urging to have a hearing test. We went to Costco to have my ears tested. After taking the test, I admitted to Lily, the Specialist, that having inserted a small hearing device in both ears, I could understand everything she and Steve said. Needless to say, I went home wearing them and sort of enjoyed them. It took a little while for me to adjust to strange objects in my ears, but I'm glad that I listened to Steve and bought them. I could hear better and rarely said "What?" thus making everyone happy that they no longer needed to constantly repeat themselves. I still went to Dr. Buchalter for my gel shots in both knees. I was thankful the baker's cysts did not reappear.

In late November 2022, Genny and Terry Ross, coming off a cruise, spent only one day and night with me as they needed to get back home for a baby shower that weekend. I was happy, as always, to have spent time with them. They are a delightful, fun-loving couple.

The day they left, my niece, Mary, arrived. Mary was going to stay with me for about a month while her bathroom was being renovated and her apartment was being painted, which she said was long overdue. I was so pleased that I had someone to talk to and share meals with; a great change. Mary and I always had a good relationship going back to her earliest childhood. I am amazed at how talented she is, a multi-linguist! She speaks not only Ukrainian but also Chinese, Japanese, French, and now Italian! Mary is also an estate planning attorney. She set up her laptop on the table in the dining room and kept in touch with her office. Peter took Mary to several yoga classes, which she enjoyed. Friday nights were spent with Steve and Peter on the Avenue, mingling with their friends. Mary stayed in the guest bedroom, but before Manya and the Howson crew arrived for the Christmas holidays, she moved into Steve's guest bedroom so that Manya and Donald would be as usual in the back guest bedroom.

When the Howsons arrived, I was totally shocked when Jamison walked up to me. He was so tall! I couldn't believe it. He was taller than his Dad, 6'2", and as handsome as ever! Beautiful Jadyn was also no longer a kid, now blossoming into a young teenager and soon-to-be "Sweet 16" on January 12th, 2023!

Both Jadyn and Jamison had some last-minute Christmas shopping to do at the Boca Mall. Manya pushed me in a wheelchair because I could not go in and out of the stores the way they did. I bought a suit at Macy's for Jamison. He looked so handsome and grown-up, 17½ years old! Manya surprised me with a triple birthday celebration. She ordered three cakes, all saying Happy Birthday. One cake had a number 98 candle for me, the second cake had a number 57 candle for Manya, and the third cake had a Sweet Sixteen for Jadyn. Leave it to Manya to do this; so different and clever! My birthday was January 3rd, 2023 (I was 98 years old), but Manya and Jadyn's birthdays are on the same day, January 12th, 2023. This was the first time I shared my birthday with them, and I was so happy we could celebrate them together.

After the holidays, Mary left to return to New York, the renovations and painting for her apartment having been completed. She and the Howsons left the same day, December 30th, to be in time to celebrate the New Year at home. For New Year's Eve, as customary, I stayed up until the ball fell at midnight in Times Square! I also had my favorite drink, Pama (pomegranate juice, vodka, and tequila mixed with cranberry raspberry soda, yum, yum!). I raised my glass to toast my departed loved ones whom I often speak to in my prayers, those few friends I'm lucky to still have around, and, of course, my beautiful family!

I needed to renew my driver's license as it would expire on my birthday, January 3rd. Steve drove me to the Driver's License Bureau where I took a visual test as well as an oral test, both of which I passed. I received a new license, which floored me. It expired in January 2030! 2030 would make me 105 years old. Hilarious! But then, one never knows. Over the years, I was frequently asked,

"What's your secret? You don't look your age and have barely any wrinkles!" I usually attribute it to "good peasant stock," but I have a secret practice accounting for my smooth facial skin, which goes back to my early childhood. I always remember that whenever my mother cracked an egg, she would smear the egg white from the shell onto my face. After the egg white dried (like a facial mask), I would rinse it off with cold water, no soap, and dry my face. My face is to this day soft to the touch, shiny and smooth. I still put egg white on my face faithfully and even got Steve to do it. Steve is now in his 70's and has barely any wrinkles which he attributes to using egg whites. After the egg whites dried, I washed my face (without soap) and applied coconut oil which acts as a moisturizer/foundation. No face-lift, just egg whites! I am now 98 years old, and I appreciate each and every waking moment and try not to whine too often about my aches and pains and occasionally feeling "loopy," being so grateful that I am still pretty lucid and able to be independent in many ways.

I feel that it is about time for me to stop writing and get into other areas requiring my attention, namely disposing of antiques and collectibles from "The Odyssey." As I end this autobiography, I must say when it came to "Recall," I sincerely did so to the best of my ability, even though, at times, events might appear foggy. As far as "Recoil" is concerned, to this day, I still recoil over the despicable events but truly "Rejoice" over the many great years of love and companionship, especially my sixty-eight years with Pete! I still remember and miss his jovial sense of humor, his kisses, loving and hugging. Ahhh, sweet memories! I rejoice in the fact that the Howsons presented me with two fantastic, amazing, articulate, and healthy-loving grandchildren, Jamison and Jadyn. I rejoice that I have both Steve and Peter living next door who never ever hesitate to help me carry out my needs and wishes so lovingly. I rejoice in that Manya and Mary (my niece) never let a day go by without calling and chatting with me. And I rejoice in having Aspen (my cat), who is a great and very vocal companion. I am so glad fate brought us together! The future is unknown, but as I said in my video to Mika (at the Know Your Value Conference), "Age is only a number, and I will do my best to keep going, hopefully reaching the ripe old age of 100, which I fully intend to do!" And a sequel to this autobiography could still be in the wings!

Photos And Newspaper Clippings:

Scribbles Booth at Toy Convention, Sept. 1951, Hotel New Yorker

POLICE SIREN—For the benefit of the New York Policewomen's Endowment Association the big city's lady gendarmes
recently staged their third annual entertainment and dance. Policewoman Mary Zaharko vividly demonstrates the transition from blue
uniform to frills. At left, she's seen as she dresses when on regular
duty. At right, she is seen in her fetching stage costume.

246

"Cops and Garters" – Policewoman's Revue, November 1957

The Brooklyn Daily Eagle (Brooklyn, New York) · Sat, Dec 5, 1953 · Page

Printed on Jan 22, 202

Old Woman Fleeced of $4,000; Con Girl Nabbed, 2d Hunted

By FRANK LYNN

The Brooklyn District Attorney's office today sought the second member of a female confidence team which allegedly fleeced a 72-year-old Brooklyn woman of $4,000.

Barbara Spencer, 22, of 35 Hamilton Place, Manhattan, was in Women's House of Detention, Manhattan, today, after being arraigned on the swindle charge in Magistrate's Court yesterday and held in $25,000 bail.

The victim of the swindle was Antonie Goepfert of 72 Highland Place. Assistant District Attorney Lewis D. Cohen pointed out that there may be other victims who have not reported the swindles to the police.

Mrs. Goepfert was window-shopping at 164th St. and Jamaica Ave. on Nov. 30 when, she charged, Miss Spencer approached her and said that she had just found a package containing $6,000 but that she didn't want to turn it over to the police.

At that moment, a confederate hurried up and began berating Miss Spencer for telling someone about the "find," according to the District Attorney's office.

Mrs. Goepfert charges the two women then decided to

PRO AND CON WIRES ON MAC ARE TALLIED

White House Promises To Tell How Many Back Senator's Stand

Washington, Dec. 5 (U.P.)—The White House promised to issue a boxscore today on whether a volley of telegrams received in response to Senator Joseph R. McCarthy's foreign policy attack favor President Eisenhower or the Senator.

Assistant Presidential Press Secretary Murray Snyder said 2,030 telegrams had been received at the White House by 7:30 o'clock last night. He said Western Union here had a backlog of 1,800 not yet relayed to the executive mansion.

McCarthy earlier branded the White House count a "grievous mistake." The Wisconsin Republican said his own "sources" at Western

split the $6,000 with her provided that she would show her good faith by withdrawing $4,000 from a $4,182.84 account at the Nassau Savings Bank, 2515 Atlantic Ave.

Mrs. Goepfert agreed and she says the trio went to the bank where, she charges, Miss Spencer withdrew the money, in cash, after Mrs. Goepfert had signed a withdrawal slip. Noting that Mrs. Goepfert's handbag was small, Miss Spencer volunteered to carry the money in her larger handbag while they journeyed to the Stuart Building in Jamaica where a "Mr. Stevens" would advise them on the disposition of the found money, the complaint stated.

The women agreed to meet Mrs. Goepfert at a nearby church ten minutes after the bank withdrawal, when the three would then proceed to the Stuart Building. They never showed up, according to the complaint.

Assistant D. A. Cohen revealed that Miss Spencer had been arrested, with a woman companion, Thursday on a jostling charge when two detectives, Doris McDonald and Mary Zaharko, say they overheard them plotting a similar scheme. He added that Miss Spencer, who was convicted for prostitution in October, 1952, is wanted for questioning concerning an $18,000 swindle in Manhattan.

to Improve

raffic Light

Daily News (New York, New York) · Fri, Aug 24, 1956 · Page 24

Printed on Jan 22, 202

(NEWS foto by Al Amy)

Arrested. Detective Mary Zaharko takes James Damas, 31, in-, to W. 47th St. police station after arresting him on pickpocket rap. He was charged with reaching into her friend's purse as they window-shopped.

Baggy Pants Trap 'Socialite' Beauty

By EDWARD MURRAIN

Red-haired Mrs. Opal Jackson, 29, who created a sensation parading in a $7,000 black diamond mink coat at the Bon Bons swank party less than a month ago, made news of another sort last Thursday.

The high fashion California model was arrested for "loitering" in the Bonwit Teller store at 721 Fifth Ave. Detectives Mary Zaharko and Mary Fitzgerald later ascertained that Mrs. Jackson was wearing a pair of baggy pants, known in the trade as "shoplifter's bloomers."

BAGGY PANTS 11

Late Thursday afternoon, the striking beauty was arraigned in Magistrates Court, and paroled in the custody of her attorney, Andrew Tyler. She will receive a hearing this Friday, Feb. 1.

AWAKENING

Mrs. Jackson, who claims to be the wife of a wealthy Los Angeles stock broker, had been received with open arms by some of New York's "400" when she arrived from the West Coast and checked into the Statler Hotel one month ago.

The rude awakening came much later, when her hosts and hostesses learned that Mrs. Jackson had been summoned here by her attorney, to map a defense against the state's charge that she lifted diamond rings from the Robert Mercade Jewelry store, 528 Park Ave., and a gem shop at the Waldorf-Astoria, shortly after registering in a luxurious Waldorf suite last November.

UNDER BAIL

She was subsequently held in $5500 bail by Magistrate Vernon Riddick, and after waiving hearing in Manhattan Felony Court, was freed to await the action of a grand jury weighing the indictment.

After a short return trip to Los Angeles, Mrs. Jackson reappeared on the New York scene as a guest of several well known socialites and celebrities.

BULLETIN

At press time Tuesday, the New York Age was informed that no word had been received from President Eisenhower by the NAACP, the National Newspaper Publishers Association, or the Montgomery Improvement Association, in answer to their appeals for the Chief Executive to visit the South and voice his protest to the Anti-Negro violence in that area.

Meanwhile the bigots keep up their theme of "bomb away" while Negro citizens pray and keep vigil on their churches and homes.

Ala. Governor Hits Violence; Posts Award

The Governor of Alabama has spoken. This time in the vein of a man attempting to uphold the law. Governor Folsom this week denounced the renewal of anti-Negro violence as "anarchy pure and simple" and posted $2,000 reward for the arrest and convic-
(Continued on page 20)

Baby Sitter 11, Expecting; L. I. Man Held

Shocks aplenty are flooding Long Island citizens these days. This time it was the announcement that an 11 year-old child hardly through playing with dolls, is to be a mother in May.

The unusual news followed doctors report after the child's foster parents requested an examination. They became worried when the girl continued to gain weight. She was examined by two doctors before the couple found the reason. Her name is being withheld because of her age.

According to detectives, the first doctor said the child was suffering from gas. Unsatisfied with that diagnosis, the couple consulted another physician, who told them the girl was six months with child.

Following this disclosure, the foster parents immediately put detectives on the trail of J. W. Thompson, 20, a hotly construction worker and father of two daughters, aged 2 and 5, for whom the mother-to-be served as a baby sitter last July.

At the time of the attack for which Thompson is being accused, the Thompson family lived at 164-22 108th Rd., South Ja...

SUSPECT FADES— AND VICTIM TOO

Left without either suspect or complainant—each of whom just walked away while the cops weren't looking—Long Island State Parkway police hopefully searched Hempstead Lake State Park, near Valley Stream, yesterday for an attempted rapist who had dragged a pretty young equestrienne from her horse and tried to attack her.

The superhighway operation began at 4:45 P.M. Saturday when two patrolmen spotted the girl's escape on the bridle path and captured the suspect after a brief chase. The cops took one suspect, but not the girl, to the Valley Stream barracks for questioning.

There, while they were busy directing other cops to pick up the suspect eased out a back door of the barracks, hopped a fence and disappeared. By the time the other cops got to the scene of the attempted attack, the girl had disappeared, too.

The three pickpockets, Morris Finkelstein, Eddie Stein and Louis Goldberg (l. to r.), reluctantly precede Detective Mary Zaharko into police station. Mary's husband, Peter, brings up rear.

Lady Cop Bags 3 Pickpockets

Report Dag, Nasser Agree on Canal But Not on Aqaba, Gaza

Returns Once Too Often

2,500 Attend PO Pay Rally

11 Hero Cons Rewarded

Hormel Heir Weds Again

Bearded George A. Hormel Jr. heir to a meat packing fortune, smiles with his bride, Kim Wadsworth, following their wedding in Las Vegas, Nev.

Says Presley Pulled 'Pistol' on Him

Memphis, Tenn., March 24

Elvis Presley displays the Hollywood grip that he said he pulled on Marine Pvt. Hershel Nixon.

Judge Okays School Police; Jansen Howls

Lady Cops at Classes Trap Wolf for Passes

Our Satellite Plan Blocked, Probers Told

MIKA BRZEZINSKI   MARY ZAHARKO
(MSNBC HOST)
              ORLANDO FLORIDA - Nov. 20, 2015
        KNOW YOUR VALUE CONFERENCE

Made in the USA
Columbia, SC
30 October 2024

45363722R00141